Additional Praise for
Real Options Analysis Course

"Dr. Mun has managed to remove the cloak of mystery from real options. While his first book dives into the theory and mathematics of the real options methodology, this new book cuts to the chase and is chock full of real-life examples that the practitioner can use for framing and analyzing real-world problems. He has created what are destined to become *the* user's manuals for anyone attempting to apply the exciting analytics of real options."

> —Jaswant Singh Sihra
> Senior Strategic Planning Advisor
> Halliburton Company

"The *Real Options Analysis Course* is an engaging hands-on reference for corporate financial engineers and corporate controllers looking for robust state-of-the-art financial methodologies to tie corporate strategy with financial asset management with the objective of creating shareholder value. It is a must study for former MBAs who have the desire to keep up with new financial analytics."

> —Professor Thoi Truong
> Oregon Graduate Institute of Technology

"Mun eliminates the 'halo effect' surrounding real options—the notion that only rocket scientists are capable of analyzing and valuing real options. The Real Options Analysis Toolkit software that he personally developed will open doors for practitioners and academicians looking to frame and solve real options problems."

> —Roberto J. Santillán, Ph.D.
> Director of the Ms.Sc. Program in Finance
> Graduate School of Business
> Instituto Tecnológico de Monterrey (México)

Real Options
Analysis Course

Founded in 1807, John Wiley & Sons is the oldest independent publishing company in the United States. With offices in North America, Europe, Australia, and Asia, Wiley is globally committed to developing and marketing print and electronic products and services for our customers' professional and personal knowledge and understanding.

The Wiley Finance series contains books written specifically for finance and investment professionals as well as sophisticated individual investors and their financial advisors. Book topics range from portfolio management to e-commerce, risk management, financial engineering, valuation and financial instrument analysis, as well as much more.

For a list of available titles, visit our Web site at www.WileyFinance.com.

Real Options
Analysis Course

Business Cases and Software Applications

JOHNATHAN MUN

WILEY

John Wiley & Sons, Inc.

Library of Congress Cataloging-in-Publication Data:
Mun, Johnathan.
    Real options analysis course : business cases and software applications / Johnathan Mun.
        p. cm.
Published simultaneously in Canada.
    ISBN 0-471-43001-3 (Cloth/CD-Rom : alk. paper)
1. Real options (Finance) I. Title: Business cases and software applications (with real options toolkit software CD-Rom). II. Title.
    HG6042 .M855 2003
    332.63—dc21
                                                                        2002153126
Printed in the United States of America.
10 9 8 7 6 5 4 3 2 1

Preface

I wrote this book with the corporate financial analyst and graduate student in mind. *Real Options Analysis Course*'s business cases, exercises, step-by-step methodologies, and applications have been adapted for and solved using the enclosed Real Options Analysis Toolkit trial software CD-ROM. It is assumed that the reader has familiarity with real options concepts as outlined in my previous book, *Real Options Analysis* (Wiley, 2002), as some of the more important concepts overlap between these books. As in the first book, I focus on the ease of use and pragmatic applications of real options and forgo many of the theoretical concepts. The idea is to demystify the black-box analytics in real options and to make transparent its concepts, methodologies, and applications. Rather than relying on stochastic Ito calculus, variance reduction, differential equations, numerical methods, or stochastic path-dependent simulations to solve real options problems, I have instead relied heavily on binomial lattices, which I have shown time and again to be reliable and produce identical results, at the limit, to the former approaches. While it is extremely easy to modify binomial lattices depending on the real options or to more accurately mirror the intricacies of actual business cases, it is extremely difficult to do so using the more advanced techniques. In the end, the more flexible and mathematically manageable approach becomes the pragmatic approach. The flexibility in the modeling approach flows well with the overall theme of this book: *"If you can think it, you can solve it!"* Finally, my intention is to reveal as much as possible in the realms of real options. A black box will remain a black box if no one can understand the concepts, despite its power and applicability. Only when the black box becomes so transparent that analysts can understand, apply, and convince others of its results and applicability will the approach receive widespread influence. It took over two decades for discounted cash flow and net present value analysis to take hold in corporate finance—then again, that was during an era of slide rules, little knowledge of corporate finance, and virtually no desktop computer software spreadsheet applications. However, it is vital to note that the software does not eliminate the analyst, as it is only a tool. Instead, the tool exists to allow the analyst to spend more time thinking and framing the real options problem—50 percent of the real options challenge is simply thinking about it, 25 percent is the modeling, and the remaining 25 percent is explaining the results to management. I am convinced that with the advent of my software, Real Options Analysis Toolkit, books such as this one (that demystifies real options, rather than cloud it with academic jargon and unnecessary complexities), and seminars and trainings like the ones I have held worldwide, the learning curve will be traversed even more quickly and real options will be accepted as widely as discounted cash flow modeling within the next few decades.

JOHNATHAN MUN, PH.D.

Denver, Colorado
JohnathanMun@cs.com
February 2003

About the Author

Dr. Johnathan C. Mun is currently the vice president of Analytical Services at Decisioneering, Inc., the makers of Real Options Analysis Toolkit and the Crystal Ball suite of products, including applications of Monte Carlo simulation, optimization, and forecasting. He heads up the development of real options and financial analytics software products, analytical consulting, training, and technical support. He is also a Visiting and Adjunct Professor and has taught courses in financial management, investments, real options, economics, and statistics at the undergraduate and the graduate M.B.A. levels. He has taught at universities all over the world, from the University of Applied Sciences (Switzerland) to Golden Gate University (California) and St. Mary's College (California). Prior to joining Decisioneering, he was a consulting manager and financial economist in the Valuation Services and Global Financial Services practice of KPMG Consulting (now Bearing Point) and a manager with the Economic Consulting Services practice at KPMG LLP. He has extensive experience in econometric modeling, financial analysis, real options, economic analysis, forecasting, and statistics. During his tenure both at Decisioneering and at KPMG Consulting, he consulted on real options and financial valuation for many Fortune 100 firms. His experience prior to joining KPMG included being department head of financial planning and analysis at Viking Inc. of FedEx, performing financial forecasting, economic analysis, and market research. Prior to that, he had also performed some financial planning and freelance financial consulting work.

Dr. Mun received his Ph.D. in finance and economics from Lehigh University, where his research and academic interests were in the areas of investment finance, econometric modeling, financial options, corporate finance, and microeconomic theory. He also has an M.B.A. from Nova Southeastern University and a B.S. in biology and physics from the University of Miami. He is certified in financial risk management (FRM) and in financial consulting (CFC), and is currently a Level III candidate for the Chartered Financial Analyst (CFA) Program. He is a member of the American Mensa, Phi Beta Kappa Honor Society, and Golden Key Honor Society, as well as several other professional organizations, including the Eastern and Southern Finance Associations, American Economic Association, and Global Association of Risk Professionals. Finally, he has written many academic articles published in the *Journal of the Advances in Quantitative Accounting and Finance, The Global Finance Journal, The International Financial Review, The Journal of Financial Analysis, Journal of the Society of Petroleum Engineers,* and *Financial Engineering News.*

Contents

Real Options
Analysis Course

CHAPTER 1

Installing the Software

INSTALLING CRYSTAL BALL MONTE CARLO SIMULATION SOFTWARE

To get started with the business cases, you first have to install the Crystal Ball® Monte Carlo simulation software. The Crystal Ball software needs to be installed prior to installing the Real Options Analysis Toolkit software covered in the next section. You do not have to install Crystal Ball if you have a previous version already installed. The version of Crystal Ball on the accompanying CD-ROM requires a minimum of Microsoft Windows 2000 or later, Microsoft Excel 97 or later, 10 MB hard drive space, and 64 MB RAM to run.

Exit all other programs before starting the installation process. To start the installation process, browse the contents of the CD-ROM. Open the *Crystal Ball Software* folder and double-click on the *setup.exe* file (Figure 1.1). You will then be greeted with an installation welcome screen as seen in

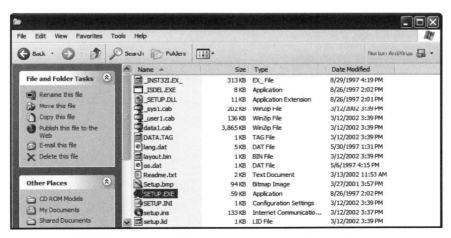

FIGURE 1.1 Setup folder contents for Crystal Ball software.

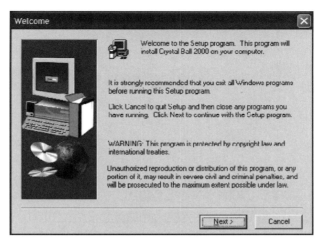

FIGURE 1.2   Program setup welcome screen.

Figure 1.2. Click on the *Next* button to continue with the installation process.

The installation process will then prompt you for your name, company name, and a registration number as seen in Figure 1.3. Leave the registration code field empty for a trial period, or enter a valid registration number if you have purchased a full version of the software. Click on the *Next* button to continue with the installation process. You will then be prompted with several installation and start-up preferences. For simplicity, select the recom-

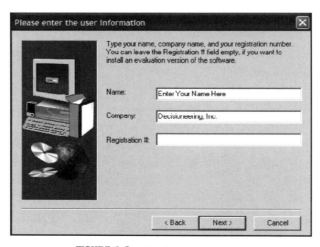

FIGURE 1.3   Registration screen.

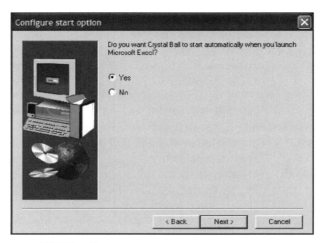

FIGURE 1.4   Start option configuration screen.

mended default setup settings, that is, set Crystal Ball to start every time Microsoft Excel is launched. Click on the *Next* button to continue with the installation process (Figure 1.4).

The installer will automatically locate the directory where Microsoft Excel resides. If you have multiple versions of Microsoft Excel and you wish to use Crystal Ball only with a particular version, then click on the *Browse* button to locate the folder with the specific version of Microsoft Excel. Otherwise, click on the *Next* button to continue (Figure 1.5). Choose the

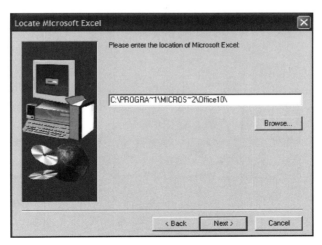

FIGURE 1.5   Microsoft Excel location prompt at setup.

destination folder to install the software. Unless there are specific reasons, such as low disk space or installing on servers, use the default installation location and click on *Next* (Figure 1.6).

You will then be prompted to select the components to install. Crystal Ball 2000 is a required component to run simulations. CB Predictor is a time-series forecasting utility. Crystal Ball Tools is a collection of power tools ranging from Tornado Charts and Sensitivity Analysis to Nonparametric Bootstrap Simulation. OptQuest for Crystal Ball is a stochastic optimization tool. Developer Kit for Crystal Ball is a collection of functions available through Visual Basic for Applications (VBA) in Microsoft Excel. Keep the default settings to select *all* the components for installation and click *Next* (Figure 1.7). When the installation is complete, you will be notified (Figure 1.8). Click on *Finish* to complete and exit the process. The entire installation process may take from 3 minutes to 10 minutes, depending on the speed of your computer.

Now, to verify that the installation procedure has been successful, click on the *Start* button in Microsoft Windows, select *Programs* and *Crystal Ball*. You will then see some supporting materials including examples and help files. Click on *Crystal Ball* to launch the software (Figure 1.9). When the software starts for the very first time, you will see an end-user license agreement (Figure 1.10). Read through the agreement and click on *Accept* to get started. If the installation process had been successful, you will see the Crystal Ball splash screen appear momentarily (Figure 1.11).

The software will also start Microsoft Excel. You should notice a new Crystal Ball icon toolbar in Microsoft Excel (Figure 1.12). In addition, three

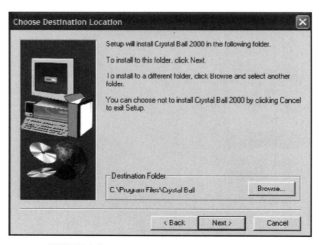

FIGURE 1.6   Choose setup location screen.

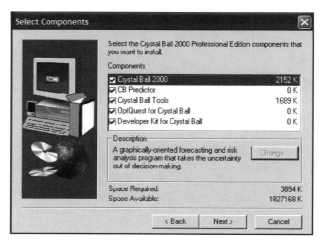

FIGURE 1.7 Component selection screen at setup.

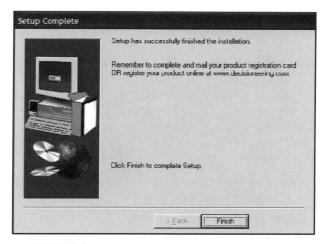

FIGURE 1.8 Setup completion verification screen.

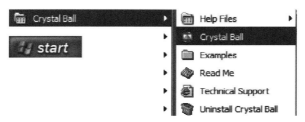

FIGURE 1.9 Location of the Crystal Ball software.

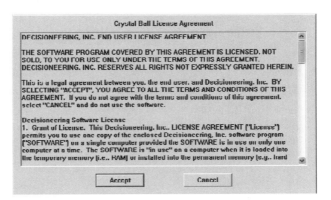

FIGURE 1.10   License acceptance screen.

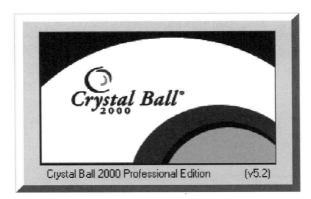

FIGURE 1.11   Crystal Ball splash screen.

FIGURE 1.12   Crystal Ball icon bar.

new menu bar items will be added to Microsoft Excel (Figure 1.13). If these elements do not appear, click on *Tools* and select *Add-Ins* (Figure 1.14).

Make sure the box beside Crystal Ball is checked and click *OK* (Figure 1.15). You are now ready to install the Real Options Analysis Toolkit software and begin the exercises. Refer to Chapter 2, Getting Started with the Software, to begin using the software.

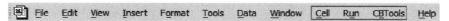

FIGURE 1.13   Crystal Ball menu bar in Microsoft Excel.

FIGURE 1.14   Menu item in Microsoft Excel.

FIGURE 1.15   Add-ins dialog box in Microsoft Excel.

INSTALLING REAL OPTIONS ANALYSIS
TOOLKIT SOFTWARE

I recommend that you install the Crystal Ball software before installing the Real Options Analysis Toolkit, and that you exit all other programs before starting the installation process. To start the installation process, browse the contents of the CD-ROM. Open the *Real Options Software* folder and double-click on the *setup.exe* file (Figure 1.16). (You need to have administrative rights before you can install the software. Please see an IT professional if you are unsure if you have these rights on the computer.)

The installer then searches your computer for the Microsoft .NET Framework, a required component to run the Real Options Analysis Toolkit software. If the Microsoft .NET Framework does not exist, you will be prompted to install it by first accepting the Microsoft licensing agreement (Figure 1.17). Confirm the installation of the Microsoft .NET Framework package by selecting *Yes* when prompted (Figure 1.18). Then, simply follow the instructions by keeping all the default settings and clicking on *Next* when prompted (Figure 1.19). You will be updated on the amount of time remaining during the installation process (Figure 1.20), and notified when the installation is complete (Figure 1.21). Depending on your system configuration, the installation process for the Microsoft .NET Framework may take from 3 minutes to 20 minutes.

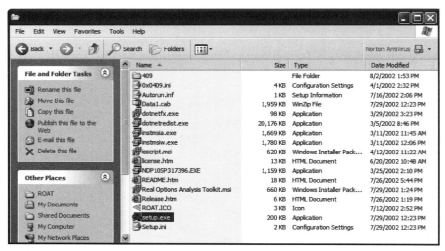

FIGURE 1.16   Setup folder contents for Real Options Analysis Toolkit software.

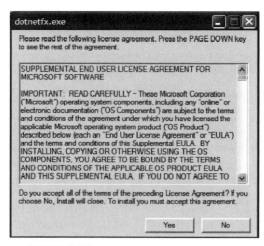

FIGURE 1.17 License acceptance screen.

FIGURE 1.18 Microsoft .NET Framework installation confirmation.

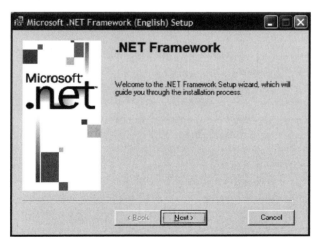

FIGURE 1.19 Microsoft .NET Framework setup screen.

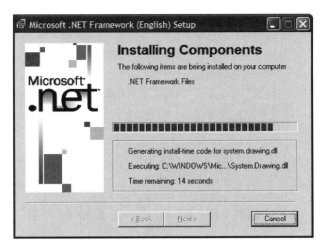

FIGURE 1.20 Microsoft .NET Setup status screen.

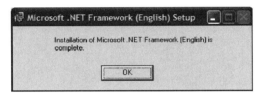

FIGURE 1.21 Microsoft .NET Setup completion verification screen.

After the Microsoft .NET Framework is installed, the Real Options Analysis Toolkit software installation starts automatically. If it does not, simply rerun the *setup.exe* file by double-clicking on the file located in the Real Options folder. Click on *Next* to continue with the installation (Figure 1.22).

Read the end-user licensing agreement and click *Yes* if you agree with the statement and to continue with the installation process (Figure 1.23). Then, enter your name and company name, and click *Next* to continue

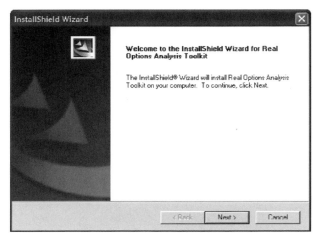

FIGURE 1.22   Real Options Analysis Toolkit software setup welcome screen.

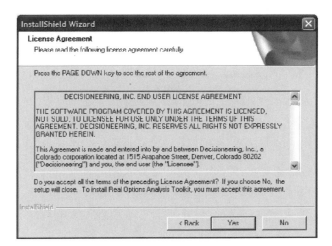

FIGURE 1.23   License acceptance screen.

(Figure 1.24). Keep the default installation location unless you are restricted by free hard drive space. Click *Next* to continue (Figure 1.25). Select *Typical* Setup Type when prompted to install all the required components as well as documentation and example files. These files are required for the exercises. Click *Next* to continue (Figure 1.26). You will be notified when the installation is complete. Restart your computer before using the software by

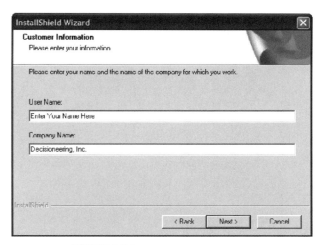

FIGURE 1.24   Registration screen.

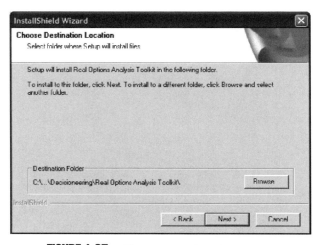

FIGURE 1.25   Choose setup location screen.

selecting *Yes* and clicking *Finish* (Figure 1.27). (Certain computer configu-
rations may require the user to reinsert the CD-ROM after rebooting is
complete.)

After restarting, verify that the installation process was successful by
clicking on *Start* in Microsoft Windows, selecting *Programs*, *Crystal Ball*,
Real Options Analysis Toolkit, and *Toolkit* (Figure 1.28). If the installation
process has been successful, the software will launch Microsoft Excel and

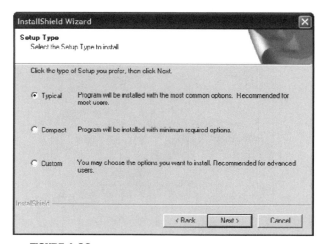

FIGURE 1.26 Component selection screen at setup.

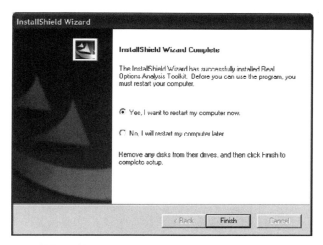

FIGURE 1.27 Setup completion verification screen.

FIGURE 1.28 Location of the Real Options Analysis Toolkit software.

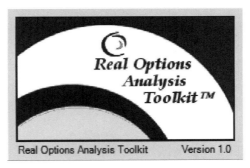

FIGURE 1.29   Real Options Analysis Toolkit splash screen.

the splash screen in Figure 1.29 appears momentarily. Then the screen in Figure 1.30 appears. When prompted for a registration number, leave it empty for a trial period or enter the full version registration number if you purchased the software. You may contact www.crystalball.com to obtain an extended trial period registration code. Refer to Chapter 2, Getting Started with the Software, on how to get started using the software.

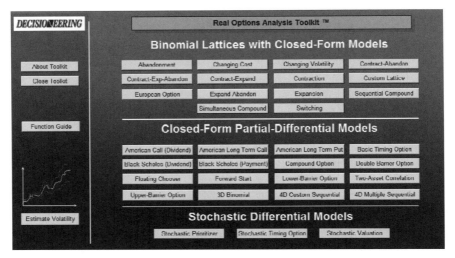

FIGURE 1.30   Real Options Analysis Toolkit software main welcome screen.

Getting Started
with the Software

GETTING STARTED WITH
CRYSTAL BALL SOFTWARE

The following exercise helps you get started using the Crystal Ball Monte Carlo simulation software. Start by opening an example spreadsheet. Click on *Start*, *Programs*, *Crystal Ball*, and choose *Examples* (Figure 2.1). The software comes with multiple sample Excel spreadsheets. Double-click on *Magazine Sales.xls* to start the example shown in Figure 2.2. The Crystal Ball splash screen in Figure 2.3 should appear momentarily.

FIGURE 2.1   Location of the Crystal Ball Software's example files.

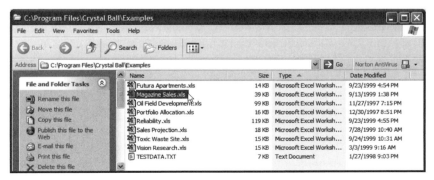

FIGURE 2.2   Contents for Crystal Ball Software's example folder.

FIGURE 2.3   Crystal Ball splash screen.

The Simulation Environment

The Crystal Ball toolbar in Figure 2.4 should appear in Microsoft Excel. To get started and to run a simple simulation, we are only concerned with three functions: *Define Assumption*, *Define Forecast*, and *Run Simulation*. Every Monte Carlo simulation analysis requires a minimum of these three sets of commands. (If the toolbar or splash screen does not appear, click on *Tools* and select *Add-Ins*. Then make sure the check box beside *Crystal Ball* is selected, and click *OK*.)

Defining an assumption means selecting a cell in Excel populated with a simple numerical entry and assigning a relevant distribution to it. Defining a forecast means to select a cell with a numerical equation and requesting Crystal Ball to capture its output results. Running a simulation means the program initiates a Monte Carlo simulation of thousands of trials (depending on the specified number of trials to run), randomly selecting numbers from the assigned distribution, and keying these random numbers into the selected assumption cell. The resulting calculations in the forecast cell are then captured in the software.

The example you opened looks at the levels of magazine checkout sales as seen in Figure 2.5. Four different magazines are listed, complete with the sales volume, retail price, and cost of goods. The resulting gross profit is then calculated. The sum of the gross profits for each magazine is calculated as $5,832.

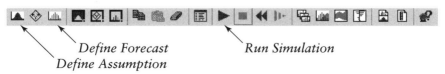

Define Forecast   *Run Simulation*
Define Assumption

FIGURE 2.4   Crystal Ball toolbar.

	Magazine A	Magazine B	Magazine C	Magazine D
Sales Volume	500	355	640	480
Retail Price	$4.95	$7.95	$3.95	$5.95
Cost of Goods	$2.20	$3.80	$1.95	$2.40
Gross Profit	$1,375	$1,473	$1,280	$1,704

Total Gross Profit: $5,832

FIGURE 2.5 Magazine checkout sales example Excel file.

Creating a Simulation

Now suppose that the projected sales volumes (the number of magazines sold) for Magazines A and B are unknown in some future period. We can perform Monte Carlo simulation on these sales volumes. First, select cell C5, which has the sales volume forecast. Click on *Define Assumption* on the Crystal Ball toolbar. A Distribution Gallery will appear, with a series of different distributions. For simplicity, assume that Magazine A's sales volume follows a triangular distribution. Select *Triangular* and click *OK* (Figure 2.6).

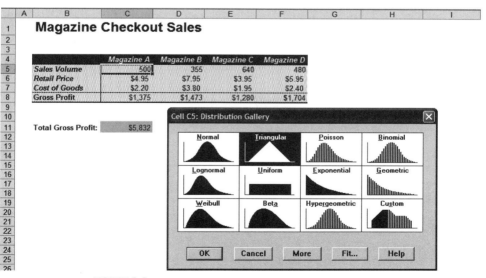

FIGURE 2.6 Magazine checkout sales example Excel file with Crystal Ball's Distribution Gallery.

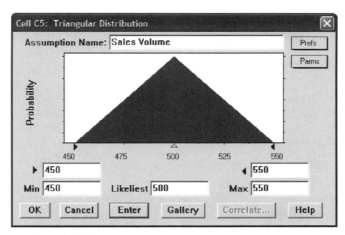

FIGURE 2.7   Triangular distribution for sales volume.

You will be prompted to enter the parameters in the triangular distribution (Figure 2.7). Suppose you know from historical sales that the worst-case scenario sales volume is 450 units, average sales volume is 500 units, and a best-case scenario is 550 units. Enter the appropriate values and click *OK*. Next, select cell D5 for the sales volume forecast of Magazine B. This time, select the *Normal* distribution as seen in Figure 2.8. You can now enter

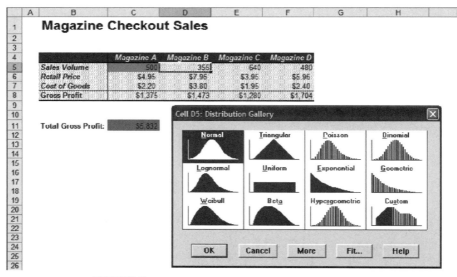

FIGURE 2.8   Magazine checkout sales example Excel file with Crystal Ball assumptions defined.

the mean and standard deviation of the normal distribution or, alternatively, you can click on the *Parms* button to locate the gallery of alternate parameters to enter. Select the *10%, 90%-tile* to change the input parameters to the 10th and 90th percentile (Figure 2.9). You can now input the relevant historical sales volumes that occurred the lowest 10 percent of the time, and the corresponding sales volume that occurred the highest 10 percent of the time. That is, 80 percent of the time, your historical sales volume was between 300 and 400 units (Figure 2.10).

Now that you have assigned distributions to the unknown variables, you will then need to define the forecast of your analysis. Select cell C11,

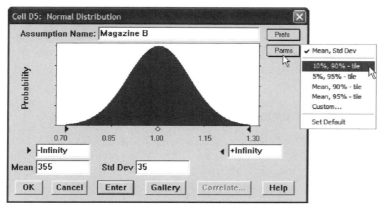

FIGURE 2.9 Crystal Ball's alternate parameters function.

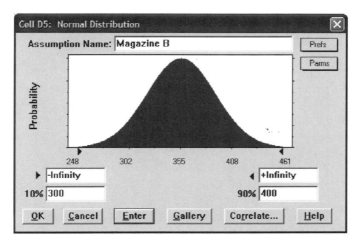

FIGURE 2.10 Crystal Ball's alternate parameters with 10th and 90th percentiles.

Cell C11: Define Forecast   ⊠

Forecast Name: Total Gross Profit

Units: Dollars

OK   Cancel   More >>   Help

FIGURE 2.11   Defining a forecast cell in Crystal Ball.

which has the total gross profit of the magazine sales. Then, click on *Define Forecast* in the Crystal Ball toolbar. Enter in the relevant name and units for this forecast. Click *OK* (Figure 2.11).

You are now ready to run a simulation. Click on the *Run Simulation* icon. The Excel spreadsheet should now come to life and a forecast chart will appear. If the forecast chart does not appear, simply click on *Run, Forecast Windows*, and select *Open All Forecasts*.

Interpreting the Simulation Results

Once the simulation process is complete, you can type 90 in the Certainty box of the forecast chart and hit enter. The 90 percent confidence interval now appears (Figure 2.12), indicating that 90 percent of the time the total gross profit of selling four magazines where the sales volumes of the first two magazines are uncertain falls between $5,522 and $6,081.

In addition, you can type in a gross revenue value, say 6,000 on the right confidence tail, hit enter and obtain an 86.80 percent certainty level, which

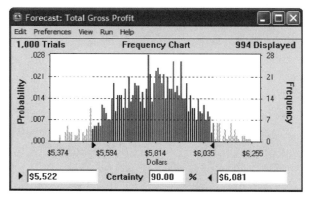

FIGURE 2.12   Forecast chart for total gross profit with a 90 percent confidence interval.

means that there is an 86.80 percent chance that total gross revenues will be below $6,000 or a 13.20 percent chance total gross revenues will exceed $6,000 (Figure 2.13). (You may need to type 100 in the certainty box before proceeding with the $6,000 example.)

Similarly, you can drag the certainty grabbers (black triangle straddling the horizontal axis in Figure 2.14) to obtain a particular certainty level or dollar confidence value. For instance, the value at risk is $5,444, such that 2 percent of the time, the worst-case scenario indicates that total gross profits will be at least this level. Other output statistics are also available by hitting the spacebar on your keyboard. For instance, the table in Figure 2.15 provides the basic statistics of the simulated total gross profit.

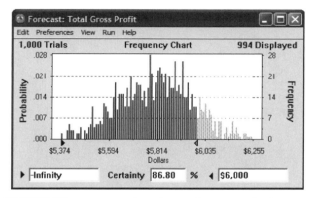

FIGURE 2.13 Forecast chart for total gross profit showing the probability of less than $6,000.

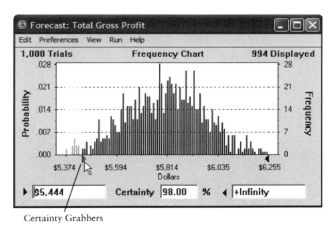

FIGURE 2.14 Forecast chart's certainty grabbers.

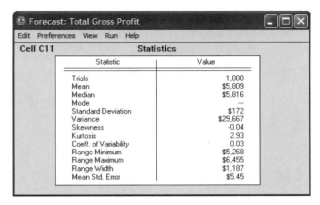

FIGURE 2.15   Forecast chart's statistics view.

GETTING STARTED WITH REAL OPTIONS ANALYSIS TOOLKIT SOFTWARE

The Modeling Interface

Click on *Start*, *Programs*, *Crystal Ball*, *Real Options Analysis Toolkit*, and select *Toolkit* (Figure 2.16). The toolkit main welcome screen now appears as illustrated in Figure 2.17. Make sure you select *Enable Macros* if prompted. The models are aggregated into three distinct categories: *Binomial Lattices with Closed-Form Models*, *Closed-Form Partial-Differential Models*, and *Stochastic Differential Models*. The first category of models uses the binomial approach, in concert with closed-form models. These two approaches are used together to confirm the analytical results. The second category of models consists purely of closed-form models or binomial lattice models performed in isolation. The last category of models focuses on stochastic-modeling techniques.

A simple example is now in order. Click on the *Abandonment* option button from the main welcome screen. The American Abandonment Option

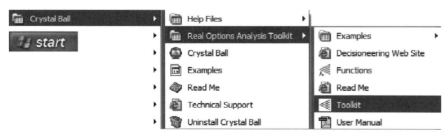

FIGURE 2.16   Location of the Real Options Analysis Toolkit software.

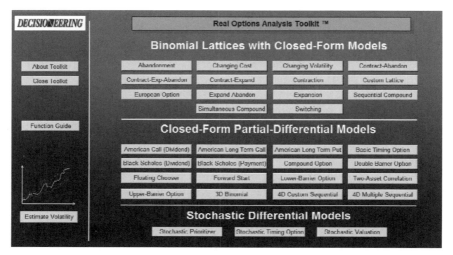

FIGURE 2.17 Real Options Analysis Toolkit software main welcome screen.

model will now appear as seen in Figure 2.18. This modeling screen is similar to most of the models in the software, that is, there is a title bar, input parameters box, intermediate calculations box, results box, Main and Help buttons, options payoff graphics, pricing and valuation lattices, and a decision lattice. Take a moment to familiarize yourself with the modeling environment. Notice that there is a Help button that will provide the user more detailed information on the model currently in use.

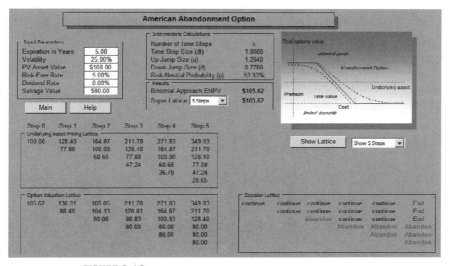

FIGURE 2.18 American Abandonment Option model.

In this example, suppose a firm owns a piece of land (or any asset, patent, or intangible) in a highly liquid and volatile market. Suppose the land is currently worth $100 million (*PV Asset Value*) in the market today. If the analyst prices the land at $100 million, it may be underpriced due to the fluctuation in the market. That is, prices can be significantly higher or lower than this $100 million value (due to the *Volatility* of 25 percent), as well as there may exist options that have not been considered (building a parking structure, building a shopping mall, leaving the land undeveloped for the future, etc.). Suppose the firm decides to hedge its bets against a potential market downside by creating an abandonment option by negotiating a contract with another firm or potential buyer, whereby for a setup fee (say, $50,000) this potential buyer agrees contractually, to purchase this piece of land from your firm at any time within the next 5 years (*Expiration in Years*) for a discounted price of $80 million (*Salvage Value*). Of course, the decision to sell the land is strictly at the prerogative of the firm that owns the land, while the potential buyer is obliged to purchase the land (to obtain the discount and the setup contractual fee). Effectively, your firm has created an abandonment option, a safety net, or an insurance policy of sorts, where if the price in the market exceeds its current levels (say, $200 million), sell the land in the market and let the contract expire (capture the upside of $100 million and lose only the $50,000 fee). Otherwise, if market prices are depressed to anything lower than the contractual salvage value (say, $50 million), call the potential buyer and execute the abandonment option, thereby reducing the risk of a downside. Hence, this insurance policy limits the minimum amount the firm will obtain selling this piece of land at $80 million. The calculated value of the land with this option is $105.62 million (*Binomial Approach ENPV*). The additional $5.62 million is the strategic abandonment option value—the price of the $80 million insurance, or the maximum value that the firm should be willing to pay to the potential buyer in order to obtain the contract. This also provides the firm with a great negotiation tool. Imagine if the counterparty does not perform this analysis but you do—providing you with competitive advantage and valuable strategic knowledge of the contract's true value.

As further illustration, if the salvage value is changed to $10 million, the option value becomes $0 and the piece of land is worth $100 million, as given such a low safety net, the market will never bear a price any lower than this $10 million and the safety net is never utilized, making the option worthless. Conversely, setting the salvage value to $300 million will change the value of the land to $300 million—this means you forget about the option and sell it immediately to the potential buyer, who is currently willing to pay you three times the market value! Finally, setting the volatility to 1 percent will yield a land value of $100 million—if uncertainty is negligible (if real estate prices hardly fluctuate, the option is not worth anything, and the price of land will probably stay at a constant $100 million for the fore-seeable future). Other related applications include putting in exit and aban-donment clauses or caveats in contracts, thereby increasing a contract's value.

Let us now look at each section in detail. The first is the Input Parame-ters section (Figure 2.19). Here, the relevant parameter can be typed in di-rectly or linked in from another spreadsheet. This area is characterized by its white background. A set of sample input parameters exists as a guide.

Entering an incorrect input (e.g., negative values or non-numeric values for certain inputs are not allowed) will yield a warning message as shown in Figure 2.20. Assuming that all the inputs are correct, the Intermediate Cal-culations section shows the time-step, up-jump size, down-jump size, and risk-neutral probability calculations for a predetermined five-step binomial lattice (Figure 2.21).

The resulting real options value calculated using the five-step binomial approach is shown in the Results section. The value shown is the Expanded Net Present Value (ENPV), which is the net present value (NPV) plus the value of the strategic option. The value for the Super Lattice calculation is set to default to five-steps, indicating the same result as the binomial five-step lattice (Figure 2.22).

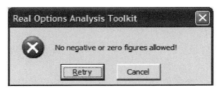

Input Parameters	
Expiration in Years	5.00
Volatility	25.00%
PV Asset Value	$100.00
Risk-Free Rate	5.00%
Dividend Rate	0.00%
Salvage Value	$80.00

FIGURE 2.19   Input Parameters for the American Abandonment Option.

Real Options Analysis Toolkit

No negative or zero figures allowed!

Retry   Cancel

FIGURE 2.20   Sample error message dialog.

Intermediate Calculations	
Number of Time Steps	5
Time Step Size (dt)	1.0000
Up Jump Size (u)	1.2840
Down Jump Size (d)	0.7788
Risk-Neutral Probability (p)	53.93%

FIGURE 2.21   Intermediate calculations for the American Abandonment Option.

FIGURE 2.22   Results from the American Abandonment Option.

The drop-down box seen in Figure 2.23 beside the Super Lattice approach provides the user a choice to change the number of steps to perform using a binomial lattice. For instance, if 1,000 steps are chosen, the results indicate that the abandonment option's ENPV is $105.87. The reader will see later that the higher the number of steps, the more granular the lattice and the higher the accuracy of the lattice results. (Manually creating a binomial lattice with 1,000 steps may take months to calculate, as compared to less than a few seconds using the software.)

Another section of interest is the Underlying Asset Pricing Lattice (Figure 2.24). This shows the simple predetermined five-step binomial lattice of the underlying asset. The Option Valuation Lattice shows the step-by-step option valuation using a process called backward induction (Figure 2.25). Please refer to my previous book, *Real Options Analysis*, for details on the specifics of creating and interpreting binomial lattices. There is also a section in the model for the Decision Lattice as shown in Figure 2.26, which calculates the optimal decision for when and if to execute the abandonment option.

Results		
Binomial Approach ENPV		**$105.62**
Super Lattice	1000 Steps ▼	**$105.87**
	5 Steps	
	10 Steps	
	50 Steps	
	100 Steps	
	300 Steps	
	500 Steps	
	1000 Steps	
	5000 Steps	

FIGURE 2.23   Super Lattice drop-down box.

Underlying Asset Pricing Lattice					
100.00	128.40	164.87	211.70	271.83	349.03
	77.88	100.00	128.40	164.87	211.70
		60.65	77.88	100.00	128.40
			47.24	60.65	77.88
				36.79	47.24
					28.65

FIGURE 2.24   Underlying Asset Pricing Lattice for the
American Abandonment Option.

Option Valuation Lattice

105.62	130.31	165.05	211.70	271.83	349.03
	88.48	104.13	128.81	164.87	211.70
		80.00	86.83	100.93	128.40
			80.00	80.00	80.00
				80.00	80.00
					80.00

FIGURE 2.25 Option Valuation Lattice for the American Abandonment Option.

Decision Lattice

continue	continue	continue	continue	continue	End
	continue	continue	continue	continue	End
		Abandon	continue	continue	End
			Abandon	Abandon	Abandon
				Abandon	Abandon
					Abandon

FIGURE 2.26 Decision Lattice for the American Abandonment Option.

The Lattice Viewer

If a higher number of time-steps is required, the user can select the relevant number of steps to show in the lattice (Figure 2.27). Clicking on *Show Lattice* will provide a view of the binomial lattice in a separate window (Figure 2.28). The underlying asset pricing lattice is shown as the first number on the lattice and the option valuation lattice as the second number. The decision lattice is also shown with different colors based on the optimal decision at each node.

Notice that the preferences on the lattice viewer can be changed by clicking on the *Tree Prefs* or *Node Prefs* icon on the toolbar. For instance, click on *Node Prefs* and deselect the *Draw Border* under the Symbol section, and *Colorize Nodes by Option Type* under the Options section, and click *OK* (Figure 2.29). The lattice viewer will change to take into account the

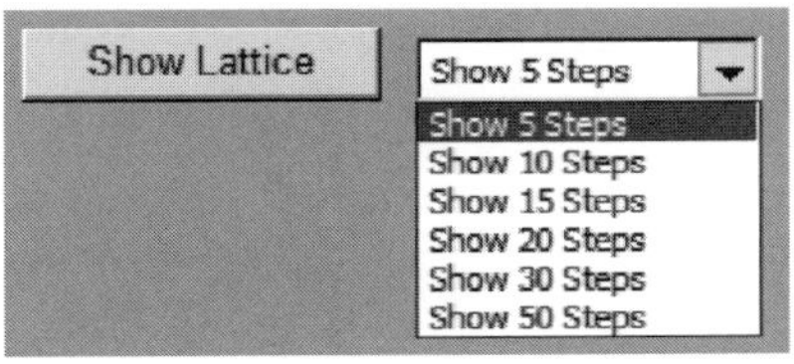

FIGURE 2.27 Show Lattice drop-down list.

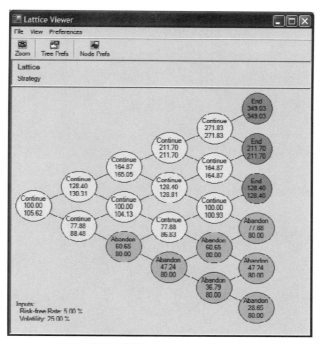

FIGURE 2.28   Lattice viewer.

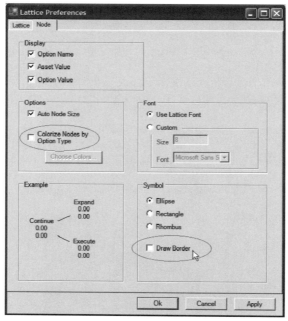

FIGURE 2.29   Lattice viewer's preferences dialog box.

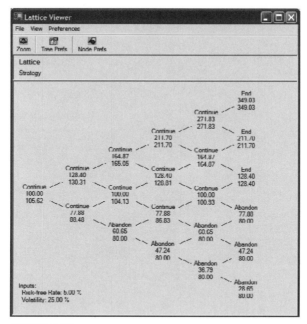

FIGURE 2.30   Lattice viewer with updated preferences.

changes in the preferences as seen in Figure 2.30. Close the lattice viewer by selecting the File, Close Window on the menu bar.

The Help Environment

In addition, the user can click on *Help* to visit the help tips for the abandonment option model. The scroll text provides the user a quick reference for the option model. In addition, moving the mouse over the numerical values with red triangular tags will provide the user additional information on what each numerical value represents (Figure 2.31). Return to the abandonment model by clicking *Close Help*. Return to the main welcome screen by clicking on *Main*. Notice that an extended user manual is also available in the software (click on *Start, Programs, Crystal Ball, Real Options Analysis Toolkit,* and select *User Manual*).

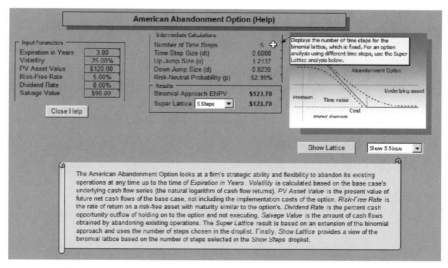

FIGURE 2.31   Help screen for the American Abandonment Option.

Solving Customized Options

Note: Foreign Excel and Windows settings may deactivate this module. To reactivate the custom lattice module, change your computer's regional settings to English USA.

From the main welcome screen, select *Custom Lattice* to launch the customized options analysis model. Click on *Step 1: Reset Sheet* to reset the spreadsheet before creating a customized option model. This step is important because any prior input parameters will be cleared from memory. Then, click on *Step 2: Enter Starting Asset Value* and you will see the dialog box in Figure 2.32 appear. Click on *OK* and enter a starting value for the pricing lattice, which is the present value of future cash flows. Type *100* and hit enter (Figure 2.33). Then, click on *Step 3: Create Pricing Lattice* and you will be prompted for more information as seen in Figure 2.34.

FIGURE 2.32   Custom Lattice's second-step message box.

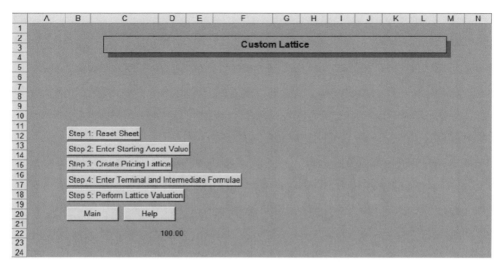

FIGURE 2.33   Custom Lattice.

FIGURE 2.34   Custom Lattice's setup dialog for creating a pricing lattice.

Enter the cell reference (e.g., D22) that contains the "*100*" value previously entered. Enter the additional parameters requested, such as volatility in percent, maturity in years, risk-free rate in percent, dividends in percent, and the number of steps. Click *Create* and the pricing lattice will be created, together with a summary of the input parameters (Figure 2.35).

Then click on *Step 4: Enter Terminal and Intermediate Formulae* to continue. A dialog box will provide further information as shown in Figure

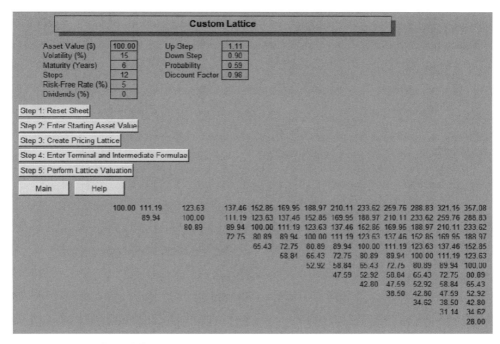

FIGURE 2.35   Custom Lattice with a calculated pricing lattice.

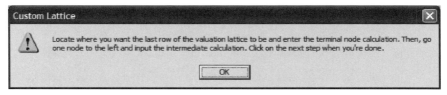

FIGURE 2.36   Custom lattice's fourth-step message box.

2.36. Click *OK*. The next step is to enter the customized valuation lattice equations, first for the terminal nodes and then for the intermediate nodes. In cell P36, type in the terminal period formula; for example, type in

$$=MAX(P22-100,0)$$

where *P22* refers to the corresponding node on the pricing lattice and 100 is the cost to execute this option. Then, in cell O36, enter in the intermediate formula (Figure 2.37); for example, type in

$$=MAX((0.5926*P36 + (1-0.5926)*P37)*0.9753, O22-100)$$

	C	D	E	F	G	H	I	J	K	L	M	N	O	P
21														
22		100.00	111.19	123.63	137.46	152.85	169.95	188.97	210.11	233.62	259.76	288.83	321.15	357.08
23			89.94	100.00	111.19	123.63	137.46	152.85	169.95	188.97	210.11	233.62	259.76	288.83
24				80.89	89.94	100.00	111.19	123.63	137.46	152.85	169.95	188.97	210.11	233.62
25					72.75	80.89	89.94	100.00	111.19	123.63	137.46	152.85	169.95	188.97
26						65.43	72.75	80.89	89.94	100.00	111.19	123.63	137.46	152.85
27							58.84	65.43	72.75	80.89	89.94	100.00	111.19	123.63
28								52.92	58.84	65.43	72.75	80.89	89.94	100.00
29									47.59	52.92	58.84	65.43	72.75	80.89
30										42.80	47.59	52.92	58.84	65.43
31											38.50	42.80	47.59	52.92
32												34.62	38.50	42.80
33													31.14	34.62
34														28.00
35														
36													221.15	257.08

FIGURE 2.37   Custom Lattice with sample terminal and intermediate calculations.

where 0.5926 is the risk-neutral probability based on the previous inputs and 0.9753 is the discount factor (top of Figure 2.35).

Then click on *Step 5: Perform Lattice Valuation* and you will be prompted with the dialog box shown in Figure 2.38. Enter or select the cell with the terminal formula (e.g., P36) and enter or select the cell with the intermediate formula (e.g., O36), enter the number of steps corresponding to the number of steps entered previously when generating the pricing lattice, and click on *Value!* to create the valuation lattice. The value of this simple option is $29.26 as shown in Figure 2.39.

Using the same approach, the user can create multiple and complex custom option types easily and effectively by merely entering the correct terminal and intermediate formulas for each successive valuation lattice. Similarly, uncertainties in pricing, demand, competition, market share, and so forth can be modeled through successive lattices.

FIGURE 2.38   Custom Lattice's setup dialog for creating a pricing lattice.

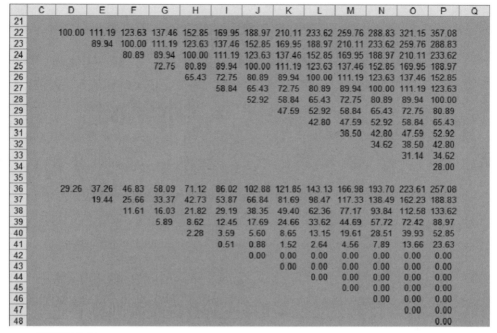

	C	D	E	F	G	H	I	J	K	L	M	N	O	P	Q
21															
22		100.00	111.19	123.63	137.46	152.85	169.95	188.97	210.11	233.62	259.76	288.83	321.15	357.08	
23			89.94	100.00	111.19	123.63	137.46	152.85	169.95	188.97	210.11	233.62	259.76	288.83	
24				80.89	89.94	100.00	111.19	123.63	137.46	152.85	169.95	188.97	210.11	233.62	
25					72.75	80.89	89.94	100.00	111.19	123.63	137.46	152.85	169.95	188.97	
26						65.43	72.75	80.89	89.94	100.00	111.19	123.63	137.46	152.85	
27							58.84	65.43	72.75	80.89	89.94	100.00	111.19	123.63	
28								52.92	58.84	65.43	72.75	80.89	89.94	100.00	
29									47.59	52.92	58.84	65.43	72.75	80.89	
30										42.80	47.59	52.92	58.84	65.43	
31											38.50	42.80	47.59	52.92	
32												34.62	38.50	42.80	
33													31.14	34.62	
34														28.00	
35															
36		29.26	37.26	46.83	58.09	71.12	86.02	102.88	121.85	143.13	166.98	193.70	223.61	257.08	
37			19.44	25.66	33.37	42.73	53.87	66.84	81.69	98.47	117.33	138.49	162.23	188.83	
38				11.61	16.03	21.82	29.19	38.35	49.40	62.36	77.17	93.84	112.58	133.62	
39					5.89	8.62	12.45	17.69	24.66	33.62	44.69	57.72	72.42	88.97	
40						2.28	3.59	5.60	8.65	13.15	19.61	28.51	39.93	52.85	
41							0.51	0.88	1.52	2.64	4.56	7.89	13.66	23.63	
42								0.00	0.00	0.00	0.00	0.00	0.00	0.00	
43									0.00	0.00	0.00	0.00	0.00	0.00	
44										0.00	0.00	0.00	0.00	0.00	
45											0.00	0.00	0.00	0.00	
46												0.00	0.00	0.00	
47													0.00	0.00	
48														0.00	

FIGURE 2.39   Custom Lattice with calculated pricing lattice and valuation lattice.

Accessing the Functions, Running Simulations, and Optimization

Note: Functions are only accessible in the full version of the software.

If the user requires access only to the functions and results, as well as to run Monte Carlo simulation or optimization, the user should then first exit the Real Options Analysis Toolkit software by exiting Excel. Open any existing Excel spreadsheet. For instance, click on *Start, Programs, Crystal Ball, Real Options Analysis Toolkit, Examples,* and choose *Simulation* (Figure 2.40). The spreadsheet shown in Figure 2.41 appears. The spreadsheet example is a simple discounted cash flow (DCF) model with the appropriate resulting NPV. Suppose this is the user's own spreadsheet that requires additional real options analysis. To perform a real options analysis on this existing model, launch the real options functions by clicking on *Start, Programs, Crystal Ball, Real Options Analysis Toolkit,* and select *Functions* (Figure 2.42). A splash screen will appear, indicating that the functions have been loaded into Excel.

Select cell D49 in the spreadsheet and click on Excel's paste function icon on the taskbar (Figure 2.43). Then, select the *Financial* category and

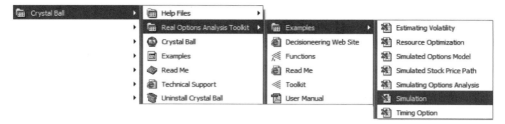

FIGURE 2.40 Location of the Real Options Analysis Toolkit software's example simulation model.

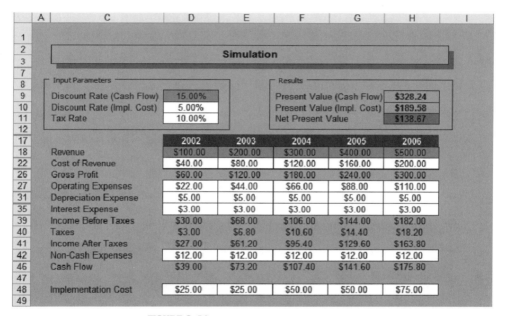

FIGURE 2.41 Sample simulation model.

FIGURE 2.42 Location of the Real Options Analysis Toolkit software's functions.

FIGURE 2.43 Excel's paste function icon.

scroll down the functions list until you come to the section that starts with the prefix *RO* (Figure 2.44). The functions with *RO* prefixes indicate the real options analysis functions that were loaded into Excel. Selecting any function on the list also provides a brief description of the function. Select the *ROBlackScholesCall* function and click *OK*.

The function arguments dialog box appears (Figure 2.45). You can now use the real options analysis function as you would any Excel function. Enter in the cell reference (H9) for the asset value, link the function to a cell (H10) for the cost value, or simply type the value in directly. When all the inputs are entered, and assuming the inputs are relevant, the results are indicated at the bottom of the dialog box. For example, the result is $212.01. Incorrect or irrelevant inputs will not yield an answer. Click *OK* and the result will be pasted into the existing Excel spreadsheet.

Note that for the expert user, the equation can be entered in directly; that is, in cell D49, the user can type (without spaces) the following and obtain the same $212.01 result:

$$=ROBlackScholesCall(H9,H10,5,D10,0.5)$$

The Real Options Analysis Toolkit Software Function Description for Excel in Chapter 9 lists all the models and corresponding input variables for all the real options analysis functions that are available.

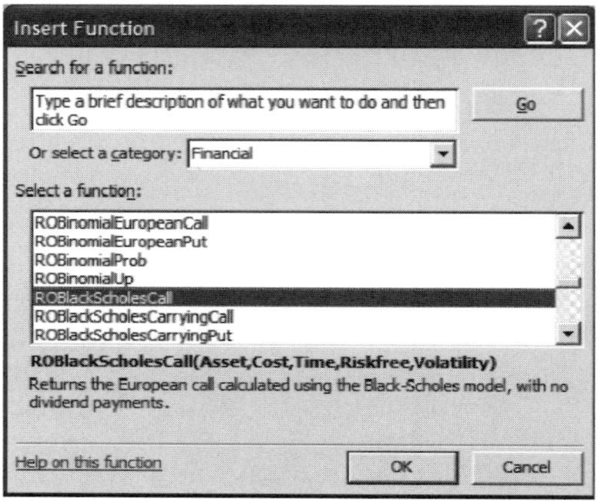

FIGURE 2.44 Microsoft Excel's insert function dialog box.

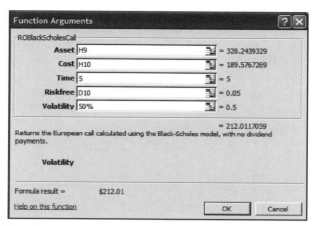

FIGURE 2.45   Microsoft Excel's function arguments dialog box for the Black-Scholes model.

Because the functions loaded are completely compatible with Microsoft Excel, the user can now perform Monte Carlo simulation or optimization using Crystal Ball. The simulation spreadsheet (Figure 2.46) used already has distributional assumptions assigned. However, the real options analysis function we pasted needs to be defined as a forecast. Select cell D49 with the

	C	D	E	F	G	H
				Simulation		
	Input Parameters			**Results**		
9	Discount Rate (Cash Flow)	15.00%		Present Value (Cash Flow)		$328.24
10	Discount Rate (Impl. Cost)	5.00%		Present Value (Impl. Cost)		$189.58
11	Tax Rate	10.00%		Net Present Value		$138.67
17		**2002**	**2003**	**2004**	**2005**	**2006**
18	Revenue	$100.00	$200.00	$300.00	$400.00	$500.00
22	Cost of Revenue	$40.00	$80.00	$120.00	$160.00	$200.00
26	Gross Profit	$60.00	$120.00	$180.00	$240.00	$300.00
27	Operating Expenses	$22.00	$44.00	$66.00	$88.00	$110.00
31	Depreciation Expense	$5.00	$5.00	$5.00	$5.00	$5.00
35	Interest Expense	$3.00	$3.00	$3.00	$3.00	$3.00
39	Income Before Taxes	$30.00	$68.00	$106.00	$144.00	$182.00
40	Taxes	$3.00	$6.80	$10.60	$14.40	$18.20
41	Income After Taxes	$27.00	$61.20	$95.40	$129.60	$163.80
42	Non-Cash Expenses	$12.00	$12.00	$12.00	$12.00	$12.00
46	Cash Flow	$39.00	$73.20	$107.40	$141.60	$175.80
48	Implementation Cost	$25.00	$25.00	$50.00	$50.00	$75.00
49	Option Value	$212.01				

FIGURE 2.46   Simulation example complete with defined assumptions and forecast.

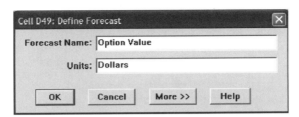

FIGURE 2.47   Defining a forecast on the calculated option value.

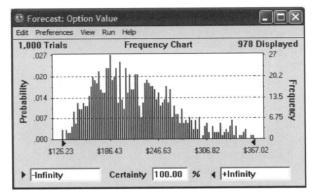

FIGURE 2.48   Forecast chart result of the option value.

option value and click on *Define Forecast* in the Crystal Ball toolbar. Provide a relevant name and units for the forecast and click *OK* (Figure 2.47). Then, click the *RUN* icon to initiate the simulation process. When the simulation is complete, the forecast chart in Figure 2.48 will be presented. The same interpretation applicable to any simulation result is also applicable here for real options.

CHAPTER 3

Framing Real Options

This chapter illustrates the simple stepwise procedures used in setting up and solving a real options problem. The analysis domain taken applies revenue forecasts and discounted cash flow (DCF) models, Monte Carlo simulation, real options analysis, resource allocation and portfolio optimization, and, finally, feedback modeling. The goals of the analysis are efficient portfolio management and continuous improvement of decisions over time (Figure 3.1).

The steps undertaken follow those illustrated in my previous book, *Real Options Analysis*, and are redefined in Figure 3.2. The decision analysis

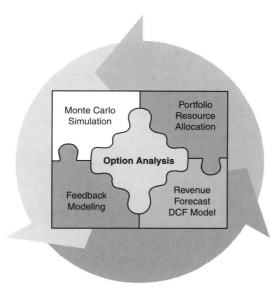

FIGURE 3.1 The analysis domain of real options.

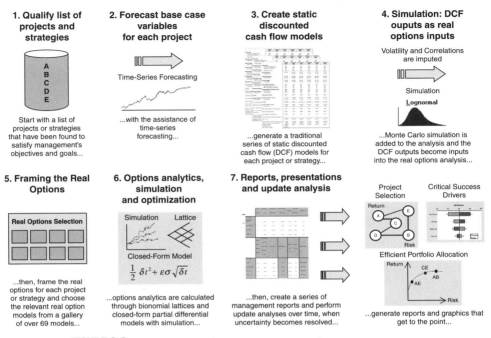

FIGURE 3.2   Decisions analysis process—procedure summary.

process is somewhat comprehensive and in the subsequent discussions, each step is broken down into substeps with examples from different industries and applications.

STEP 1: QUALIFY LIST OF PROJECTS AND STRATEGIES

In the first step, the analyst starts off with a list of qualified projects, that is, projects that have been through qualitative screening by management. Having met preset criteria, whether they are strategic visions or goals of the company, these are the projects that need to be analyzed. These projects may of course be different courses of actions, initiatives, or strategies. Here, management must understand the forces that drive their business decisions. Figure 3.3 shows an example of some forces that drive decision analysis in the energy sector, including growth in demand, heightened competition, volatile prices and supplies, and industry consolidation.

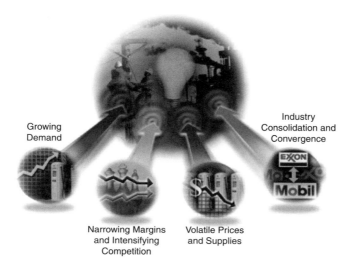

Growing
Demand

Industry
Consolidation and
Convergence

Narrowing Margins
and Intensifying
Competition

Volatile Prices
and Supplies

FIGURE 3.3   Forces driving change in the energy sector.

Having gone through this exercise, management may decide on projects and strategies that strengthen their competitive positioning, hedging downside price drops, or they may cut costs to compensate for narrowing margins or engage in mergers and acquisition. The projects and strategies that have been found to support management's goals, the firm's mission, or short-term tactical advantage will be qualified and allowed to proceed to the next step.

STEP 2: FORECAST BASE-CASE VARIABLES FOR EACH PROJECT

For each of these strategies or projects, the base-case net present value (NPV) analysis is performed, as indicated in steps two and three. This analysis could be done in terms of the market, income, or cost approach, using something akin to a DCF model. In certain circumstances, the analyst may elect to perform some intermediate steps such as time-series forecasting and simulation to predict future revenue and cost streams. Depending on the availability of historical data, some fancy econometric, forecasting, regression, time-series, cross-sectional, or stochastic model may be constructed for this purpose. Table 3.1 shows an example applying Crystal Ball Predictor to assist in the forecasting of revenues given historical data. The resulting revenue forecasts account for seasonality effects and the software

TABLE 3.1 Time-Series Forecasting

Historical Data		Forecast	
Date	Revenues	Date	Revenues
Q1 1997	30	Q1 2003	202.27
Q2 1997	35	Q2 2003	210.25
Q3 1997	42	Q3 2003	217.26
Q4 1997	49	Q4 2003	230.30
Q1 1998	50	Q1 2004	231.80
Q2 1998	57	Q2 2004	239.86
Q3 1998	63	Q3 2004	246.81
Q4 1998	72	Q4 2004	260.60
Q1 1999	80	Q1 2005	261.33
Q2 1999	85	Q2 2005	269.47
Q3 1999	92	Q3 2005	276.37
Q4 1999	112	Q4 2005	290.90
Q1 2000	120	Q1 2006	290.85
Q2 2000	135	Q2 2006	299.08
Q3 2000	144	Q3 2006	305.93
Q4 2000	156	Q4 2006	321.20
Q1 2001	153	Q1 2007	320.38
Q2 2001	166	Q2 2007	328.69
Q3 2001	178	Q3 2007	335.48
Q4 2001	180	Q4 2007	351.50
Q1 2002	178		
Q2 2002	185		
Q3 2002	190		
Q4 2002	200		

Note: Periodicity is quarterly and seasonality is four.

automatically inserts probability distributions around the future forecast values. See Chapter 7 for details.

STEP 3: CREATE STATIC DCF MODELS FOR EACH CASE

These initial steps encapsulate the traditional approach. Using the revenues and cost structures coupled with conventional accounting principles, the analyst would then calculate the NPV of the projects or strategies. Occasionally, other financial metrics may be used, such as an internal rate of return (IRR) or some form of return on investment (ROI) measure. In most cases,

Simple Discounted Cash Flow Model		

Input Parameters

Discount Rate (Cash Flow)	15.00%
Discount Rate (Impl. Cost)	5.00%
Tax Rate	10.00%

Results

Present Value (Cash Flow)	**$1,265.09**
Present Value (Impl. Cost)	**($865.90)**
Net Present Value	**$399.20**

Year	2003	2004	2005	2006	2007
Revenue	$860.08	$979.07	$1,098.06	$1,217.06	$1,336.05
Adjustment to Revenue	$51.60	$97.91	$197.65	$316.43	$467.62
Cost of Revenue	$86.01	$97.91	$109.81	$121.71	$133.60
Royalties Paid	$43.00	$48.95	$164.71	$182.56	$200.41
Gross Profit	$679.46	$734.30	$625.90	$596.36	$534.42
Operating Expenses	$135.89	$146.86	$125.18	$119.27	$106.88
Depreciation Expense	$10.00	$10.00	$10.00	$10.00	$10.00
Interest Expense	$100.00	$100.00	$100.00	$100.00	$100.00
Income Before Taxes	$433.57	$477.44	$390.72	$367.09	$317.54
Taxes	$43.36	$47.74	$39.07	$36.71	$31.75
Income After Taxes	$390.21	$429.70	$351.65	$330.38	$285.78
Non-Cash Expenses	$4.30	$4.90	$16.47	$18.26	$20.04
Cash Flow	$394.51	$434.59	$368.12	$348.63	$305.82
Implementation Cost	($200.00)	($200.00)	($200.00)	($200.00)	($200.00)

FIGURE 3.4   A Simple DCF model.

a decision will be made based on these deterministic results. Figure 3.4 shows a simplified DCF model.

Obviously, more complex models can also be built, where the analyst may create multiple work sheets to estimate the volume and prices for different product lines for this strategy, and link the results into this DCF model. These different product lines may be correlated to one another or cannibalize each other's market share. In addition, the price and quantity estimated may be negatively correlated, following an elastic demand curve. The direct and indirect operating costs of these product lines may also follow a U-shaped average total cost curve over time, to account for diminishing marginal returns, and so on. Suffice it to say, the analyst can create a very simple model or a highly sophisticated model for this DCF analysis. Either way, the process integrity is kept.

STEP 4: MONTE CARLO SIMULATION—DCF OUTPUTS BECOME REAL OPTIONS INPUTS

In more advanced financial analysis, a highly recommended step for the real options approach is the application of Monte Carlo simulation. Based on some sensitivity analysis, the analyst decides which input variables to the DCF model previously constructed are most vulnerable to risks and sudden exogenous and systemic shocks. A powerful tool for calculating static sensitivities is the use of a Tornado Diagram in Crystal Ball, as seen in Figure 3.5.

Using historical data, the analyst can take the time-series or cross-sectional data and fit them to a multitude of different distributions, for those variables that have been found to be stochastic and uncertain, and, at the same time, the resulting NPV or IRR are highly sensitive to, based on the Tornado analysis. The analyst may also opt to use management assumptions, hunches, experience, or economic behaviors of variables to make the distributional determination of these so-called Critical Success Factors. The DCF model is then simulated. The result is a distribution of the variable of interest, for example, the NPV. Instead of obtaining single-point estimates, the analyst now has a probability distribution of outcomes, indicating with what probabilities certain outcomes will most likely occur. Based on this Monte Carlo simulation, certain intrinsic variables key to the real options analysis are calculated and imported into the real options analysis. These key variables that flow out of the simulation procedures include the volatility of the underlying variable, typically the lognormal returns on the future free cash flows; the implied cross-correlation pairs between the underlying projects; and the expected present value of cash flows. Figure 3.6 illustrates a simulated DCF model using Crystal Ball Professional. Notice that a multitude of tweaks can be applied here. The analyst may wish to account for multiple stochastic variables and influences. For example, competitive effects, cannibalization from other products, and market saturation effects

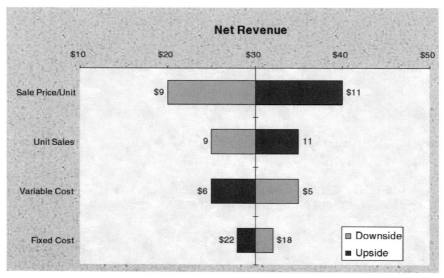

FIGURE 3.5 Sample Tornado Diagram.

Monte Carlo Simulation		

Input Parameters

		Results		
Discount Rate (Cash Flow)	15.00%	Present Value (Cash Flow)	$1,265.09	
Discount Rate (Impl. Cost)	5.00%	Present Value (Impl. Cost)	($865.90)	
Tax Rate	10.00%	Net Present Value	$399.20	

Year	**2003**	**2004**	**2005**	**2006**	**2007**
Revenue	$860.08	$979.07	$1,098.06	$1,217.06	$1,336.05
Adjustment to Revenue	$51.60	$97.91	$197.65	$316.43	$467.62
Cost of Revenue	$86.01	$97.91	$109.81	$121.71	$133.60
Royalties Paid	$43.00	$48.95	$164.71	$182.56	$200.41
Gross Profit	$679.46	$734.30	$625.90	$596.36	$534.42
Operating Expenses	$135.89	$146.86	$125.18	$119.27	$106.88
Depreciation Expense	$10.00	$10.00	$10.00	$10.00	$10.00
Interest Expense	$100.00	$100.00	$100.00	$100.00	$100.00
Income Before Taxes	$433.57	$477.44	$390.72	$367.09	$317.54
Taxes	$43.36	$47.74	$39.07	$36.71	$31.75
Income After Taxes	$390.21	$429.70	$351.65	$330.38	$285.78
Non-Cash Expenses	$4.30	$4.90	$16.47	$18.26	$20.04
Cash Flow	$394.51	$434.59	$368.12	$348.63	$305.82
Implementation Cost	($200.00)	($200.00)	($200.00)	($200.00)	($200.00)

Adjustment to Revenue:	**2003**	**2004**	**2005**	**2006**	**2007**
Competitive Effects	1.00%	2.00%	3.00%	4.00%	5.00%
Cannibalization Effects	5.00%	8.00%	10.00%	12.00%	15.00%
Market Saturation	0.00%	0.00%	5.00%	10.00%	15.00%

Volatility Measure:					
Logarithmic Returns		0.0968	-0.1660	-0.0544	-0.1310
Volatility	11.67%				

FIGURE 3.6   Applying Monte Carlo simulation on a DCF model.

(product lifecycle) all can be stochastically accounted for in the model. In contrast, more advanced stochastic uncertainties can be modeled through the use of interacting and correlated stochastic processes. To illustrate, suppose the project under consideration is a utility power plant. The revenues generated are simply the multiplication of prices and quantity demanded. However, prices may be modeled after a mean-reversion with Poisson jump-diffusion stochastic process, while quantity demanded may be modeled as an impulse-response function process, but negatively correlated to the price of electricity. This negative correlation only holds for a particular price trench when the price elasticity of demand is highly elastic, but drops off at a lower price level (Figure 3.6).

These interacting stochastic processes and variables should not be modeled separately in a real options approach but modeled together, flowing into and through a DCF model. The DCF model will filter out all the interacting relationships, causalities, correlations, and co-movements among variables. Otherwise, modeling these stochastic variables in real options lattices will yield mathematically intractable models—each stochastic variable will now have its own binomial lattice, and modeling n stochastic variables will yield a 2^n-*nomial*. For instance, modeling 2 stochastic variables will yield a quadranomial with 4 branches on a lattice at each node, and 5 variables a 32-branch multinomial lattice! The mathematical complexity involved in calculating a 32-branch multinomial lattice is staggering and should not be attempted. In contrast, the analyst can model in as many stochastic variables as he or she chooses in the DCF using Monte Carlo simulation, watch how they interact with each other through the DCF, and capture the resulting cash-flow stream as input into the real options modeling paradigm.

STEP 5: FRAMING THE REAL OPTIONS

Now that the DCF models have been created for the projects that survived an initial management screening process, what next? Which projects should undergo a real options analysis? Should all projects be scrutinized this closely? The answer comes in several parts:

- Projects that are close to at-the-money or slightly in-the-money or slightly out-of-the-money will benefit most from a real options analysis.
- Projects that are lumped together and hard to separate or prioritize from a DCF standpoint can benefit greatly from real options analysis.
- Projects that face great uncertainty in the future but yet possess an element of flexibility to hedge against downsides and capture the upside premiums can benefit greatly from real options analysis.
- Projects that by themselves produce little value but when viewed in their entirety, accounting for strategic downstream opportunities they create, can benefit greatly from real options analysis.

One powerful visualization method to observe the "clumping" of project valuation is the use of a three-dimensional (3D) option space as shown in Figure 3.7. The horizontal axis is a measure of a project's profitability index (Q-Ratio), that is, the ratio of the sum of present value of future net cash flows to the sum of the present value of investment or implementation costs. The former is discounted at a market-risk adjusted discount rate of return and the latter using the risk-free rate, to account for differences between market risk and private risks. A Q-Ratio greater than one means that the NPV is positive and the project is financially feasible and profitable, whereas a Q-Ratio less than one means the NPV is negative. Break-even projects have a Q-Ratio of one.

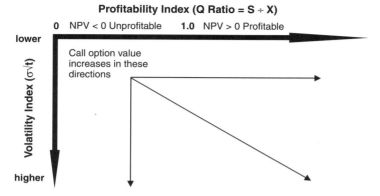

FIGURE 3.7 Option value in 3D space. The option value increases with increases in the volatility and value to cost.

The vertical axis measures the volatility index, essentially the standard deviation of the NPV or IRR value after performing Monte Carlo simulation, multiplied by the square root of the project's maturity in years. The project's maturity in years can be calculated either as the amount of time left to implement the project, or the project's economic life. Either way, as long as the calculation is applied consistently across all projects, the volatility index indicates a project's uncertainty, adjusted for time. A higher volatility index implies a higher option value but a potentially risky project. Figure 3.8 illustrates a completed 3D option space matrix.

Projects can then be classified into different regions (invest now, invest later, and so forth) depending on where they fall in the 3D space as well as management's risk and investment preferences. Notice that Figure 3.8 has a

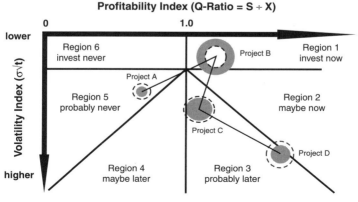

FIGURE 3.8 Project portfolio in 3D option space.

width (profitability index), height (volatility index), and depth (size of the circles, indicative of the projects' relative benefits and costs); hence, the name 3D option space matrix.

Plotting projects' profitability and volatility indexes is the first step in the real options framing exercise. The reason is that projects that are deep in-the-money should be executed immediately anyway (subject to budget constraints), and additional analyses are unnecessary. For instance, spending $1 million to make $100 million guaranteed is a "no-brainer" and should be implemented immediately. All the real options analysis in the world will not yield any more significant value. Conversely, deep out-of-the-money projects should not compel the analyst to perform any more in-depth analyses using real options as the project is so unprofitable, all the uncertainties and strategic options in the world are useless in justifying its existence. However, projects that are close to at-the-money or slightly in-the-money or slightly out-of-the-money should be considered for real options analytics. This decision is so, especially in the case where projects tend to clump or cluster together, making it difficult to distinguish which projects ought to be selected. This clustering together is where the 3D option space matrix provides valuable insights into which projects ought to undergo more real options scrutiny. In addition, the real options value tables, implied volatility tables, and dividend impact tables in Chapter 10 will help the analyst identify, at least as a first pass, projects that have significant strategic value.

The next step is to thoroughly understand your project and the strategic benefits it creates, as well as the inherent flexibilities. For instance, Figures 3.9 and 3.10 show the existence of several types of strategic real options

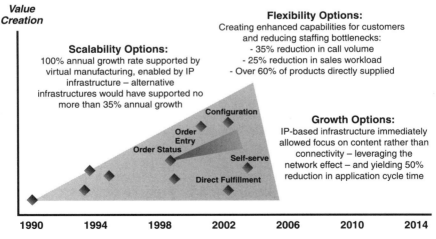

FIGURE 3.9   Strategic real options for an intellectual property (IP) infrastructure.

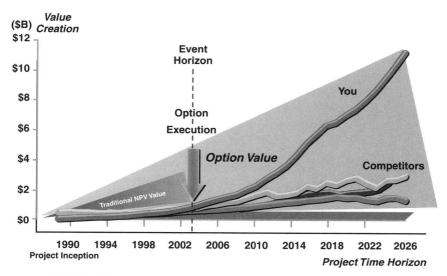

FIGURE 3.10 Timescale of an infrastructure investment real option.

inherent in an intellectual property infrastructure project, as well as the projected benefits based on a timescale. Framing these strategic options include the identification of real strategic flexibilities and options for a project and categorizing them into different groups of options.

As another example, Figure 3.11 shows the types of real options that exist in a pharmacology research and development (R&D) project.

On occasion, strategy trees are an invaluable tool in framing the time-dependent options that exist in a project. The use of strategy trees is especially important in the R&D world, where the existence of multiple phases is commonplace. For example, Figure 3.12 shows a simple two-stage R&D process, where the second stage depends on the success of the first stage, creating a sequential compound option. (See the examples of sequential compound options in later chapters of this book to learn how to solve the option.)

Figures 3.13 and 3.14 illustrate more complex R&D cases, where there are multiple stages in the R&D process. In pharmaceutical R&D, there are usually three phases in the R&D process, prior to FDA approval and market launch. In other high-tech industries, the R&D process follows a stage-gate process, with multiple stages. In the more complex sequential compound options world, at certain stages, different options may emerge; for instance, the project can only be abandoned after the first phase, or contracted starting the second phase (sufficient intellectual property has been

Timing

Delaying a product launch and major investment until more is learned about the strength of demand. It may be that the risk avoided by waiting to invest has greater value than the sales that might be forfeited by postponing.

Growth

Initial investment to build a manufacturing and sales facility in a foreign country for the new product produced through this new technology may lead to an opportunity to sell the entire firm's range of products through an established sales network. The investment would thus create growth options that have value above and beyond the returns generated by the initial recombinant insulin operation.

Phases

If the firm decides that its portfolio management and review process should include options analysis, you can stage the investment to allow options for continuing, delaying, or abandoning.

Exit and Abandonment

Early drug development holds numerous options to abandon if the compound does not look to be successful. The exit option increases the value of the project because it reduces the size of the investment at risk.

Learning

Before the firm launches its new drug advertising campaign across the United States, you release ads on a limited number of markets in select cities and then refine the marketing plans based on what is learned.

Expansion

Launch the injectable drug preparation to preserve dominant position in the marketplace while an inhalable drug preparation completes the final stages of development.

FIGURE 3.11   Framing real options in pharmacology.

developed only after the first two stages such that the company can license off its patent rights, etc.), or at a certain phase, the technology is mature enough such that it can be spun off into other ancillary products, thereby creating additional value to the existing project.

On occasion, strategy trees look similar to decision trees where probabilities of occurrence are created, as in Figure 3.15. Recall from my previous book, *Real Options Analysis*, that decision trees are a valuable tool, useful in setting up and visualizing real options strategies but cannot and should not be used to value real options projects. This restriction is due to the subjective probability estimates required on each branch of a tree, as well as

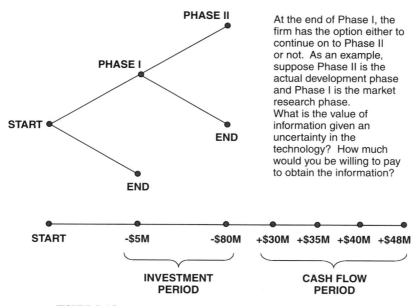

At the end of Phase I, the firm has the option either to continue on to Phase II or not. As an example, suppose Phase II is the actual development phase and Phase I is the market research phase.
What is the value of information given an uncertainty in the technology? How much would you be willing to pay to obtain the information?

PHASE II

PHASE I

START

END

END

START   -$5M   -$80M   +$30M   +$35M   +$40M   +$48M

INVESTMENT PERIOD   **CASH FLOW PERIOD**

FIGURE 3.12   Simple two-stage R&D real options process.

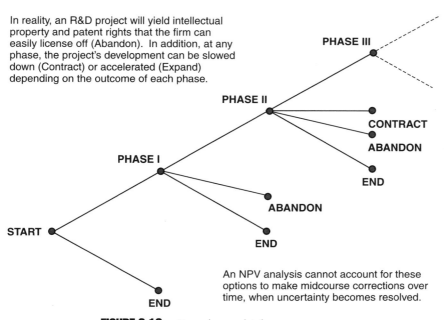

In reality, an R&D project will yield intellectual property and patent rights that the firm can easily license off (Abandon). In addition, at any phase, the project's development can be slowed down (Contract) or accelerated (Expand) depending on the outcome of each phase.

PHASE III

PHASE II

CONTRACT

ABANDON

END

PHASE I

ABANDON

START

END

END

An NPV analysis cannot account for these options to make midcourse corrections over time, when uncertainty becomes resolved.

FIGURE 3.13   Complex multiple-stage process.

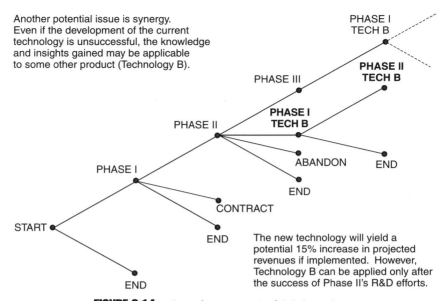

Another potential issue is synergy. Even if the development of the current technology is unsuccessful, the knowledge and insights gained may be applicable to some other product (Technology B).

The new technology will yield a potential 15% increase in projected revenues if implemented. However, Technology B can be applied only after the success of Phase II's R&D efforts.

FIGURE 3.14 Complex customized R&D options.

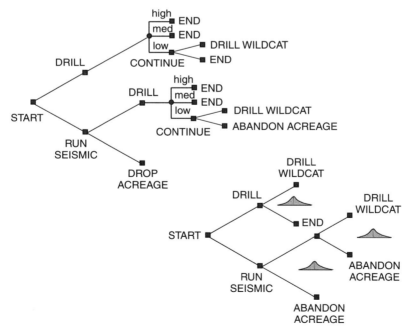

FIGURE 3.15 Strategy tree with probabilities in oil and gas.

different market risk-adjusted discount rates required on each node of the tree. The errors in estimation compound significantly and the resulting expected value calculated will be in error.

Instead, if probabilities of success are required in the analysis, rather than making subjective guesses and scenarios (high, medium, and low estimates in the market) as seen in the upper decision tree in Figure 3.15, these subjective guesses should be collapsed into distributions of outcomes using Monte Carlo simulation and applied in the DCF models. For instance, use a Triangular distribution on the revenues and run 10,000 simulation trials—this provides a higher level of accuracy as simulation run in this instance is simply recreating 10,000 scenarios based on these probabilities as opposed to running only 3 scenarios. In addition, any number of other probabilistic or stochastic variables can also be modeled and their interactions, co-movements, or correlations can also be modeled easily, using Monte Carlo simulation (see the lower decision tree in Figure 3.15).

After identifying the real options in each project, the dynamics of the uncertainty and corresponding flexibility inherent in the projects should be determined. For example, Figure 3.16 shows the application of a feedback loop to model the qualitative and quantitative critical success drivers and uncertainty drivers in the project. Using techniques such as feedback loops and

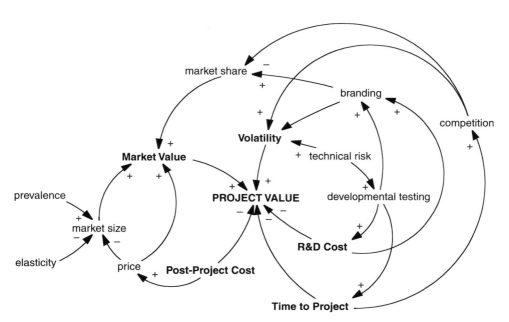

FIGURE 3.16 Feedback loops and influence diagrams.

influence diagrams (similar to feedback loops but the influence of uncertainty does not loop back to itself over time), the required uncertainties can be determined and modeled back into the DCF. Based on this approach, all relevant data can then be collected, estimated, or simulated in the model.

STEP 6: OPTIONS ANALYTICS, SIMULATION, AND OPTIMIZATION

The next step is to apply the options analytics based on the real options framed. The remainder of this book focuses primarily on solving the different types of real options analytically as well as using the Real Options Analysis Toolkit software. Refer to the relevant sections for the real options you are attempting to solve.

Once the real options analysis is performed, the 3D option space can then be revisited. For instance, Figure 3.17 shows the effects of having real options in different projects, and how their strategic positions have changed.

If multiple projects exist, the options analysis can be further enhanced using portfolio resource optimization. Figure 3.18 shows the use of Crystal Ball's OptQuest software to perform stochastic optimization (stochastic optimization refers to an optimization process where the uncertainties are first simulated thousands of times using Monte Carlo simulation, and the outputs are then optimized, then the whole process is repeated hundreds of times).

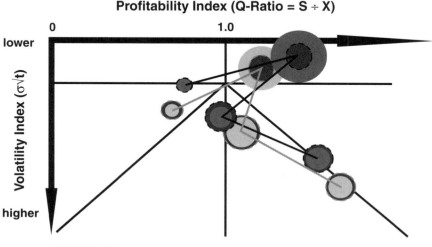

FIGURE 3.17 3D options space matrix with real options value.

Simulation	Maximize Objective ENPV Mean	Requirement NPV 400 <= Percentile (90)	Royalty 2003	Royalty 2004	Royalty 2005	Royalty 2006	Royalty 2007
1	448.454	438.697	5.0000E-02	5.0000E-02	0.137500	0.137500	0.125000
2	479.014	475.329	5.5933E-02	5.2216E-02	0.107451	0.101703	0.115646
11	500.154	444.145	6.4312E-02	5.0000E-02	0.100000	0.100000	0.185688
31	502.071	442.340	5.9495E-02	5.0000E-02	0.100000	0.100000	0.190505
Best: 40	506.812	446.872	5.0000E-02	5.0000E-02	0.100000	0.100000	0.200000
Current: 42	472.386	446.553	6.1028E-02	6.2347E-02	0.110937	0.102989	0.162699

Status — Time Remaining: 4:26 — Simulation: 43 — Optimization File — UnNamed.opt — Crystal Ball Simulation: Step by Step Analysis.xls — Optimizing...

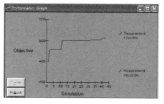

FIGURE 3.18 Portfolio and resource optimization.

Optimization is used to efficiently allocate resources across multiple projects subject to resource and budget constraints, where the best combination of projects that maximizes returns and minimizes risks can be ascertained. In addition, a predefined probability of success can also be imputed into the optimization process, as a requirement of the final allocation. Other uses of optimization includes finding the optimal royalty rates paid on some intellectual property, or to select a portfolio of say 15 projects from a list of 500 initial projects.

STEP 7: REPORTS, PRESENTATIONS, AND UPDATE ANALYSIS

The final results are then presented to management. See *Real Options Analysis* for detailed examples on the questions management most frequently ask as well as the approaches to broach a potentially complex subject to management in an expositionally easy way. Finally, after all is said and done, the real options value is the value of strategic flexibility in an uncertain world, (otherwise, if everything is certain, uncertainty and hence volatility reverts to zero, and real options value approaches zero, making the DCF approach a special case of the real options analysis) and when uncertainty becomes resolved over time, management can capture upside swings or limit downside crashes through real options hedging by executing a project's flexibility. Hence, when uncertainty becomes resolved through the passage of time, the real options analysis needs to be updated and revisited with new information. Real options analysis assumes a continued improvement and continued monitoring of strategic projects, and as such, update analysis is required.

CHAPTER 4

The Basics of Financial Modeling

FINANCIAL ANALYSIS

The most common approach in financial analysis is the use of discounted cash flow (DCF) analysis. In using DCF analysis, several conventions require consideration: continuous versus periodic discrete discounting, midyear versus end-of-year convention, and beginning-of-period versus end-of-period discounting.

Continuous Versus Periodic Discrete Discounting

The discounting convention is important when performing a DCF analysis. Using the same compounding period principle, future cash flows can be discounted using the effective annualized discount rate. The same applies to compounding present values to future values. For instance, suppose an annualized discount rate of 30 percent is used on a $100 cash flow. Depending on the compounding periodicity, the calculated present value and future value differ (Table 4.1).

To illustrate this point further, a $100 deposit in a 30 percent interest-bearing account will yield $130 at the end of one year if the interest

TABLE 4.1   Future and Present Value Table with Different Compounding and Discounting Periodicities

Periodicity	Periods/ Year	Effective Interest (%)	Future Value ($)	Present Value ($)
Annual	1	30.00	130.00	76.92
Quarterly	4	33.55	133.55	74.88
Monthly	12	34.49	134.49	74.36
Daily	365	34.97	134.97	74.09
Continuous		34.99	134.99	74.08

compounds once a year. However, if interest is compounded quarterly, the deposit value increases to $133.55 due to the additional interest-on-interest compounding effects. For instance:

Value at the end of the first quarter = $100.00(1 + 0.30/4)^1 = $107.50
Value at the end of the second quarter = $107.50(1 + 0.30/4)^1 = $115.56
Value at the end of the third quarter = $115.56(1 + 0.30/4)^1 = $124.23
Value at the end of the fourth quarter = $124.23(1 + 0.30/4)^1 = $133.55

That is, the annualized discount rate for different compounding periods is its effective annualized rate, calculated as

$$\left(1 + \frac{discount}{periods}\right)^{periods} - 1$$

For the quarterly compounding interest rate, the effective annualized rate is

$$\left(1 + \frac{30.00\%}{4}\right)^4 - 1 = 33.55\%$$

Applying this rate for the year, we have $100(1 + 0.3355) = $133.55.

This analysis can be extended for monthly, daily, or any other periodicities. In addition, if the interest rate is assumed to be continuously compounding, the continuous effective annualized rate should be used, where

$$\lim_{periods \to \infty} \left(1 + \frac{discount}{periods}\right)^{periods} - 1 = e^{discount} - 1$$

For instance, the 30 percent interest rate compounded continuously yields $e^{0.3} - 1 = 34.99\%$. Notice that as the number of compounding periods increases, the effective interest rate increases until it approaches the limit of continuous compounding.

The annually, quarterly, monthly, and daily compounding is termed discrete periodic discounting, as compared to the continuous-compounding approach using the exponential function. In summary, the higher the number of compounding periods, the higher the future value and the lower the present value of a cash flow payment. When applied to DCF analysis, if the discount rate calculated using a weighted average cost of capital (WACC) is continuously compounding (e.g., interest payments and cost of capital are continuously compounding), then the net present value (NPV) calculated may be overoptimistic if discounted discretely.

End-of-Year Versus Midyear Convention

In the conventional DCF approach, cash flows occurring in the future are discounted back to the present value and summed, to obtain the NPV of a project. These cash flows are usually attached to a particular period in the future, measured usually in years, quarters, or months. The time line in Figure 4.1 illustrates a sample series of cash flows over the next 5 years, with an assumed 20 percent discount rate. Because the cash flows are attached to an annual time line, they are usually assumed to occur at the end of each year, that is, $500 will be recognized at the end of the first full year, $600 at the end of the second year, and so forth. This situation is termed the full-year discounting convention.

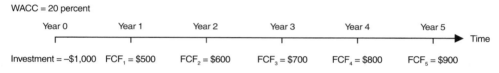

FIGURE 4.1   Cash-flow stream.

$$NPV = -\$1000 + \frac{\$500}{(1 + 0.2)^1} + \frac{\$600}{(1 + 0.2)^2} + \frac{\$700}{(1 + 0.2)^3} + \frac{\$800}{(1 + 0.2)^4}$$

$$+ \frac{\$900}{(1 + 0.2)^5} = \$985$$

However, under usual business conditions, cash flows tend to accrue throughout the entire year and do not arrive in a single lump sum at the end of the year. In this case, the midyear convention should be applied, that is, the $500 cash flow gets accrued over the entire first year and should be discounted at 0.5 years, rather than 1.0 years. Using this midpoint approach assumes that the $500 cash flow comes in equally over the entire year.

$$NPV = -\$1,000 + \frac{\$500}{(1 + 0.2)^{0.5}} + \frac{\$600}{(1 + 0.2)^{1.5}} + \frac{\$700}{(1 + 0.2)^{2.5}} + \frac{\$800}{(1 + 0.2)^{3.5}}$$

$$+ \frac{\$900}{(1 + 0.2)^{4.5}} = \$1,175$$

End-of-Period Versus Beginning-of-Period Discounting

Another approach to consider is to forecast cash flows with more granular periodicities, that is, instead of using annual cash flows, use forecast cash flows based on quarterly or monthly periods. In addition, discounting may

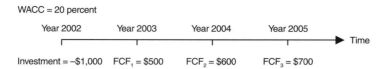

WACC = 20 percent

Year 2002   Year 2003   Year 2004   Year 2005

Investment = –$1,000   FCF$_1$ = $500   FCF$_2$ = $600   FCF$_3$ = $700

FIGURE 4.2   Cash-flow stream for 3 years.

also involve the use of end-of-period versus beginning-of-period discounting. Suppose the cash-flow series are generated on a time line such as the one shown in Figure 4.2. Further assume that the valuation date is January 1, 2002. The $500 cash flow can occur either at the beginning of the first year (January 1, 2003) or at the end of the first year (December 31, 2003). The former requires the discounting of one year; the latter, the discounting of two years. If the cash flows are assumed to roll in equally over the year (that is, from January 1, 2002 to January 1, 2003), the discounting should be for only 0.5 years.

In retrospect, suppose that the valuation date is December 31, 2002, and the cash-flow series occurs at January 1, 2003 or December 31, 2003. The former requires no discounting, while the latter requires a 1-year discounting using an end-of-year discounting convention. In the midyear convention, the cash flow occurring on December 31, 2003, should be discounted at 0.5 years. Therefore, it is clear from these illustrations that the discounting convention is important, as are the forecast dates of each cash-flow occurrence.

Exercise: DCF Model

Open the Excel file *Workbook Exercise (DCF Model).xls* from the enclosed CD-ROM. Using the discrete and continuous discounting conventions, and assuming a 20 percent discount rate, calculate the present value of cash flows and NPV of the following cash flows, and complete the analysis.

Discounted Cash Flow Analysis						
Discount Rate	20%					
		Discrete Discounting				
Year	2002	2003	2004	2005	2006	2007
Revenues		$100	$200	$300	$400	$500
Operating Expenses		$10	$20	$30	$40	$50
Net Income		$90	$180	$270	$360	$450
Investment Costs	($450)					
Free Cash Flow	($450)	$90	$180	$270	$360	$450
Present Value of Cash Flow						
Net Present Value						

			Continuous Discounting			
Year	2002	2003	2004	2005	2006	2007
Revenues		$100	$200	$300	$400	$500
Operating Expenses		$10	$20	$30	$40	$50
Net Income		$90	$180	$270	$360	$450
Investment Costs	($450)					
Free Cash Flow	($450)	$90	$180	$270	$360	$450
Present Value of Cash Flow						
Net Present Value						

MONTE CARLO SIMULATION

Simulation is any analytical method that is meant to imitate a real-life system, especially when other analyses are too mathematically complex or too difficult to reproduce. Spreadsheet risk analysis uses both a spreadsheet model and simulation to analyze the effect of varying inputs based on outputs of the modeled system. One type of spreadsheet simulation is Monte Carlo simulation, which randomly generates values for uncertain variables over and over to simulate a real-life model, based on some predefined probability distributions.

A simulation calculates numerous scenarios of a model by repeatedly picking values from the probability distribution for the uncertain variables and using those values for the event. As all those scenarios produce associated results, each scenario can have a forecast. Forecasts are events (usually with formulas or functions) that you define as important outputs of the model, such as totals, net profit, or gross expenses. The following exercises provide the reader instructions for creating and running Monte Carlo simulations using Excel to simulate a stock price path, as well as instructions for using Decisioneering, Inc.'s Crystal Ball Monte Carlo simulation software to perform risk analysis on a DCF model.

Exercise: Simulation I (Simulating a DCF Model)

Open the Excel file *Workbook Exercise (Simulation I).xls* from the enclosed CD-ROM. Using the spreadsheet, create a DCF model and calculate the present value of cash flows, present value of implementation costs, and the NPV.

Monte Carlo Simulation

Input Parameters

Discount Rate (Cash Flow)	
Discount Rate (Impl. Cost)	
Tax Rate	

Results

Present Value (Cash Flow)	
Present Value (Impl. Cost)	
Net Present Value	

	2002	2003	2004	2005	2006
Revenue					
Cost of Revenue					
Gross Profit					
Operating Expenses					
Depreciation Expense					
Interest Expense					
Income Before Taxes					
Taxes					
Income After Taxes					
Non-Cash Expenses					
Cash Flow					
Implementation Cost					

Use these assumptions in the model:

- Discount Rate for cash flows is 15 percent
- Discount Rate for implementation cost is 7 percent
- Tax Rate is 40 percent
- Revenue in 2002 is $100, growing $100 every year
- Cost of Revenue is fixed at 25 percent of revenues
- Operating Expense is fixed at 10 percent of revenues
- Depreciation Expense is fixed at 50 percent of operating expenses
- Interest Expense is fixed at 5 percent of revenues
- Non-Cash Expense is fixed at $10 every year
- Implementation Cost is $20 in 2002, growing $20 every year after that

Now add Monte Carlo simulation using Crystal Ball. Define these assumptions: Discount Rate of cash flows follows a normal distribution with a mean of 15 percent and a standard deviation of 1.5 percent; and Revenue follows a uniform distribution with a ±10 percent from the mean revenue provided previously (i.e., year 2002's revenues follow $90 minimum and $110 maximum values using a uniform distribution). Define the NPV as the forecast result and run 1,000 simulation trials.

Exercise: Simulation II (Simulating a Stock Price Path)

Another use of Monte Carlo simulation is forecasting a stochastic process, for example, a stock price path. Open the Excel file *Workbook Exercise (Simulation II).xls* from the enclosed CD-ROM. Assuming a 100 percent annualized stock-return volatility, 8 percent mean growth returns, and a $100 starting stock price, simulate a stock price path for the period of January 1, 2001 to April 30, 2001, on a weekly basis, using a Geometric Brownian Motion stochastic process. Recreate this following analysis. Remember to press the F9 function key repeatedly to simulate different price paths. See *Real Options Analysis* for details on Geometric Brownian Motions.

Simulated Stock Price Path			

Stock returns annualized volatility	Annualized mean growth of returns	Starting stock price at time 0	Calculated periodic volatility
100.00%	8.00%	$100.00	13.87%

Simulate	Date	Value
	01-Jan-01	$100.00
0.5014	08-Jan-01	$107.11
0.7518	15-Jan-01	$118.44
0.4664	22-Jan-01	$126.28
1.9135	29-Jan-01	$159.98
0.7381	05-Feb-01	$176.60
-0.7137	12-Feb-01	$169.40
0.4923	19-Feb-01	$170.52
-0.5082	26-Feb-01	$158.77
-1.8518	05-Mar-01	$118.24
0.6272	12-Mar-01	$128.71
-1.4103	19-Mar-01	$103.73
-0.5980	26-Mar-01	$95.29
-0.3994	02-Apr-01	$90.16
0.1685	09-Apr-01	$92.41
1.9986	16-Apr-01	$118.16
-1.6219	23-Apr-01	$91.77
1.7050	30-Apr-01	$113.60

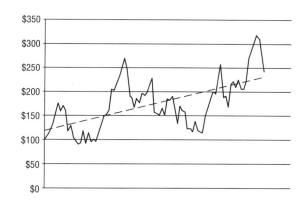

VOLATILITY ESTIMATES

Probably one of the most difficult input parameters to estimate in a real options analysis is the volatility of cash flows. A review is presented of several methods used to calculate volatility, together with a discussion of their potential advantages and shortcomings.

Logarithmic Cash-Flow Returns Approach

The logarithmic cash-flow returns approach calculates the volatility using the individual future cash-flow estimates and their corresponding logarithmic returns, as illustrated in Table 4.2. Starting with a series of forecast future cash flows, convert them into relative returns. Then take the natural logarithms of these relative returns. The standard deviation of these natural logarithm returns is the volatility of the cash-flow series used in a real options analysis. Notice that the number of returns is one less than the total number of periods. That is, for time periods 0 to 5, we have six cash flows but only five cash-flow returns (Table 4.2).

TABLE 4.2   Logarithmic Cash Flow

Time Period	Cash Flows	Cash-Flow Relative Returns	Natural Logarithm of Cash-Flow Returns (X)
0	$100	—	—
1	$125	$125/$100 = 1.25	ln($125/$100) = 0.2231
2	$ 95	$ 95/$125 = 0.76	ln($ 95/$125) = –0.2744
3	$105	$105/$ 95 = 1.11	ln($105/$ 95) = 0.1001
4	$155	$155/$105 = 1.48	ln($155/$105) = 0.3895
5	$146	$146/$155 = 0.94	ln($146/$155) = –0.0598

The volatility estimate is then calculated as

$$volatility = \sqrt{\frac{1}{n-1} \sum_{i=1}^{n} (x_i - \bar{x})^2} = 25.58\%$$

where n is the number of X's, and $\bar{x}$ is the average X value. Clearly there are advantages and shortcomings to this simple approach. This method is very easy to implement, and Monte Carlo simulation is not required in order to obtain a single-point volatility estimate. This approach is mathematically valid and is widely used in estimating volatility of financial assets. However, for real options analysis, there are several caveats that deserve closer attention, including when cash flows are negative over certain time periods. That is, the relative returns will be a negative value, and the natural logarithm of a negative value does not exist. Hence, the volatility measure does not fully capture the possible cash-flow downside and may produce erroneous results. In addition, autocorrelated cash flows (estimated using time-series forecasting techniques) or cash flows following a static growth rate will yield volatility estimates that are erroneous. Great care should be taken in such instances. To solve the negative cash flow situation, simply shift the negative cash flows to positive values. Arithmetic translation of adding values to all cash flows and making them positive will only shift the expected returns, but keep constant the second moment or volatility. Finally, initial occurrences of negative cash flows should be regarded as different phases and analyzed as staged or phased investments with different volatilities. The same rules apply to autocorrelated cash flows with periods of positive and negative values.

Monte Carlo simulation can also be used in creating the DCF model that is used to calculate the cash flows, thereby running thousands of trials and reducing the risk of obtaining a single erroneous volatility estimate. Performing a Monte Carlo simulation at the DCF level is highly appropriate because a distribution of volatilities can be obtained and used as input into a real options analysis. The results of such an analysis will then yield a forecast distribution of real options values, with its relevant probabilities of occurrence, rather than a single-point estimate.

Logarithmic Present-Value Approach

The logarithmic present-value approach collapses all future cash-flow estimates into two sets of present values, one for the first time period and another for the present time. The steps are seen below. The calculations assume a constant 10 percent discount rate. The cash flows are discounted all the way to Time 0 and again to Time 1. Then the values are summed, and the following logarithmic ratio is calculated:

$$X = \ln\left(\frac{\sum_{i=1}^{n} PVCF_i}{\sum_{j=0}^{m} PVCF_j}\right)$$

where $PVCF_{ij}$ is the present value of future cash flows at different time periods i and j (Table 4.3).

In the example above, X is simply $ln(\$514.31/\$567.56) = -0.0985$. Using this X value, perform a Monte Carlo simulation on the DCF model (simulate the individual cash flows) and obtain the resulting forecast distribution of X.

TABLE 4.3 Logarithmic Present Value

Time Period	Cash Flows	Present Value at Time 0	Present Value at Time 1
0	$100	$\dfrac{\$100}{(1 + 0.1)^0} = \$100.00$	—
1	$125	$\dfrac{\$125}{(1 + 0.1)^1} = \$113.64$	$\dfrac{\$125}{(1 + 0.1)^0} = \$125.00$
2	$ 95	$\dfrac{\$95}{(1 + 0.1)^2} = \$ 78.51$	$\dfrac{\$95}{(1 + 0.1)^1} = \$ 86.36$
3	$105	$\dfrac{\$105}{(1 + 0.1)^3} = \$ 78.89$	$\dfrac{\$105}{(1 + 0.1)^2} = \$ 86.78$
4	$155	$\dfrac{\$155}{(1 + 0.1)^4} = \$105.87$	$\dfrac{\$155}{(1 + 0.1)^3} = \$116.45$
5	$146	$\dfrac{\$146}{(1 + 0.1)^5} = \$ 90.65$	$\dfrac{\$146}{(1 + 0.1)^4} = \$ 99.72$
SUM		$567.56	$514.31

The standard deviation of the forecast distribution of X is the volatility estimate used in the real options analysis. It is important to note that only the numerator is simulated while the denominator remains unchanged.

The downside to estimating volatility this way is that the approach requires Monte Carlo simulation, but the calculated volatility measure is a single-digit estimate, as compared to the logarithmic cash-flow approach, which yields a distribution of volatilities that will in turn yield a distribution of calculated real options values. The main objection to using this method is its dependence on the variability of the discount rate used. For instance, we can expand the X equation as follows:

$$X = \ln\left(\frac{\displaystyle\sum_{i=1}^{n} PVCF_i}{\displaystyle\sum_{j=0}^{m} PVCF_j}\right) = \ln\left(\frac{\dfrac{CF_1}{(1 + D)^0} + \dfrac{CF_2}{(1 + D)^1} + \dfrac{CF_3}{(1 + D)^2} + \ldots + \dfrac{CF_N}{(1 + D)^{N-1}}}{\dfrac{CF_0}{(1 + D)^0} + \dfrac{CF_1}{(1 + D)^1} + \dfrac{CF_2}{(1 + D)^2} + \ldots + \dfrac{CF_N}{(1 + D)^N}}\right)$$

where D represents the constant discount rate used. Here, we see that the cash-flow series CF for the numerator is offset by one period, and the discount factors are also offset by one period. Therefore, by performing a Monte Carlo simulation on the cash flows alone versus performing a Monte

Carlo simulation on both cash-flow variables as well as the discount rate will yield very different X values. The main critique of this approach is that in a real options analysis, the variability in the present value of cash flows is the key driver of option value and not the variability of discount rates used in the analysis. Modifications to this method include duplicating the cash flows and simulating only the numerator cash flows, thereby providing different numerator values but a static denominator value for each simulated trial, while keeping the discount rate constant. This approach reduces the measurement risks of autocorrelated cash flows and negative cash flows.

This approach is analogous to stock price simulations where the theoretical stock price is the sum of all future dividend cash payments. In Real Options, these cash payments are the free cash flows. Thus, the sum of free cash flows present valued to time zero is the current stock price (asset value), and at time one, the stock price in the future. The natural logarithm of the ratio of these sums is analogous to the logarithmic returns of stock prices. As stock price at time zero is known while the future stock price is uncertain, simulate only the uncertain future stock price.

Management Assumption Approach

Another approach to estimating volatility is through management assumptions. For instance, suppose management assumes that the present value of a particular project follows a lognormal distribution with a mean of $44 million. In addition, management assumes that this expected value can fluctuate between $30 million and $60 million. These values represent the worst-case 10 percent probability and best-case 90 percent probability (Figure 4.3).

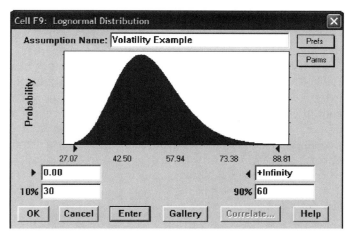

FIGURE 4.3 Lognormal distribution assumption in Crystal Ball with alternate parameters.

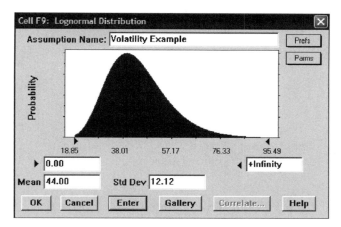

FIGURE 4.4   Calculated lognormal distribution in Crystal Ball.

Using Crystal Ball's Monte Carlo simulation software, the percentile inputs seen in Figure 4.4 are calculated using the software. The corresponding standard deviation is computed as $12.12 million. Hence, the volatility estimate is $12.12/$44.00 or 27.55 percent. This calculation is done with Crystal Ball's Define Assumption function, choosing the alternate parameters (Parms) command, and entering the relevant percentiles. In addition, Chapter 10, Real Options Tables, provides an excellent set of implied volatility tables that are well suited for these types of management approach to estimating volatilities.

Annualizing Volatility

Regardless of the approach taken, the volatility estimate used in a real options analysis has to be an annualized volatility. Depending on the periodicity of the raw cash flow used, the volatility calculated should be converted into annualized values using $\sigma \sqrt{T}$, where T is the number of periods in a year. For instance, if the calculated volatility using monthly cash-flow data is 10 percent, the annualized volatility is $10\% \sqrt{12} = 35\%$. This figure should be used in the real options analysis. Similarly, T is 365 for daily data, 4 for quarterly data, 2 for semiannual data, and 1 for annual data. Annualizing is important because volatility is assumed, in an options paradigm, to grow at the rate of the square root of stepping time.

Explaining Volatilities

Now that you know how to estimate volatilities, how on earth do you explain what it actually means to management? Management usually understands what probabilities mean. As a matter of fact, they feel more comfortable looking at a decision tree filled with probabilities of outcomes or probabilities of a project being successful, and so forth, than to talk about volatilities. Provide them a volatility value of 35 percent and all is lost, or so you think. There is a very simple, powerful, and yet logical explanation to volatilities.

Figure 4.5 shows a simple Crystal Ball forecast chart. On the vertical axis are the probabilities of occurrence given a particular value on the horizontal axis. Obviously, the wider the distribution, the higher the standard deviation or volatility of this distribution, and the corresponding probabilities get reallocated to the tails of the distribution. In other words, volatility and probabilities are related, as seen in this graph. For instance, Figure 4.6 illustrates the forecast statistics where the resulting standard deviation (a measure of volatility) is calculated as 34.52.

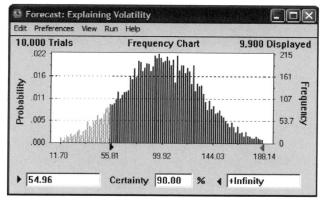

FIGURE 4.5 Forecast chart showing probabilities and volatility.

Statistics	
Statistic	Value
Trials	10,000
Mean	99.45
Median	99.57
Mode	---
Standard Deviation	34.52
Variance	1,191.67
Skewness	-0.04
Kurtosis	2.98
Coeff. of Variability	0.35
Range Minimum	-29.26
Range Maximum	231.88
Range Width	261.15
Mean Std. Error	0.35

FIGURE 4.6 Forecast statistics showing the volatility/standard deviation level.

To further illustrate the relationship, suppose management assumes that there is a 10 percent probability that a particular project will be successful or break even, and the break-even level is set at $55 million. Using Crystal Ball's alternate parameters function, the custom level is chosen for 10 percentile and 99 percentile (Figure 4.7).

The assign distribution dialog in Figure 4.8 shows the distribution with a 10 percent confidence at $55 million. Reverting back to the mean and standard deviation view, Figure 4.9 shows the resulting standard deviation is calculated as 34.65, in agreement with the simulated values (rounded, of course).

Using this simple yet effective approach, an analyst can explain to management that volatilities are nothing but the counterparts of probabilities. As

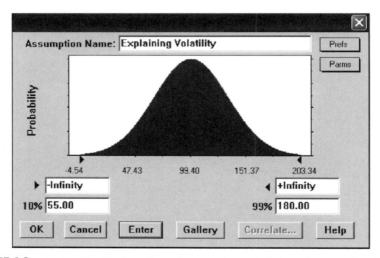

FIGURE 4.7   Crystal Ball's custom parameters dialog box.

FIGURE 4.8   Assign distribution chart showing the probability of success/breakeven.

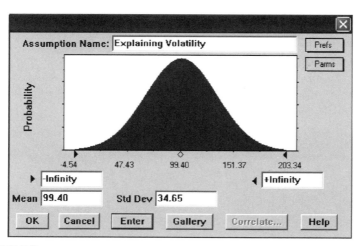

FIGURE 4.9   Assign distribution chart showing standard deviation/volatility.

a matter of fact, there is a perfect statistical and mathematical exactness to this relationship. Taking this idea a few steps further, the same approach can be used to estimate the volatility of any uncertain variable given its probabilities of occurrence, and vice versa. However, in a real options modeling paradigm, volatilities are used instead of probabilities as the latter tend to be more subjective and prone to guesstimates. When used on a large decision tree, errors in estimating probabilities will compound and the resulting expected values on the tree will be erroneous. In addition, volatilities are much more exact and powerful in the sense that when you model multiple stochastic and uncertain variables using Monte Carlo simulation and force these simulated values through a DCF model, the model will account for specific causalities, correlations, interrelationships, and co-movements among these many variables. The resulting cash-flow stream is distilled from these interactions. Hence, calculating the volatility based on this final flow of events as captured by the cash-flow stream is more accurate, accounting for all uncertainties and all their interactions. Otherwise, more advanced Bayesian updating and reversal and combinatoric approaches would have to be applied on a decision tree as well as all the interacting relationships among probabilities have to be known ahead of time, making the use of simple probabilities inappropriate, inexact, and unnecessarily difficult.

Exercise: Volatility Estimates

Open the Excel file *Workbook Exercise (Volatility Estimate).xls* from the enclosed CD-ROM. Using the cash-flow assumptions from the graphic, calculate the annualized volatility assuming the cash flows have an annual periodicity.

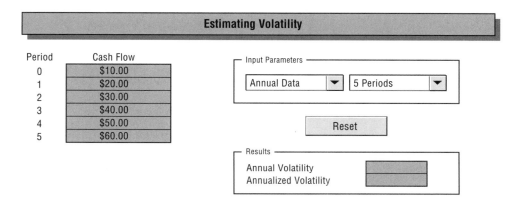

What would happen if the cash flows are on a monthly periodicity instead? What happens if the cash flow in Period 0 is –$10 instead?

CHAPTER 5

The Basics of Real Options

BINOMIAL LATTICES

In the binomial-lattice world, several basic similarities are worth mentioning. No matter the types of real options problems you are trying to solve, if the binomial lattice approach is used, the solution can be obtained in one of two ways. The first is the use of risk-neutral probabilities, and the second is the use of market-replicating portfolios. Throughout this book, the former approach is used. The use of a market-replicating portfolio is more difficult to understand and apply, but the results obtained from replicating portfolios are identical to those obtained through risk-neutral probabilities. Accordingly, it does not matter which method is used; nevertheless, application and expositional ease should be emphasized.

Market-replicating portfolios' predominant assumptions are that there are no arbitrage opportunities and that there exist a number of traded assets in the market that can be obtained to replicate the existing asset's payout profile. A simple illustration is in order here. Suppose you own a portfolio of publicly traded stocks that pay a set percentage *dividend* per period. You can, in theory, assuming no trading restrictions, taxes, or transaction costs, purchase a second portfolio of several *nondividend-paying* stocks and replicate the payout of the first portfolio of *dividend-paying* stocks. You can, for instance, sell a particular number of shares per period to replicate the first portfolio's dividend payout amount at every time period. Hence, if both payouts are identical although their stock compositions are different, the value of both portfolios should then be identical. Otherwise, there will be arbitrage opportunities, and market forces will tend to make them equilibrate in value. This scenario makes perfect sense in a financial-securities world where stocks are freely traded and highly liquid. However, in a real-options world where physical assets and firm-specific projects are being valued, financial purists would argue that this assumption is hard to accept, not to mention that the mathematics behind replicating portfolios are also more difficult to apply.

Compare the use of replicating portfolios to a risk-neutral probability approach. Simply stated, instead of using a risky set of cash flows and discounting them at a risk-adjusted discount rate akin to the discounted cash-flow (DCF) models, you can instead easily risk-adjust the probabilities of specific cash flows occurring at specific times. Thus, using these risk-adjusted probabilities on the cash flows lets you discount these cash flows (whose risks have now been accounted for) at the risk-free rate. This situation is the essence of binomial lattices as applied in valuing options. The results that are obtained are identical.

Let us now see how easy it is to apply risk-neutral valuation. In any options model, there is a minimum requirement of at least two lattices. The first lattice is always the lattice of the underlying asset, while the second lattice is the option valuation lattice. No matter what real options model is of interest, the basic structure almost always exists, taking the form:

$$\text{Inputs: } S, X, \sigma, T, rf, q$$

$$u = e^{\sigma\sqrt{\delta t}} \quad \text{and} \quad d = e^{-\sigma\sqrt{\delta t}} = \frac{1}{u}$$

$$p = \frac{e^{(rf-q)(\delta t)} - d}{u - d}$$

The basic inputs are the present value of the underlying asset (S), present value of implementation cost of the option (X), annualized volatility of the natural logarithm of the underlying free cash-flow returns in percent (σ), time to expiration in years (T), annualized risk-free rate or the rate of return on a riskless asset (rf), and continuous annualized dividend outflows in percent (q). In addition, the binomial lattice approach requires two additional sets of calculations, the up and down factors (u and d) as well as a risk-neutral probability measure (p). We see from the equations above that the up factor is simply the exponential function of the cash-flow volatility multiplied by the square root of time-steps or stepping time (δt). Time-steps or stepping time is simply the timescale between steps. That is, if an option has a 1-year maturity and the binomial lattice that is constructed has 10 steps, each time-step has a stepping time of 0.1 years. The volatility measure is an annualized value; multiplying it by the square root of time-steps breaks it down into the time-step's equivalent volatility. The down factor is simply the reciprocal of the up factor. In addition, the higher the volatility measure, the higher the up and down factors. This reciprocal magnitude ensures that the lattices are recombining because the up and down steps have the same magnitude but different signs; at places along the future path these binomial bifurcations must meet.

The second required calculation is that of the risk-neutral probability, defined simply as the ratio of the exponential function of the difference between risk-free rate and dividend, multiplied by the stepping time less the down factor, to the difference between the up and down factors. This risk-neutral probability value is a mathematical intermediate and by itself has no particular meaning. One major error that real options users commit is to extrapolate these probabilities as some kind of subjective or objective probabilities that a certain event will occur. Nothing is further from the truth. There is no economic or financial meaning attached to these risk-neutralized probabilities save that they are an intermediate step in a series of calculations. Armed with these values, you are now on your way to creating a binomial lattice of the underlying asset value, shown in Figure 5.1.

Starting with the present value of the underlying asset at time zero (S_0), multiply it by the up (u) and down (d) factors as shown above, to create a binomial lattice. Remember that there is one bifurcation at each node, creating an up and a down branch. The intermediate branches are all recombining. This evolution of the underlying asset shows that if the volatility is zero, in a deterministic world where there are no uncertainties, the lattice would be a straight line, and a DCF model will be adequate because the value of the option or flexibility is also zero. In other words, if volatility (σ) is zero, then the up ($u = e^{\sigma\sqrt{\delta t}}$) and down ($d = e^{-\sigma\sqrt{\delta t}}$) jump sizes are equal

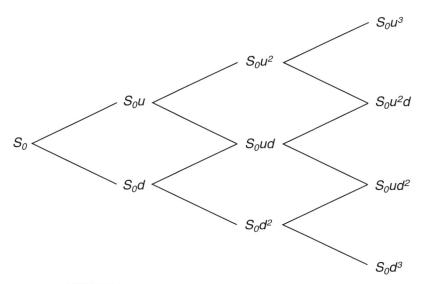

FIGURE 5.1 Recombining lattice with three time-steps.

to one. It is because there are uncertainties and risks, as captured by the volatility measure, that the lattice is not a straight horizontal line but comprises up and down movements. It is this up and down uncertainty that generates the value in an option. The higher the volatility measure, the higher the up and down factors as previously defined, the higher the potential value of an option as higher uncertainties exist and the potential upside for the option increases.

Exercise: Creating and Solving Lattices

Open the Excel file *Workbook Exercise (Creating and Solving Lattices).xls* from the enclosed CD-ROM. Using the risk-neutral approach, calculate the stepping time, up and down steps, and the risk-neutral probability. Then create an underlying asset lattice and solve the American option value using the option valuation lattice below. If you require detailed assistance in solving lattices, refer to Chapter 6 of *Real Options Analysis* ("Granularity" heads to "Precision" section).

Creating and Solving Lattices

Assumptions

Asset Value ($)	$100.00
Implementation Cost ($)	$80.00
Maturity (Years)	5.00
Risk-free Rate (%)	5.00%
Dividends (%)	0.00%
Volatility (%)	25.00%
Lattice Steps	5

Intermediate Calculations

Stepping-Time (dt)	
Up Step-Size (up)	
Down Step-Size (down)	
Risk-neutral Probability (prob)	

Results

Lattice Results	

Underlying Asset Lattice

Option Valuation Lattice

GRANULARITIES IN LATTICES

Another key concept in the use of binomial lattices is the idea of steps and precision. For instance, if a 5-year real options project is valued using five steps, each time-step size (δt) is equivalent to one year. Conversely, if 50 steps are used, then δt is equivalent to 0.1 year per step. Recall that the up and down step sizes were $e^{\sigma\sqrt{\delta t}}$ and $e^{-\sigma\sqrt{\delta t}}$, respectively. The smaller δt is, the smaller the up and down steps, and the more granular the lattice values will be.

Suppose that a European financial call option has a stock price of $100 and a strike price of $100 expiring in 1 year. Further, suppose that the corresponding risk-free rate is 5 percent and the calculated volatility of historical logarithmic returns is 25 percent. Because the option pays no dividends and is exercisable only at termination, a Black-Scholes equation will suffice. The call option value calculated using the Black-Scholes equation is $12.3360, which is obtained by

$$Call = S\Phi\left[\frac{\ln(S \ / \ X) + (r + \sigma^2 \ / \ 2)T}{\sigma\sqrt{T}}\right] - Xe^{-rf(T)}\Phi\left[\frac{\ln(S \ / \ X) + (r - \sigma^2 \ / \ 2)T}{\sigma\sqrt{T}}\right]$$

$$= 100\Phi\left[\frac{\ln(100 \ / \ 100) + (0.05 + 0.25^2 \ / \ 2)1}{0.25\sqrt{1}}\right] - 100e^{-0.05(1)} \times$$

$$\Phi\left[\frac{\ln(100 \ / \ 100) + (0.05 - 0.25^2 \ / \ 2)1}{0.25\sqrt{1}}\right]$$

$$= 100\Phi[0.325] - 95.13\Phi[0.075] = 100(0.6274) - 95.13(0.5298) = 12.3360$$

Compare the Black-Scholes results with those obtained using a binomial-lattice approach.

Black-Scholes model: $12.3360

Binomial Approach

5 Steps:	$12.7946
10 Steps:	$12.0932
20 Steps:	$12.2132
50 Steps:	$12.2867
100 Steps:	$12.3113
1,000 Steps:	$12.3335
10,000 Steps:	$12.3358
50,000 Steps:	$12.3360

Notice that as the number of steps increases, the binomial-lattice results approach the Black-Scholes result. That is, at the limit, when the number of steps approaches infinity, the time between steps approaches zero, the results are identical. Research has shown that 1,000 steps are sufficient for a good estimate in most real options problems. Although the Black-Scholes model is only applicable in very specific circumstances (no dividend payments are allowed and it is applicable to European-type options only), it is used here to illustrate the convergence of results between closed-form models (Black-Scholes type models) and binomial lattices. As shown in later chapters, the Black-Scholes model has limited applications, and abuse and misuse of this model will yield highly inaccurate and misleading results.

Exercise: Granularity in Lattices

Open the Excel file *Workbook Exercise (Granularity in Lattices).xls* from the enclosed CD-ROM. Using the input assumptions provided below, calculate a 5-step and 10-step lattice of the underlying asset. What are your observations? Redo the question on your own with a 20-step lattice and compare the 5-step lattice with the 20-step lattice. Something interesting happens here, as the factor size of going from 5 to 20 steps is 4, the square root of the stepping-time factor size is 2, which means that the same values appear every two steps, interspersed with intermediate granularities.

Granularity in Lattices

Assumptions

Asset Value ($)	$100.00
Implementation Cost ($)	$90.00
Maturity (Years)	5.00
Risk-free Rate (%)	5.00%
Dividends (%)	0.00%
Volatility (%)	20.00%
Small Lattice Steps	5
Large Lattice Steps	10

Intermediate Calculations

	5-Step	10-Step
Stepping-Time (dt)		
Up Step-Size (up)		
Down Step-Size (down)		
Risk-neutral Probability (prob)		

Underlying Asset Lattice (5 Steps)

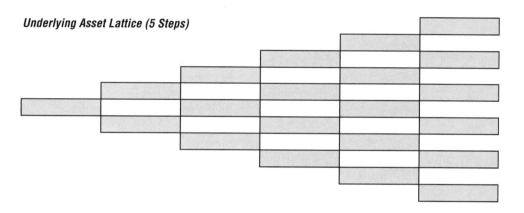

Underlying Asset Lattice (10 Steps)

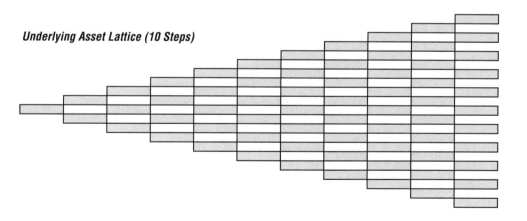

Exercise: European Option

Open the Excel file *Workbook Exercise (European Option).xls* from the enclosed CD-ROM. Calculate the European call option by completing the following lattices and assuming that these assumptions hold:

European Option Calculations

Assumptions

Asset Value ($)	$100.00
Implementation Cost ($)	$100.00
Maturity (Years)	1.00
Risk-free Rate (%)	5.00%
Dividends (%)	0.00%
Volatility (%)	25.00%
Lattice Steps	5

Intermediate Calculations

Stepping-Time (dt)	
Up Step-Size (up)	
Down Step-Size (down)	
Risk-neutral Probability (prob)	

Results

Lattice Results	
Black-Scholes Results	

Underlying Asset Lattice

Option Valuation Lattice

Decision Lattice

Exercise: American Option

Open the Excel file *Workbook Exercise (American Option).xls* from the enclosed CD-ROM. Calculate the American call option by completing the lattices below, assuming that the assumptions in the graphic hold:

American Option Calculations

Assumptions

Asset Value ($)	$100.00
Implementation Cost ($)	$80.00
Maturity (Years)	3.00
Risk-free Rate (%)	5.00%
Dividends (%)	12.00%
Volatility (%)	35.00%
Lattice Steps	5

Intermediate Calculations

Stepping-Time (dt)	
Up Step-Size (up)	
Down Step-Size (down)	
Risk-neutral Probability (prob)	

Results

Lattice Results	

Underlying Asset Lattice

Option Valuation Lattice

Decision Lattice

Change the input parameters in the American option exercise to match the previous European option exercise. What happens to the results? How do you reconcile the similarities and differences? Notice that the European option result is the same as the American option result when no dividends exist. This result means that it is never optimal to execute an American option early when no dividends exist. However, when a dividend exists, both American and European options become less valuable. The American option does, though, have a higher value than the European option due to its ability to execute early, which now becomes optimal.

Exercise: Risk-Neutral Probability Versus Market-Replicating Portfolio

In this exercise, solve the American call option using the risk-neutral probability approach, and then solve the same option using the market-replicating portfolio approach. For the market-replicating portfolio approach, assume a continuous discounting factor. Verify that the theory holds such that both approaches results in identical call option values. Which approach is simpler to apply?

For both approaches, assume these parameters: asset value = $100, strike cost = $100, maturity = 3 years, volatility = 10 percent, risk-free rate = 5 percent, dividends = 0 percent, and steps = 3.

Part I: Risk-Neutral Probability
Calculate the intermediate values and fill in the boxes:

Stepping Time (dt) = [＿＿＿＿]
Up Jump-Size (up) = [＿＿＿＿]
Down Jump-Size $(down)$ = [＿＿＿＿]
Risk-Neutral Probability $(prob)$ = [＿＿＿＿]

Underlying Asset Lattice

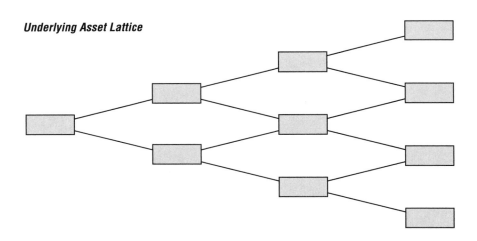

Option Valuation Lattice

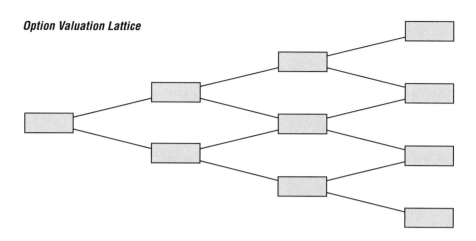

Calculated American call option value = $ [   ]

Part II: Market-Replicating Portfolio Approach

Underlying Asset Lattice

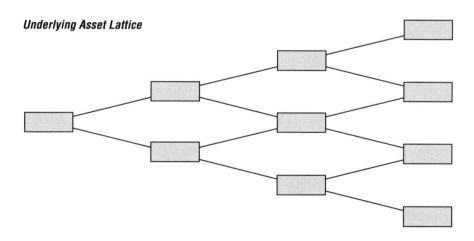

Use the following formulas:

- Hedge ratio (h): $h_{i-1} = (C_{up} - C_{down}) / (S_{up} - S_{down})$

- Debt load (D): $D_{i-1} = S_i(h_{i-1}) - C_i$

- Call value (C) at node i: $C_i = S_i(h_i) - D_i e^{-rf(\delta t)}$

- Risk-adjusted probability (q): $q_i = (S_{i-1} - S_{down}) / (S_{up} - S_{down})$

obtained assuming $S_{i-1} = q_i S_{up} + (1 - q_i)S_{down}$. This means that $S_{i-1} = q_i S_{up} + S_{down} - q_i S_{down}$ and $q_i[S_{up} - S_{down}] = S_{i-1} - S_{down}$ so we get $q_i = (S_{i-1} - S_{down}) / (S_{up} - S_{down})$.

Step 1: Get the call values at the terminal nodes. As we assume the strike prices are \$100 at all terminal nodes, we get (all values in \$)

$$C_{3UU} = \max\ [\ \boxed{}\ ] = \boxed{}$$
$$C_{3UD} = \max\ [\ \boxed{}\ ] = \boxed{}$$
$$C_{3DU} = \max\ [\ \boxed{}\ ] = \boxed{}$$
$$C_{3DD} = \max\ [\ \boxed{}\ ] = \boxed{}$$

Step 2: Get the hedge ratios for the terminal branches.

$$h_{2U} = \boxed{} \qquad h_{2M} = \boxed{} \qquad h_{2D} = \boxed{}$$

Step 3: Get the debt load for the terminal branches.

$$D_{2U} = S_{3UU}(h_{2U}) - C_{3UU} = \boxed{} = \boxed{}$$
$$D_{2M} = S_{3UD}(h_{2M}) - C_{3UD} = \boxed{} = \boxed{}$$
$$D_{2L} = S_{3DU}(h_{2D}) - C_{3DU} = \boxed{} = \boxed{}$$

Step 4: Get the call values one node back, $t = 2$.

$$C_{2U} = S_{2U}(h_{2U}) - D_{2U}(e^{-rf(\delta t)}) \quad = \boxed{} \quad = \boxed{}$$

$$C_{2M} = S_{2M}(h_{2M}) - D_{2M}(e^{-rf(\delta t)}) \quad = \boxed{} \quad = \boxed{}$$

$$C_{2D} = S_{2D}(h_{2D}) - D_{2D}(e^{-rf(\delta t)}) \quad = \boxed{} \quad = \boxed{}$$

Step 5: Get the hedge ratios for the one branch back, $t = 1$.

$$h_{1U} = \boxed{}$$

$$h_{1D} = \boxed{}$$

Step 6: Get the debt load for one branch back, $t = 1$.

$$D_{1U} = S_{2U}(h_{1U}) - C_{2U} = \boxed{} \quad = \boxed{}$$
$$D_{1D} = S_{2D}(h_{1D}) - C_{2D} = \boxed{} \quad = \boxed{}$$

Step 7: Get the call values one node back.

$$C_{1U} = S_{1U}(h_{1U}) - D_{1U}(e^{-rf(\delta t)}) = \boxed{} \quad = \boxed{}$$

$$C_{1D} = S_{1D}(h_{1D}) - D_{1D}(e^{-rf(\delta t)}) = \boxed{} \quad = \boxed{}$$

Step 8: Get the hedge ratios for two branches back, $t = 0$.

$$h_0 = \boxed{}$$

Step 9: Get the debt load for two branches back, $t = 0$.

$$D_0 = S_1(h_0) - C_{1U} = \boxed{} = \boxed{}$$

Step 10: Get the call value at $t = 0$, the option value of this analysis.

$$C_0 = S_0(h_0) - D_0(e^{-rf(\delta t)}) = \boxed{} = \boxed{}$$

Make sure the option value calculated in Step 10 is identical to the result obtained using the risk-neutral probability approach.

STATE-PRICING APPROACH TO SOLVING A EUROPEAN OPTION

Another approach that is useful in solving a real options problem is the application of state pricing. The state-pricing approach is fairly similar to the binomial-lattice approach. The exception being that the up and down jumps do not have to be symmetrical. The following exercise illustrates how a state-pricing approach yields similar answers to a binomial-lattice approach at the limit. The results converge at $32.504 using the closed-form American approximation model, state-pricing approach with 10,000 steps and binomial approach using 10,000 steps (Figure 5.2). The example assumes a $100 asset value, $100 implementation cost, 5-year expiration, 5 percent risk-free rate, and 25 percent in volatility. The following exercise looks at the steps required to solve a state-pricing European option model using five steps. These examples have important theoretical ramifications. Closed-form models, like the Black-Scholes, rely on some fairly restrictive assumptions (which are often violated), as do market-replicating portfolios, binomial lattices, and state-pricing approaches. However, while each methodology's assumptions are different, they yield identical results at the limit. This similarity implies that these restrictive assumptions are negligible and inconsequential when used in a Real Options context, and that they are only important in theoretical extrapolations, not in applied circumstances.

Black-Scholes Model	$32.504				
State-Pricing Model	$32.713	$31.753	$32.428	$32.489	$32.496	$32.504
Binomial Model	$33.164	$31.986	$32.452	$32.493	$32.499	$32.504
Steps	5	10	100	500	1,000	10,000

FIGURE 5.2   Comparison of approaches and time-steps.

When using the binomial approach, the up jump, down jump, and risk-neutral probability are calculated. Instead, when using the state-pricing approach, an up-state price and down-state price are calculated. The equations used in the state-pricing approach are:

$$\text{Up State} = \frac{rf(\delta t) - down}{up - down} e^{-rf(\delta t)}$$

$$\text{Down State} = \frac{up - rf(\delta t)}{up - down} e^{-rf(\delta t)}$$

Here, rf is the risk-free rate, δt is the time between steps, up is the absolute up-jump increment, and down is the absolute down-jump increment. For example, suppose the asset value is $100.00 but jumps to $128.40 and $77.88 in the first up and down jumps, the binomial up jump is hence 1.2840 and the down jump is 0.7788. In contrast, the state-price absolute up-jump increment is calculated as ($128.40 – $100.00) / $100.00 = 28.40 percent and the absolute down-jump increment is ($77.88 – $100.00) / $100.00 = –22.12 percent. Then, using these up and down increments, calculate the up-state and down-state values. Using these up-state and down-state values, calculate the expected value of the valuation lattice back to the starting time. The resulting value is the real options results using the state-pricing approach.

Exercise: State-Pricing Approach

Open the Excel file *Workbook Exercise (State Pricing).xls* from the enclosed CD-ROM. Verify that the answer is indeed $32.713. Using the state-pricing approach, solve this real options problem.

European Option Calculations – State Pricing Approach

Assumptions

Asset Value ($)	$100.00
Implementation Cost ($)	$100.00
Maturity (Years)	5.00
Risk-free Rate (%)	5.00%
Dividends (%)	0.00%
Volatility (%)	25.00%
Lattice Steps	5

Intermediate Calculations

Stepping-Time (dt)	
Up Step-Size (up)	
Down Step-Size (down)	
Up Jump Increment	
Down Jump Increment	
Up State Price	
Down State Price	

Results

State Pricing Approach	
Binomial Lattice Approach	
Black-Scholes Results	

Underlying Asset Lattice

State Prices Lattice

TRINOMIAL LATTICES AND AMERICAN OPTIONS

Building and solving a trinomial lattice is similar to building and solving a binomial lattice, complete with the up/down jumps and risk-neutral probabilities. However, the recombining trinomial lattice below is more complicated to build. The results stemming from a trinomial lattice are the same as those from a binomial lattice at the limit, but the lattice-building complexity is much higher for trinomial or multinomial lattices. Hence, the examples thus far have been focusing on the binomial lattice, due to its simplicity and applicability. It is difficult enough to create a three-time-step trinomial lattice as shown below; imagine having to keep track of the number of nodes, bifurcations, and which branch recombines with which, in a very large lattice. The equations relevant to developing a trinomial lattice depend on the up-jump size (u), down-jump size (d), risk-neutral probabilities for the low branch (p_L), middle branch (p_M), and high branch (p_H).

$$u = e^{\sigma\sqrt{3\delta t}} \quad \text{and} \quad d = e^{-\sigma\sqrt{3\delta t}}$$

$$p_L = \frac{1}{6} - \sqrt{\frac{\delta t}{12\sigma^2}}\left[r - q - \frac{\sigma^2}{2}\right]$$

$$p_M = \frac{2}{3}$$

$$p_H = \frac{1}{6} + \sqrt{\frac{\delta t}{12\sigma^2}}\left[r - q - \frac{\sigma^2}{2}\right]$$

The trinomial lattice follows the configuration shown in Figure 5.3.

The only reason to use a trinomial lattice is because the level of convergence to the correct option value is achieved quicker than using a binomial lattice. At the limit, both the binomial and trinomial lattices yield the same result, as seen below. Notice how the trinomial lattice yields the correct option value with fewer steps while it takes more steps for a binomial lattice (Figure 5.4). No matter the number of options solved, binomial lattices and trinomial lattices will both yield the same results at the limit.

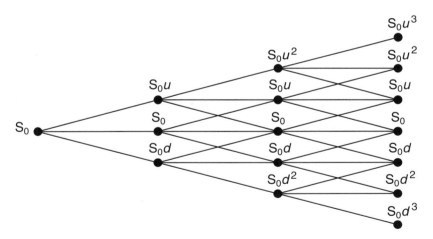

FIGURE 5.3 Generic three-step trinomial lattice.

American Approximation Model	$29.78				
Binomial Model	$30.73	$29.22	$29.72	$29.77	$29.78
Trinomial Model	$29.22	$29.50	$29.75	$29.78	$29.78
Steps	5	10	100	1,000	5,000

FIGURE 5.4 Comparison of approaches and time-steps.

Exercise: Trinomial Lattices

Open the Excel file *Workbook Exercise (Trinomial) Lattice.xls* from the enclosed CD-ROM. Using the formulas for building a trinomial lattice above, solve this American call option using a three-step trinomial lattice. Verify the results using the same assumptions by applying a three-step and four-step binomial lattice.

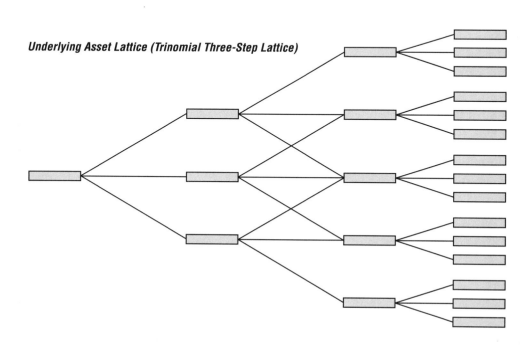

American Option Calculations (Trinomial Lattice)

Assumptions

Asset Value ($)	$100.00
Implementation Cost ($)	$100.00
Maturity (Years)	3.00
Risk-free Rate (%)	5.00%
Dividends (%)	0.00%
Volatility (%)	35.00%
Lattice Steps	3

Intermediate Calculations

Stepping-Time (dt)
Up Step-Size (up)
Down Step-Size (down)

High Branch Probability (P_H)
Middle Branch Probability (P_M)
Low Branch Probability (P_L)

Results

Lattice Results

Underlying Asset Lattice (Trinomial Three-Step Lattice)

Option Valuation Lattice (Trinomial Three-Step Lattice)

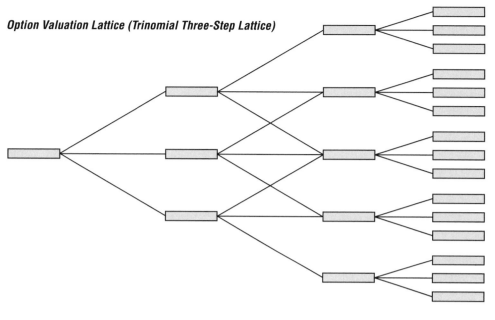

┌─ Intermediate Calculations ─────────────────────────────┐
│ Steps (N)   │ 3.0000 │
│ Stepping-Time (dt)   │   │
│ Up Step-Size (up)   │   │
│ Down Step-Size (down)   │   │
│ Risk-neutral Probability (prob)   │   │
└──┘

Underlying Asset Lattice (Binomial Three-Step Lattice)

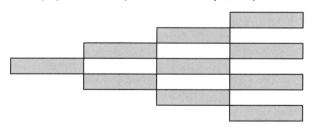

Option Valuation Lattice (Binomial Three-Step Lattice)

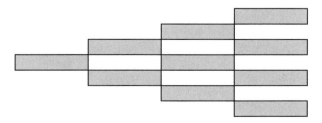

┌─ Intermediate Calculations ──────────────────────────────┐
│ Steps (N)   ┌──────────┐ │
│ Stepping-Time (dt)   │ 4.0000   │ │
│ Up Step-Size (up)   ├──────────┤ │
│ Down Step-Size (down)   ├──────────┤ │
│ Risk-neutral Probability (prob)   └──────────┘ │
└──┘

Underlying Asset Lattice (Binomial Four-Step Lattice)

Option Valuation Lattice (Binomial Four-Step Lattice)

CHAPTER 6

Real Options Business Cases

OPTION TO ABANDON

Suppose a pharmaceutical company is developing a particular drug. However, due to the uncertain nature of the drug's development progress, market demand, success in human and animal testing, and FDA approval, management decides that it will create a strategic abandonment option. That is, at any time period within the next 5 years of development, management can review the progress of the research and development effort and decide whether to terminate the drug development program. After 5 years, the firm would have either succeeded or completely failed in its drug development initiative, and there exists no option value after that time period. If the program is terminated, the firm can potentially sell off its intellectual property rights of the drug in question to another pharmaceutical firm with which it has a contractual agreement. This contract with the other firm is exercisable at any time within this period, at the whim of the firm owning the patents.

Using a traditional discounted cash flow (DCF) model, you find the present value of the expected future cash flows discounted at an appropriate market risk-adjusted discount rate to be $150 million. Using Monte Carlo simulation, you find the implied volatility of the logarithmic returns on future cash flows to be 30 percent. The risk-free rate on a riskless asset for the same time frame is 5 percent, and you understand from the intellectual property officer of the firm that the value of the drug's patent is $100 million contractually, if sold within the next 5 years. For simplicity, you assume that this $100 million salvage value is fixed for the next 5 years. You attempt to calculate how much this abandonment option is worth and how much this drug development effort on the whole is worth to the firm. By virtue of having this contractual safety net of being able to abandon drug development, the value of the project is worth more than its net present value (NPV). You decide to use a closed-form approximation of an American put option because the option to abandon drug development can be exercised at any time up to the expiration date. You also decide to confirm the value of the closed-form analysis with a binomial lattice calculation. With these assumptions, do the following exercises, answering the questions that are posed:

1. Solve the abandonment option problem analytically and confirm the results using the software. Then solve the same problem, but assume that the dividend rate is 2 percent, and the original salvage value of $100 at Year 0 grows at an annual rate of 3 percent starting in the first year. (Use the templates following.) Finally, confirm the initial results using the Real Options Analysis Toolkit software.
2. Select the right choice for each of the following:
   a. Increases in maturity (increase/decrease) the abandonment option value.
   b. Increases in volatility (increase/decrease) the abandonment option value.
   c. Increases in asset value (increase/decrease) the abandonment option value.
   d. Increases in risk-free rate (increase/decrease) the abandonment option value.
   e. Increases in dividend (increase/decrease) the abandonment option value.
   f. Increases in salvage value (increase/decrease) the abandonment option value.
3. Verify the results using the software's closed-form *American Long-Term Put Option Approximation* model.
4. Using the *Custom Lattice*, build and solve the abandonment option.
5. Use the *Black-Scholes* model to benchmark the results.
6. Apply 1,000 steps using the software's binomial lattice.
   a. How different are the results as compared to the five-step lattice?
   b. How close are the closed-form results compared to the 1,000-step lattice?
7. Apply a 3 percent continuous dividend yield to the 1,000-step lattice.
   a. What happens to the results?
   b. Does a dividend yield increase or decrease the value of an abandonment option? Why?
8. Assume that the salvage value increases at a 10 percent annual rate. Show how this can be modeled using the software's *Custom Lattice*.

Analytical Solutions

The figures below show the results of your analysis using a binomial approach, where the calculated value of the abandonment option is $6.6412 million (five time-steps). First, to obtain the results for the abandonment option, calculate and complete the following.

Stepping Time
Up Step-Size (up)
Down Step-Size (down)
Risk-neutral Probability (prob)

The first lattice, the lattice of the underlying asset, is shown below. All the required calculations and steps in the underlying asset lattice are based on the up factor and down factor. Complete the lattice showing all your calculation steps.

Underlying Asset Lattice

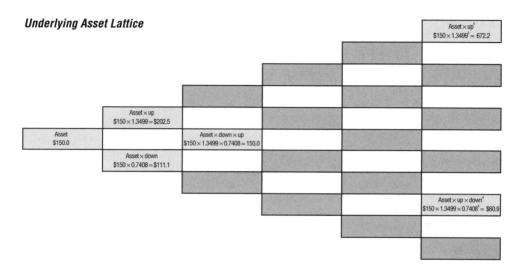

Creating the option valuation lattice proceeds in two steps: the valuation of the terminal nodes and the valuation of the intermediate nodes using a process called backward induction. In the first underlying asset lattice, the values are created in a forward multiplication of up and down factors, from left to right. For the second lattice, the option valuation lattice, the calculation proceeds in a backward manner starting from the terminal nodes, that is, the nodes at the end of the lattice are valued first, going from right to left.

The circled terminal node (denoted A) reveals a value of $672.2, which can be obtained through the value maximization of abandonment versus continuation. At the end of 5 years, the firm has the option both to sell off and to abandon its existing drug program or to continue developing. Obviously, management will choose the strategy that maximizes profitability. The value of abandoning the drug program is equivalent to selling the patent rights at the predetermined $100 million value. The value of continuing with development can be found in the underlying asset lattice evolution, which is $672.2 million. The profit-maximizing decision is to continue development; hence, we have the value $672.2 million on that node (denoted A). Similarly, for the terminal node B, we see that the value of abandoning at that time is $100 million as compared to $60.99 from the underlying asset lattice. Hence, the decision at that node is to abandon the project, and the profit-maximizing value of that node becomes the abandonment value of $100 million. This result is very easy to understand because if the underlying asset value of pursuing the drug development is high (node A), it is wise to continue with the development. Otherwise, if circumstances force the value of the development effort down to such a low level as specified by node B, then it is more optimal to abandon the project and cut the firm's losses. This action of course assumes that management will execute the optimal profit-maximizing behavior of abandoning the project when it is optimal to do so rather than hanging on to it.

Moving on to the intermediate nodes, we see that node C is calculated as $273.3 million. At this particular node, the firm again has two options: to abandon at that point or not to abandon, thereby keeping the option to abandon open and available for the future in the hopes that when things seem less rosy, the firm has the ability to execute the option and abandon the development program. The value of abandoning is again the $100 million in salvage value. The value of continuing is simply the discounted weighted average of potential future option values using the risk-neutral probability. Calculate the option to abandon by completing the option valuation lattice.

Option Valuation Lattice

Max(Abandon, End)
Max($100, $672.2)
Decision: End at $672.2
(A)

Max(Abandon, Open)
Max($100, $273.3)
Decision: End at $273.3
(C)

Max(Abandon, End)
Max($100, $60.9)
Decision: Abandon at $100.0
(B)

By having a safety net or way out for management under dire circumstances, the project is worth more than its static value of $[   ] million. This is the static NPV without flexibility, the $[   ] million is the real options value, and the combined value of $[   ] million is the ENPV (Expanded NPV) value or NPV+O (NPV with real options flexibility value), the correct total value of this drug development program. Clearly, modifications to the lattice analysis can be done to further mirror actual business conditions. For instance, the abandonment salvage value can change over time, which can simply be instituted through changing the salvage amount at the appropriate times with respect to the nodes on the lattice. Changes in abandonment salvage value can be caused by an inflation adjustment, a growth or decline in the value of the intellectual property over time, and so forth.

Exercise: Abandonment Option

Open the Excel file *Workbook Exercise (Abandonment Option).xls* from the enclosed CD-ROM. Solve the same abandonment option using binomial lattices. However, add a 2 percent dividend rate and change the salvage value by a 3 percent growth rate per year, starting in the first year. Complete these lattices.

Creating and Solving an Abandonment Option

Assumptions

Asset Value ($)	$150.00
Maturity (Years)	5.00
Risk-free Rate (%)	5.00%
Dividends (%)	2.00%
Volatility (%)	30.00%
Lattice Steps	5
Salvage Value ($)	$100.00
Growth Rate (%)	3.00%

Intermediate Calculations

Stepping-Time (dt)	
Up Step-Size (up)	
Down Step-Size (down)	
Risk-neutral Probability (prob)	

Results

Lattice Results	

Underlying Asset Lattice

Salvage Values

Option Valuation Lattice

Decision Lattice

Software Solutions

1. Solve the abandonment option problem analytically and confirm the initial results using the software.

The value of the project is $156.64 million. $150 million is the NPV, and $6.64 million comes from the strategic abandonment option.

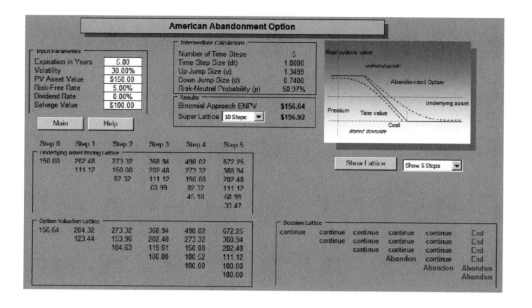

2. Select the right choice for each of the following:

    a. Increases in maturity increase the abandonment option value.
    b. Increases in volatility increase the abandonment option value.
    c. Increases in asset value decrease the abandonment option value.
    d. Increases in risk-free rate decrease the abandonment option value.
    e. Increases in dividend decrease the abandonment option value.
    f. Increases in salvage value increase the abandonment option value.

3. Verify the initial results using the software's closed-form *American Long-Term Put Option Approximation* model.

    The closed-form result is $6.98 million compared to $6.64 million using a five-step binomial analysis.

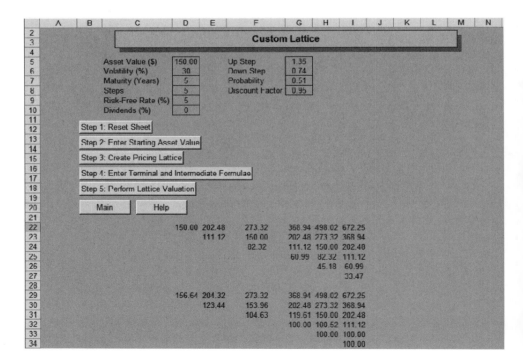

American Long-Term Put Option Approximation

Inputs		Upside	Downside
Asset Value	$150.00	-1.5037	2.0097
Implementation Cost	$100.00	2.6789	-2.1791
Time to Maturity	5.00	0.4896	-0.5345
Risk-Free Rate	5.00%	-0.4148	0.4438
Dividend Rate	0.00%	0.0000	0.0000
Volatility	30.00%	1.9459	-1.8005
Closed Form Approx.	$6.98		
Binomial Approach 5 Steps	$6.64	Reset to Original	

+/-10% Sensitivity   Show Lattice   Show 5 Steps

Main   Help

4. Using the *Custom Lattice*, build and solve the abandonment option. *The* Custom Lattice *replicates the results from the American Abandonment Option model, with $6.64 million for the abandonment option value. The underlying asset pricing and valuation lattices' inputs are shown here.*

Custom Lattice

Asset Value ($)	150.00	Up Step	1.35
Volatility (%)	30	Down Step	0.74
Maturity (Years)	5	Probability	0.51
Steps	5	Discount Factor	0.95
Risk-Free Rate (%)	5		
Dividends (%)	0		

Step 1: Reset Sheet

Step 2: Enter Starting Asset Value

Step 3: Create Pricing Lattice

Step 4: Enter Terminal and Intermediate Formulae

Step 5: Perform Lattice Valuation

Main   Help

150.00	202.48	273.32	368.94	498.02 672.25
	111.12	150.00	202.48	273.32 368.94
		82.32	111.12	150.00 202.48
			60.99	82.32 111.12
				45.18 60.99
				33.47

156.64	204.32	273.32	368.94	498.02 672.25
	123.44	153.96	202.48	273.32 368.94
		104.63	119.61	150.00 202.48
			100.00	100.52 111.12
				100.00 100.00
				100.00

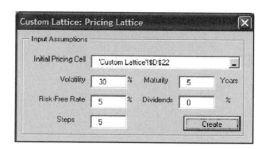

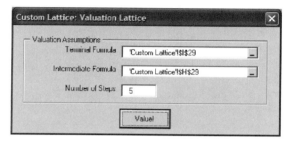

5. Use the *Black-Scholes* model to benchmark the results.

The Black-Scholes *put option value is calculated to be $6.09, providing somewhat of a decent benchmark for an abandonment option in this example. However, be aware that the* Black-Scholes *model fails miserably as a benchmark for other options (e.g., expansion options).*

European Black-Scholes Model with Dividend

Inputs		Call Upside	Call Downside	Put Upside	Put Downside
PV Asset	$150.00	13.7512	-13.3712	-1.2488	1.6288
Implementation Cost	$100.00	-5.5711	5.9474	2.2169	-1.8406
Time to Maturity	5.00	2.2382	-2.3404	0.3153	-0.3688
Risk-Free Rate	5.00%	1.4334	-1.4458	-0.4895	0.5257
Dividend Rate	0.00%	0.0000	0.0000	0.0000	0.0000
Volatility	30.00%	1.7617	-1.6182	1.7617	-1.6182
Call Option	**$78.21**				
Put Option	**$6.09**		Reset to Original		

Instantaneous Sensitivities	
Asset (Delta)	0.9053
Cost (Xi)	-0.5759
Time (Tau)	-4.5759
Risk-Free Rate (Rho)	2.8795
Vega (Volatility)	0.5655

+/-10% Sensitivity

| Main | Help |

6. Apply 1,000 steps using the software's binomial lattice.
   a. How different are the results as compared to the five-step lattice? *The results are fairly close to a five-step lattice, yielding $7.0878 million as compared to $6.6412 million.*
   b. How close are the closed-form results compared to the 1,000-step lattice? *Closed-form solutions ($6.9756 million) are also fairly close to the 1,000-step lattice ($7.0878 million).*

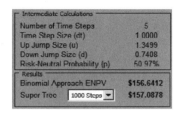

7. Apply a 3 percent continuous dividend yield on the 1,000-step lattice.
   a. What happens to the results? *The resulting option analysis results decrease.*
   b. Does a dividend yield increase or decrease the value of an abandonment option? *The option value decreases due to the leakage in asset value as specified by the 3 percent continuous dividend yield. Dividends increase a **financial** put option's value but reduce an abandonment **real option** value because in real options, dividends (e.g., annual taxes, maintenance costs, operating expenses) are only incurred when the option is kept open and not abandoned.*

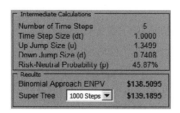

8. Assume that the salvage value increases at a 10 percent annual rate. Show how this can be modeled using the software's *Custom Lattice* function.
   To incorporate this changing salvage value, create a row between the lattice of the underlying asset and the option valuation lattice. This row has the salvage value increasing over time.

		150.00	202.48	273.32	368.94 498.02 672.25	
			111.12	150.00	202.48 273.32 368.94	
				82.32	111.12 150.00 202.48	
					60.99 82.32 111.12	
					45.18 60.99	
					33.47	
Salvage Value	100.00	110.00		121.00	133.10 146.41 161.05	
	176.19	217.03		278.38	368.94 498.02 672.25	
		152.16		175.94	213.34 273.32 368.94	
				143.34	155.47 173.28 202.48	
					145.72 153.20 161.05	
					153.20 161.05	
					161.05	

OPTION TO EXPAND

Suppose a growth firm has a static valuation of future profitability using a DCF model (in other words, the present value of the expected future cash flows discounted at an appropriate market risk-adjusted discount rate) that is found to be $400 million. Using Monte Carlo simulation, you calculate the implied volatility of the logarithmic returns on the projected future cash flows to be 35 percent. The risk-free rate on a riskless asset for the next 5 years is found to be yielding 7 percent. Suppose that the firm has the option to expand and double its operations by acquiring its competitor for a sum of $250 million at any time over the next 5 years. What is the total value of this firm, assuming that you account for this expansion option?

You decide to use a closed-form approximation of an American call option because the option to expand the firm's operations can be exercised at any time up to the expiration date. You also decide to confirm the value of the closed-form analysis with a binomial lattice calculation. Do the following exercises, answering the questions that are posed:

1. Solve the expansion option problem analytically. Then verify the original results using the Real Options Analysis Toolkit software.
2. Rerun the original expansion option problem using the software for 100 steps, 300 steps, and 1,000 steps. What are your observations?
3. Show how you would use the *American Long-Term Call Option Approximation* model to estimate and benchmark the results from an expansion option. How comparable are the results?
4. Show the different levels of expansion factors but still yielding the same expanded asset value of $800. Explain your observations in terms of why the expansion value changes, and why the *Black-Scholes* and *American Long-Term Option Approximation* models are insufficient to capture the fluctuation in value.
   a. Use an expansion factor of 2.00 and an asset value of $400.00 (yielding an expanded asset value of $800).

   b. Use an expansion factor of 1.25 and an asset value of $640.00 (yielding an expanded asset value of $800).

   c. Use an expansion factor of 1.50 and an asset value of $533.33 (yielding an expanded asset value of $800).

   d. Use an expansion factor of 1.75 and an asset value of $457.14 (yielding an expanded asset value of $800).

5. Add a dividend yield, and see what happens. Explain your findings.

   a. What happens when the dividend rate equals or exceeds the risk-free rate?

   b. What happens to the accuracy of closed-form solutions such as the *Black-Scholes* and *American Long-Term Call Option Approximation* models?

6. What happens to the decision to expand if a dividend yield exists?

Analytical Solutions

The figures below show the results of your analysis using a binomial approach, where you calculate the value of the expansion option as $638.3 million using five time-steps. Solve the expansion option by first completing the calculations on stepping time and step sizes.

Stepping Time	
Up Step-Size (up)	
Down Step-Size (down)	
Risk-neutral Probability (prob)	

Then complete the underlying asset lattice. The only required computation here is the up and down step sizes calculated previously.

Underlying Asset Lattice

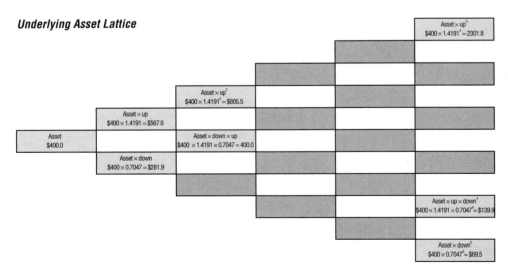

Asset × up⁵
$400 × 1.4191⁵ = 2301.8

Asset × up²
$400 × 1.4191² = $805.5

Asset × up
$400 × 1.4191 = $567.6

Asset
$400.0

Asset × down × up
$400 × 1.4191 × 0.7047 = 400.0

Asset × down
$400 × 0.7047 = $281.9

Asset × up × down⁴
$400 × 1.4191 × 0.7047⁴ = $139.9

Asset × down⁵
$400 × 0.7047⁵ = $69.5

Next, calculate the expansion option by completing the option valuation lattice below. The sample circled terminal node (denoted D) reveals a value of $4,353.7, which can be obtained through the value maximization of expansion versus continuation. At the end of 5 years, the firm has the option to acquire the competition and expand its existing operations or not. Obviously, management will choose the strategy that maximizes profitability. The value of acquiring and expanding its operations is equivalent to doubling its existing capacity of $2,301.8 obtained from the underlying asset lattice. Hence, the value of acquiring and expanding the firm's operations is double this existing capacity less any acquisition costs or 2($2,301.8) – $250 = $4,353.6 million (rounded). The value of continuing with existing business operations can be found in the underlying asset lattice, which is $2,301.8 million. The profit-maximizing decision is to acquire the firm for $250 million; hence, we have the value $4,353.6 million on that node (denoted D). Similarly, for the terminal node E, we see that the value of continuing existing operations at that time is $69.5 million from the underlying asset lattice. In comparison, by expanding its operations through acquisition, the value is only 2($69.5) – $250 = –$111 million. Hence, the decision at that node is to continue with existing operations without expanding, and the profit-maximizing value on that node is $69.5 million. This result is intuitive because if the underlying asset value of pursuing existing business operations is such that it is very high based on current market conditions (node D), then it is wise to double the firm's operations through acquisition of the competitor. Otherwise, if circumstances force the value of the firm's operations down to such a low level as specified by node E, then it is more optimal to continue with the existing business and not worry about expanding because the project will be a loser at that point.

Moving on to the intermediate nodes, we see that node F is calculated as $1,408.4 million. At this particular node, the firm again has two options: to expand its operations at that point or to keep the option to expand open for the future in the hopes that when the market is up, the firm has the ability to execute the option and acquire its competitor. The value of expanding at that node is 2($805) – $250 = $1,361 million (rounded). The value of continuing is simply the discounted weighted average of potential future option values using the risk-neutral probability. Because the risk adjustment is performed on the probabilities of future option cash flows, the discounting can be done using the risk-free rate. That is, for the value of keeping the option alive and open, we have

$$[(P)(\$\boxed{}) + (1 - P)(\$\boxed{})]\exp[(-\boxed{})(\boxed{})] = \$1,408.4 \text{ million}$$

which is higher than the expansion value. This assumes a 7 percent risk-free rate *rf*, and a time-step δt of 1. Calculate the expansion option by completing the following option valuation lattice.

Option Valuation Lattice

Max(Expand, End)
Max($4353.7, $2301.8)
Decision: Expand at $4353.7
(D)

Max(Expand, Open)
Max($1361.0, $1408.4)
Decision: End at $1408.4
(F)

Max(Expand, End)
Max(-$111.0, $69.5)
Decision: End at $69.5
(E)

By not executing the acquisition today but still having an option for management given great market and economic outlook to acquire the competitor, then the firm is worth more than its static value of $[____] million, which is the static NPV without flexibility. The $[____] million is the real options value and the combined value of $[____] million is the ENPV (Expanded NPV) or NPV+O (NPV with real options flexibility value), the correct total value of this firm. The real options value is worth an additional [____] percent of existing business operations. If a real options approach is not used, the firm will be undervalued because it has a strategic option to expand its current operations but not an obligation to do so and will most likely not do so unless market conditions deem it optimal. The firm has in essence hedged itself against any potential downside if it were to acquire the competitor immediately without regard for what may potentially happen in the future. Having an option and sometimes keeping this option open are valuable given a highly uncertain business environment. Clearly, to mirror actual business conditions, the cost of acquisition can change over time, and the expansion factor (doubling its operations) can also change as business conditions change. All these variables can be accounted for in the lattice.

Exercise: Expansion Option (American Expansion Option)

Open the Excel file *Workbook Exercise (Expansion Option I).xls* from the enclosed CD-ROM. Using the same assumptions, solve the expansion option by hand and complete these lattices.

Assumptions

Asset Value ($)	$400.00
Implementation Cost ($)	$250.00
Maturity (Years)	5.00
Risk-free Rate (%)	7.00%
Dividends (%)	0.00%
Volatility (%)	35.00%
Lattice Steps	5
Expansion Factor	2.00

Intermediate Calculations

Stepping-Time (dt)	1.0000
Up Step-Size (up)	1.4191
Down Step-Size (down)	0.7047
Risk-neutral Probability (prob)	51.49%

Results

Lattice Results	$638.30

This exercise assumes a static expansion factor.

Underlying Asset Lattice

Option Valuation Lattice

Decision Lattice

Exercise: Expansion Option (Growing Expansion Rate)

Open the Excel file *Workbook Exercise (Expansion Option II).xls* from the enclosed CD-ROM. Change the risk-free rate to 8 percent, and the expansion factor to 1.50 but growing at a 10 percent annual rate starting in Year 1. Solve the expansion option by completing these lattices.

Creating and Solving an Expansion Option II

Assumptions

Asset Value ($)	$400.00
Implementation Cost ($)	$250.00
Maturity (Years)	5.00
Risk-free Rate (%)	8.00%
Dividends (%)	2.00%
Volatility (%)	35.00%
Lattice Steps	5
Expansion Factor	1.50
Expansion Growth Rate	10.00%

Intermediate Calculations

Stepping-Time (dt)	
Up Step-Size (up)	
Down Step-Size (down)	
Risk-neutral Probability (prob)	

Results

Lattice Results	

This exercise assumes a dynamic expansion factor.

Underlying Asset Lattice

Expansion Values

Option Valuation Lattice

Decision Lattice

111

Exercise: Expansion Option (Competitive Risks)

Open the Excel file *Workbook Exercise (Expansion Option III).xls* from the enclosed CD-ROM. Use the same input parameters as in the original problem, but now assume that the competitor's cash flow has a 25 percent volatility instead of the firm's 35 percent. Show how this different risk parameter between the firm and its competitor can be accounted for using binomial lattices.

Creating and Solving an Expansion Option III

Assumptions

	Your Firm	Competition
Asset Value ($)	$400.00	$400.00
Implementation Cost ($)	$250.00	
Maturity (Years)	5.00	
Risk-free Rate (%)	7.00%	
Dividends (%)	0.00%	
Volatility (%)	35.00%	25.00%
Lattice Steps	5	

Intermediate Calculations

	Your Firm	Competition
Stepping-Time (dt)		
Up Step-Size (up)		
Down Step-Size (down)		
Risk-neutral Probability (prob)		

Results

Lattice Results	

This exercise assumes a dynamic expansion factor that depends on a competitive firm growing at different rates.

Firm's Underlying Asset Lattice

Competitor's Underlying Asset Lattice

Expansion Factors

Option Valuation Lattice

Decision Lattice

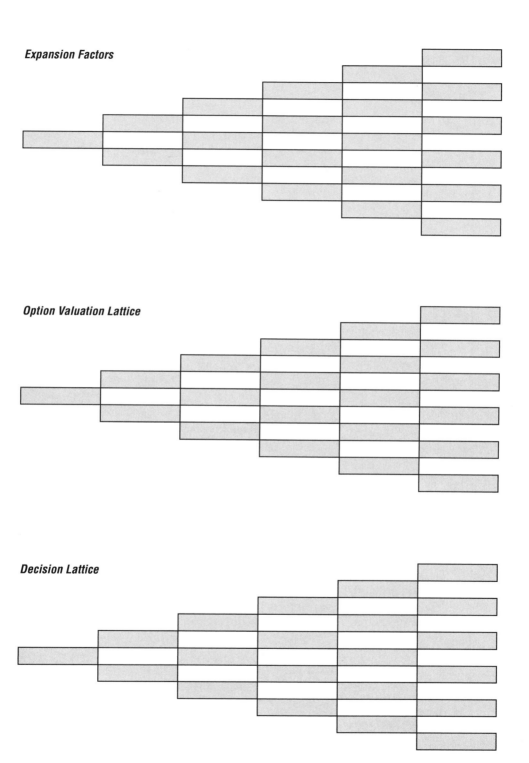

Software Solutions

1. Solve the expansion option problem analytically. Then verify the original results using the Real Options Analysis Toolkit software.

The option value is $88.30, because the binomial lattice's $638.30 includes the $88.30 option value and $550.00 NPV (expansion of 2.0 times $400.00 asset value less the implementation cost of $250).

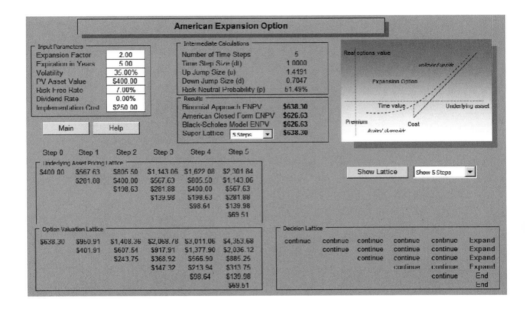

2. Rerun the expansion option problem using the software for 100 steps, 300 steps, and 1,000 steps. What are your observations?

The expansion option results converge at around $638, confirming the robustness of results. This means that convergence is achieved in this problem very early.

Super Lattice (100 steps)   = $638.7315
Super Lattice (300 steps)   = $638.8634
Super Lattice (1,000 steps) = $638.8700

3. Show how you would use the *American Long-Term Call Option Approximation* model to estimate and benchmark the results from an expansion option. How comparable are the results?

American Long-Term Call Option Approximation

Inputs		Upside	Downside
Asset Value	$800.00	79.3170	-79.0394
Implementation Cost	$250.00	-16.3924	16.6654
Time to Maturity	5.00	6.5067	-6.7414
Risk-Free Rate	7.00%	5.7026	-5.8716
Dividend Rate	0.00%	0.0000	0.0000
Volatility	35.00%	1.9773	-1.3812
Closed Form Approx.	$626.63		
Binomial Approach 5 Steps	$625.93		

Reset to Original

▲▼ +/-10% Sensitivity   Show Lattice   Show 5 Steps

Main   Help

The American Long-Term Call Option Approximation *model is a decent benchmark, providing similar magnitudes in value ($600 range). Notice that the asset value in the* American Long-Term Call Option Approximation *model is set to the expanded asset value of $800 ($400 base case asset value multiplied by the expansion factor of 2.0).*

4. Show the different levels of expansion factors but still yielding the same expanded asset value of $800. Explain your observations in terms of why the expansion value changes, and why the *Black-Scholes* and *American Long-Term Call Option Approximation* models are insufficient to capture the fluctuation in value.

The closed-form solutions do not change, but the values of the expansion option values using the binomial approach do. The closed-form models do not provide good benchmarks, as the correct expansion option values are shown using the binomial approach.

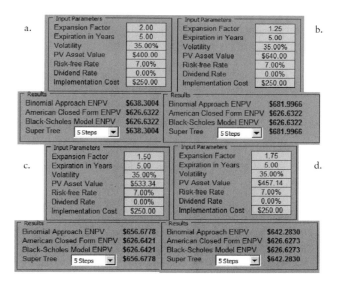

5. Add a dividend yield, and see what happens. Explain your findings.

    a. What happens when the dividend rate equals or exceeds the risk-free rate?

    b. What happens to the accuracy of closed-form solutions such as the *Black-Scholes* and *American Long-Term Call Option Approximation* models?

The higher the dividend yield, the higher the opportunity cost of holding the option open for future expansion. Hence, the asset value diminishes over the maturity period. Therefore, the option value decreases as dividend yield increases. The diminishing returns hit the maximum level when the dividend yield equals the risk-free rate. That is, once dividend yield equals or exceeds the risk-free rate, the value of the option reverts to the NPV of $550. This result is calculated using the $400 asset value expanding at 2.0 times, yielding $800 expanded asset value, less the $250 cost of expansion, yielding a net of $550. The Black-Scholes *model is inappropriate for dividend yields exceeding the risk-free rate and hence provides a bad benchmark because the* Black-Scholes *is applicable only for* European Options *and not* American Expansion Options, *especially when a dividend yield exists.* European Option *models underestimate* American Option *models when a dividend yield exists.*

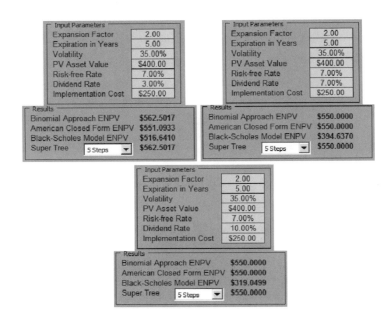

6. What happens to the decision to expand if a dividend yield exists?

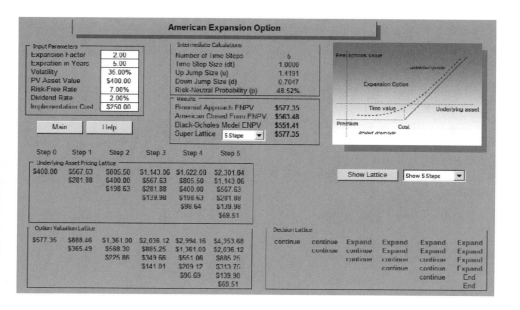

> *With a dividend yield or opportunistic cash outflow, it is optimal to exercise the option prior to expiration.*

OPTION TO CONTRACT

You work for a large aeronautical manufacturing firm that is unsure of the technological efficacy and market demand of its new fleet of long-range supersonic jets. The firm decides to hedge itself through the use of strategic options, specifically an option to contract 50 percent of its manufacturing facilities at any time within the next 5 years.

Suppose that the firm has a current operating structure whose static valuation of future profitability using a DCF model (in other words, the present value of the expected future cash flows discounted at an appropriate market risk-adjusted discount rate) is found to be $1 billion. Using Monte Carlo simulation, you calculate the implied volatility of the logarithmic returns on the projected future cash flows to be 50 percent. The risk-free rate on a riskless asset for the next 5 years is found to be yielding 5 percent.

Suppose the firm has the option to contract 50 percent of its current operations at any time over the next 5 years, thereby creating an additional $400 million in savings after this contraction. This savings is achieved through a legal contractual agreement with one of its vendors, who has agreed to take up the firm's excess capacity and space. At the same time, the firm can scale back its existing workforce to obtain this level of savings.

A closed-form approximation of an American option can be used, because the option to contract the firm's operations can be exercised at any time up to the expiration date and can be confirmed with a binomial lattice calculation. Do the following exercises, answering the questions that are posed:

1. Solve the contraction option problem analytically and using the software. Then add a 2 percent dividend rate and a 50 percent contraction factor that grows at a −5 percent growth rate. Finally, confirm the original results using the software.
2. Modify the continuous dividend payout rate until the option breaks even for a five-step lattice. What observations can you make at this break-even point?
3. Use the *American Long-Term Put Option Approximation* model to benchmark the contraction option. What are the input parameters?
4. How can you use the *American Abandonment Option* model as a benchmark to estimate the contraction option? If it is used, are the resulting option values comparable?
5. Change the contraction factor to 0.7, and answer Question 4. Why are the answers different?

Analytical Solutions

The following figures show the step-by-step analysis using a binomial approach to solve the contraction option, which is calculated to be $105.61 million using a five-time-step lattice. To begin the analysis, calculate and complete the required values in the following.

Stepping Time
Up Step-Size (up)
Down Step-Size (down)
Risk-neutral Probability (prob)

Then complete the underlying asset lattice. The only required computation here is the up and down step sizes calculated previously.

Underlying Asset Lattice

						Asset × up[1] $1000 × 1.6487[5] = $12182.5
					Asset × up[4] $1000 × 1.6487[4] = $7389.1	
				Asset × up[3] $1000 × 1.6487[3] = $4481.7		
			Asset × up[2] $1000 × 1.6487[2] = $2718.2			
		Asset × up $1000 × 1.6487 = $1648.7				
Asset $1000.0			Asset × down × up $1000 × 1.6487 × 0.6065 = 1000.0			
	Asset × down $1000 × 0.6065 = $606.5					
					Asset × up × down[3] $1000 × 1.6487 × 0.6065[3] = $368.0	
						Asset × up × down[4] $1000 × 1.6487 × 0.6065[4] = $223.1
						Asset × down[5] $1000 × 0.6065[5] = $82.1

The next step is to calculate the option valuation lattice using the values calculated in the underlying asset lattice. We see that the sample terminal node (denoted G) reveals a value of $12,183 (rounded), which can be obtained through the value maximization of contraction versus continuation. At the end of 5 years, the firm has the option to contract its existing operations or not, thereby letting the option expire. Obviously, management will choose the strategy that maximizes profitability. The value of contracting 50 percent of its operations is equivalent to half of its existing operations plus the $400 million in savings. Hence, the value of contracting the firm's operations is

$$0.5(\$\boxed{}) + \$\boxed{} = \$\boxed{} \text{ million}$$

The value of continuing with existing business operations can be found in the underlying asset lattice, which is $12,183 million. The profit-maximizing decision is to continue with the firm's current level of operations at $12,183 million on that node (denoted G). Similarly, for the terminal node H, we see that the value of continuing existing operations at that time is $82 million from the underlying asset lattice. In comparison, by contracting its operations to 50 percent, the value is 0.5($82) + $400 = $441. Hence, the decision at that node is to contract operations by 50 percent and the profit-maximizing value on that node is $441 million. This result is intuitive, because if the underlying asset value of pursuing existing business operations is such that it is very high based on current good operating conditions (node G), then it is wise to continue its current levels of operation. Otherwise, if circumstances force the value of the firm's operations down to such a low level as specified by node H, then it is optimal to contract the existing business by 50 percent.

Moving on to the intermediate nodes, we see that node I is calculated as $2,734 million. At this particular node, the firm again has two options, to contract its operations at that point or not to contract, thereby keeping the option to contract available and open for the future in the hopes that when the market is up, the firm has the ability to execute the option and contract its existing operations. The value of contracting at that node is 0.5($2,718) + $400 = $1,759 million. The value of continuing is simply the discounted weighted average of potential future option values using the risk-neutral probability. As the risk adjustment is performed on the probabilities of future option cash flows, the discounting can be done using the risk-free rate. That is, for the value of keeping the option alive and open, we have

$$[(P)(\$\boxed{}) + (1 - P)(\$\boxed{})]\exp[(-\boxed{})(\boxed{})] = \$2,734 \text{ million}$$

which is higher than the contraction value. This result assumes a 5 percent risk-free rate *rf*, and a time-step δt of 1. Using the backward induction technique, the lattice is back-calculated to the starting point to obtain the value of $\boxed{}$ million. Because the value obtained through a DCF is $1,000 million for current existing operations, the option value of being able to contract 50 percent of its operations is $\boxed{}$ million. The $1,000 million is the static NPV without flexibility, the $\boxed{}$ million is the real options value, and the combined value of $\boxed{}$ million is the ENPV (Expanded NPV) value or NPV+O (NPV with real options flexibility value), the correct total value of this manufacturing initiative. The real options value is worth an additional $\boxed{}$ percent of existing business operations. If a real options approach is not used, the manufacturing initiative will be undervalued.

Option Valuation Lattice

	Max(Contract, End)
	Max($6491, $12183)
	Decision: End at $12183

Max(Contract, Open)
Max($4095, $7389)
Decision: Open at $7389 (G)

Max(Contract, End)
Max($2741, $4482)
Decision: End at $4482

Max(Contract, Open)
Max($1759, $2734)
Decision: Open at $2734 (I)

Max(Contract, End)
Max($441, $82)
Decision: Contract at $441 (H)

Exercise: Contraction Option

Open the Excel file *Workbook Exercise (Contraction Option).xls* from the enclosed CD-ROM. Use the same input parameters provided in the example but add a 2 percent dividend rate that grows at a –5 percent rate annually. Solve this modified contraction option by completing these lattices.

Creating and Solving a Contraction Option

Assumptions

Asset Value ($)	$1,000.00
Maturity (Years)	5.00
Risk-free Rate (%)	5.00%
Dividends (%)	2.00%
Volatility (%)	50.00%
Lattice Steps	5
Savings ($)	$400.00
Contraction Factor	0.50
Contraction Growth Rate (%)	–5.00%

Intermediate Calculations

Stepping-Time (dt)	
Up Step-Size (up)	
Down Step-Size (down)	
Risk-neutral Probability (prob)	

Results

Lattice Results	

This exercise assumes a dynamic contraction factor.

Underlying Asset Lattice

Contraction Factors

Option Valuation Lattice

Decision Lattice

Software Solutions

1. Solve the contraction option problem using the software.

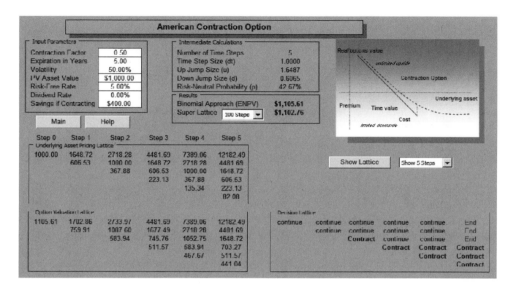

2. Modify the continuous dividend payout rate until the option breaks even. What observations can you make at this break-even point?

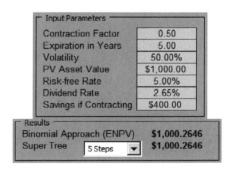

A higher dividend outflow reduces the value of the contraction option. The break-even point for this 50 percent contraction option is about 50 percent of the risk-free rate. Any dividend outflows greater than this break-even point make the option worthless.

3. Use the *American Long-Term Put Option Approximation* model to benchmark the contraction option. What are the input parameters?

American Long-Term Put Option Approximation

Inputs		Upside	Downside
Asset Value	$500.00	-9.1776	10.6648
Implementation Cost	$400.00	20.8100	-19.3293
Time to Maturity	5.00	4.0250	-4.4876
Risk-Free Rate	5.00%	-3.0764	3.2152
Dividend Rate	0.00%	0.0000	0.0000
Volatility	50.00%	14.6289	-14.8839
Closed Form Approx.	$102.23		
Binomial Approach 5 Steps ▼	$105.61		Reset to Original

+/-10% Sensitivity   Show Lattice   Show 5 Steps ▼

Main   Help

The abandonment option can be estimated using the American Long-Term Put Option Approximation *model. The asset value is modified to the initial asset value multiplied by the contraction factor. The results from a 100-step (not shown here) binomial lattice ($102.7565) approach the closed-form approximation value ($102.2278).*

4. How can you use the *American Abandonment Option* model as a benchmark to estimate the contraction option? Are the resulting option values comparable?

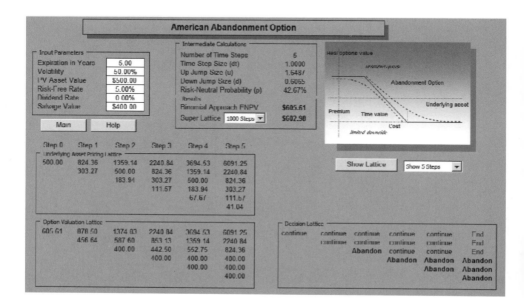

The benchmark option value using the American Abandonment Option *model closely approximates the contraction option when the asset value is replaced by the initial asset value of $1,000 multiplied by the contraction factor of 0.5, resulting in $500 of contracted asset value. However, this benchmark is applicable only for a narrow range of results. Using the results from the* American Abandonment Option *model, the asset value is $500 while the calculated value from a binomial lattice is $605.61, or a net of $105.61 in option value. This result is comparable to the $105.61 in the* American Contraction Option *model.*

5. Change the contraction factor to 0.7, and answer Question 4. Why are the answers different?

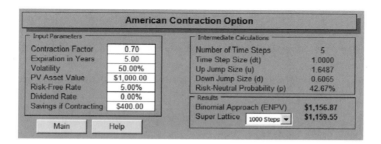

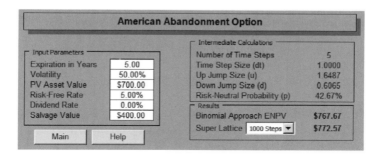

At a higher contraction factor of 70 percent with an unchanged savings rate of $400, the contraction option has a higher value because by only contracting a little (30 percent), the same savings can be incurred. The potential for more contraction occurs. In contrast, a higher asset value with the same abandonment savings means that the abandonment occurrence is less as it is less optimal to abandon, reducing the value of the abandonment option. Therefore, in general, an abandonment option analysis does not provide a good benchmark for a contraction option.

OPTION TO CHOOSE

Suppose a large manufacturing firm decides to hedge itself through the use of strategic options. Specifically, it has the option to choose among three strategies: (1) expanding its current manufacturing operations; (2) contracting its manufacturing operations; or (3) completely abandoning its business unit at any time within the next 5 years. Suppose the firm has a current operating structure whose static valuation of future profitability using a DCF model (in other words, the present value of the future cash flows discounted at an appropriate market risk-adjusted discount rate) is found to be $100 million.

Using Monte Carlo simulation, you calculate the implied volatility of the logarithmic returns on the projected future cash flows to be 15 percent. The risk-free rate on a riskless asset for the next 5 years is found to be yielding 5 percent annualized returns. Suppose the firm has the option to contract 10 percent of its current operations at any time over the next 5 years, thereby creating an additional $25 million in savings after this contraction. The expansion option will increase the firm's operations by 30 percent, with a $20 million implementation cost. Finally, by abandoning its operations, the firm can sell its intellectual property for $100 million. Do the following exercises, answering the questions that are posed:

1. Solve the option to choose (contract, expand, and abandon) problem analytically and using the software. Then redo the problem by adding a 2 percent dividend rate, 2.50 expansion factor, $120 expansion cost, and $50 contraction savings. Finally, verify the results using the Real Options Analysis Toolkit software.
2. Recalculate the option value only for an expansion option.
3. Recalculate the option value only for a contraction option.
4. Recalculate the option value only for an abandonment option.
5. Compare the results of the sum of these three individual options in Questions 2 through 4 with the results obtained in Question 1 using the option to choose (contract, expand, and abandon).
   a. Why are the results different?
   b. Which value is correct?
6. Prove that if there are many interacting options and if there is a single dominant strategy, then the value of the project's option value approaches this dominant strategy's value; that is, perform the following steps, then compare and explain the results.
   a. Reduce the expansion cost to $1.
   b. Increase the contraction savings to $100.
   c. Increase the salvage value to $150.
   d. What inferences can you make based on these results?

Analytical Solutions

A five-step binomial lattice calculation is used here, and the real options value is calculated as $19.03 million using five time-steps. To begin the analysis, calculate and complete the required values.

Stepping Time	
Up Step-Size (up)	
Down Step-Size (down)	
Risk-neutral Probability (prob)	

The first lattice, the lattice of the underlying asset, is shown next. Notice that for a chooser option like this example, no closed-form models are available. The best that an analyst can do is to use the binomial approach. Calculate and complete the underlying asset lattice.

Underlying Asset Lattice

Asset $\times$ up^5
$\$100 \times 1.1618^5 = \$211.7$

Asset $\times$ up^4
$\$100 \times 1.1618^4 = \$182.2$

Asset $\times$ up^3
$\$100 \times 1.1618^3 = \$156.8$

Asset $\times$ up^2
$\$100 \times 1.1618^2 = \$134.9$

Asset $\times$ up
$\$100 \times 1.1618 = \$116.2$

Asset
$\$100$

Asset $\times$ down $\times$ up
$\$100 \times 1.1618 \times 0.8607 = 100.0$

Asset $\times$ down
$\$100 \times 0.8607 = \$86.1$

Asset $\times$ down^2
$\$100 \times 0.8607^2 = \$74.1$

Asset $\times$ up $\times$ down^3
$\$100 \times 1.1618 \times 0.8607^3 = \$74.1$

Asset $\times$ down^3
$\$100 \times 0.8607^3 = \$63.8$

Asset $\times$ up $\times$ down^4
$\$100 \times 1.1618 \times 0.8607^4 = \$63.8$

Asset $\times$ down^4
$\$100 \times 0.8607^4 = \$54.9$

Asset $\times$ down^5
$\$100 \times 0.8607^5 = \$47.2$

The second step is to calculate the option valuation lattice as shown below using the values calculated in the underlying asset lattice. Calculate the value of the chooser option by completing the option valuation lattice.

Option Valuation Lattice

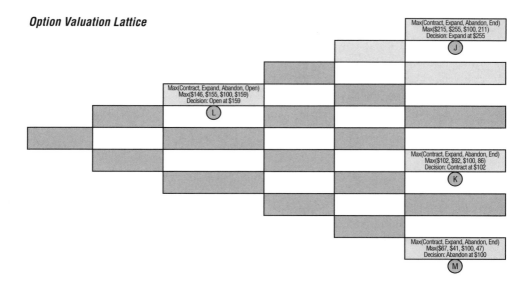

We see that the sample terminal node (denoted J) reveals a value of $255.2, which can be obtained through the value maximization of expansion, contraction, abandonment, and continuation. At the end of 5 years, the firm has the option to choose how it wishes to continue its existing operations through these options. Obviously, management will choose the strategy that maximizes profitability. The value of abandoning the firm's business unit is $100 million. The value of expansion is

[   ] ($[   ]) − $[   ] = $[   ] million

The value of contracting 10 percent of its operations is equivalent to 90 percent of its existing operations plus the $25 million in savings. Hence, the value of contracting the firm's operations is

[   ] ($[   ]) + $[   ] = million

The value of continuing with existing business operations can be found in the underlying asset lattice evolution, which is $[   ] million. The profit-maximizing decision is to expand the firm's current level of operations at $[   ] million on that node (denoted J).

Similarly, for the terminal node K, we see that the value of contracting existing operations at that time is the maximum value of $[   ] million; that is, by contracting the firm's operations by 10 percent, the value is

[   ] ($[   ]) + $[   ] = $[   ] million

In comparison, continuing operations is valued at $[____] million, the abandonment strategy is valued at $[____] million, and the expansion strategy is valued at

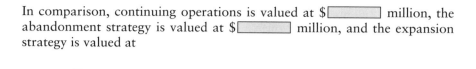

[____] ($[____]) – $[____] = $[____] million

This result is intuitive because if the underlying asset value of pursuing existing business operations is such that it is very high based on current market demand (node J), then it is wise to expand the firm's current levels of operation. Otherwise, if circumstances force the value of the firm's operations down to such a low level as specified by node K, then it is more optimal to contract the existing business by 10 percent. At any time below level K, for instance, at node M, it is better to abandon the business unit altogether.

Moving on to the intermediate nodes, we see that node L is calculated as $158.8 million. At this particular node, the firm again has four options: (1) to expand, (2) to contract, (3) to abandon its operations, or (4) not to execute anything, thus keeping these options open for the future. The value of contracting at that node is 0.9($134.9) + $25 = $146.5 million (rounded). The value of abandoning the business unit is $100.0 million. The value of expanding is 1.3($134.99) – $20 = $155.4 million. The value of continuing is simply the discounted weighted average of potential future option values using the risk-neutral probability. As the risk adjustment is performed on the probabilities of future option cash flows, the discounting can be done using the risk-free rate. That is, for the value of keeping the option alive and open, we have

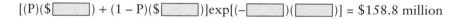

$[(P)(\$[]) + (1 - P)(\$[])]\exp[(-[])([])] = \$158.8$ million

which is the maximum value. This assumes a 5 percent risk-free rate *rf*, and a time-step *δt* of 1. Using this backward induction technique, the lattice is calculated back to the starting point to obtain the value of $[____] million. As the present value of the underlying is $[____] million, the real options value is $[____] million. In comparison, if we use the Black-Scholes model to solve the problem, we obtain an incorrect value of $14.42 million. If the project is analyzed separately, we get differing and misleading results as seen here:

Abandonment option only	$ 6.32 million
Contraction option only	$15.00 million
Expansion option only	$14.49 million
Sum of all individual options	$35.81 million

Clearly, valuing a combination of real options by performing them individually and then summing them yields wildly different and incorrect results. We need to account for the interaction of option types within the same project as we have done earlier. The reason why the sum of individual options does not equal the interaction of the same options is due to the mutually exclusive and independent nature of these specific options. That is, the firm can never both expand and contract on the same node at the same time, or expand and abandon on the same node at the same time, and so forth. This mutually exclusive behavior is captured using the option to choose (contract, expand, and abandon) mentioned earlier. If performed separately on a particular node in the lattice, the expansion option analysis may indicate that it is optimal to expand, while the contraction option analysis may indicate that it is optimal to contract, and so forth, thereby creating a higher total value. However, in an option to choose (contract, expand, and abandon), the interaction among the three options precludes this higher total value from happening, and the option is not overvalued, because in the example, multiple option executions cannot occupy the same state. However, in more advanced real options problems, this multiple interaction in a single state is highly desired.

Exercise: Option to Choose (Contract, Expand, and Abandon)

Open the Excel file *Workbook Exercise (Chooser Option).xls* from the enclosed CD-ROM. Use the input assumptions below and solve this modified option to choose (contract, expand, and abandon) by completing the three lattices.

Creating and Solving a Chooser Option

Assumptions

Asset Value ($)	$100.00
Maturity (Years)	5.00
Risk-free Rate (%)	7.00%
Dividends (%)	2.00%
Volatility (%)	25.00%
Lattice Steps	5
Expansion Factor	2.50
Expansion Cost ($)	$120.00
Contraction Factor	0.90
Contraction Savings ($)	$50.00
Salvage Value ($)	$100.00

Intermediate Calculations

Stepping-Time (dt)	
Up Step-Size (up)	
Down Step-Size (down)	
Risk-neutral Probability (prob)	

Results

Lattice Results	

Underlying Asset Lattice

Option Valuation Lattice

Decision Lattice

Software Solutions

1. Solve the option to choose (contract, expand, and abandon) problem using the software. *The option value is $19.03 ($119.03 ENPV less $100.00 PV Asset Value).*

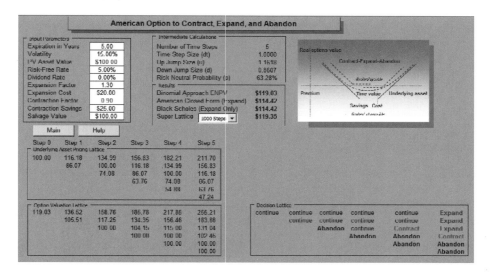

2. Recalculate the option value only for an expansion option. *The option value is $14.49 ($114.49 ENPV less $100.00 PV Asset Value).*

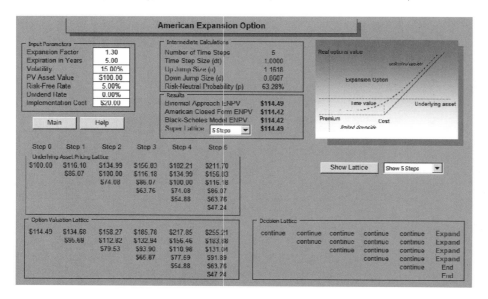

3. Recalculate the option value only for a contraction option. *The option value is $15.00 ($115.00 ENPV less $100.00 PV Asset Value).*

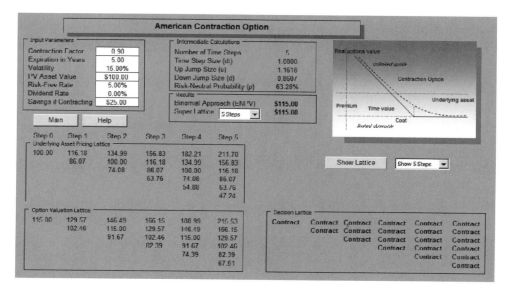

4. Recalculate the option value only for an abandonment option. *The option value is $6.32 ($106.32 ENPV less $100.00 PV Asset Value).*

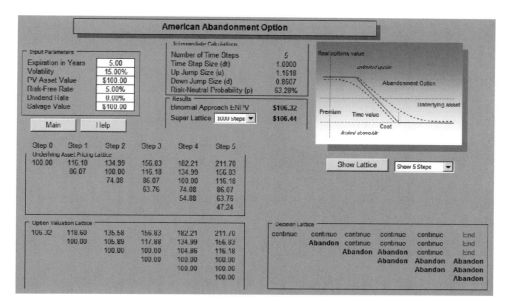

5. Compare the results of the sum of these three individual options in Questions 2 through 4 with the results obtained in Question 1 using the option to choose (contract, expand, and abandon).

a. Why are the results different?

The option to choose is $19.03, compared to $35.81 ($14.49 + $15.00 + $6.32) for the sum of all three individual options. The results are different because of the mutually exclusive and independent characteristics of these real options. That is, at each node, management can only execute one of three options, not two or three options at the same time. By valuing the options separately, for instance, on certain nodes at the terminal period, each of the three options are executed at the same time, which cannot happen in reality.

b. Which value is correct?

The option to choose result is correct because it avoids any complications of redundant option values and multiple option executions.

6. Prove that if there are many interacting options, and if there is a single dominant strategy, the value of the project's option value approaches this dominant strategy's value; that is, perform the following steps, then compare and explain the results.

a. Reduce the expansion cost to $1.

Reducing the expansion cost to $1 means that it becomes more optimal to expand, thereby making expansion the dominant strategy. The resulting option analysis value is $130.48, which approximates the expansion option value alone, of $129 (the 1.3 expansion factor multiplied by the $100 asset value less $1 implementation cost). The remaining $1.48 comes from the other options as well as the errors stemming from using only 5 steps in the binomial lattice.

b. Increase the contraction savings to $100.

With such a high salvage value, it is optimal to abandon the project more often. Thus, the abandonment option is the dominant strategy. The resulting real options analysis provides a value of $190 (0.9 contraction factor multiplied by $100 plus the $100 savings value). The rest of the option values are insignificant.

c. Increase the salvage value to $150.

Similarly, with the high salvage value of $150, it is optimal to abandon the project more often. The resulting value is $150, indicating that abandonment is the optimal strategy.

d. What inferences can you make based on these results?

If there are a few dominant real options strategies in an analysis, the value of the strategic options approaches these dominant strategy values. Valuing too many options is sometimes irrelevant because dominated strategies tend to have little value and will not change the results of the analysis.

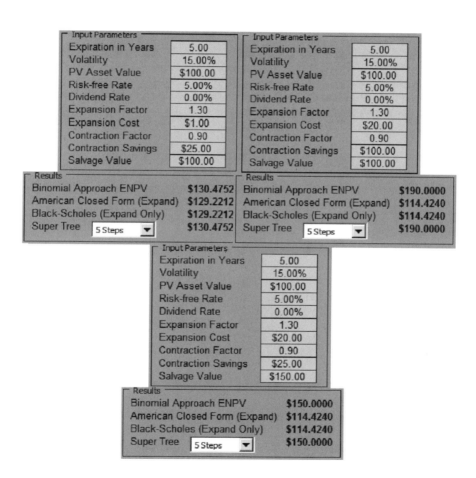

COMPOUND OPTIONS

In a compound option analysis, the value of the option depends on the value of another option. For instance, a pharmaceutical company currently going through a particular FDA drug approval process has to go through human trials. The success of the FDA approval depends heavily on the success of human testing, both occurring at the same time. Suppose that the former costs $900 million and the latter $500 million. Further suppose that both phases occur simultaneously and take 5 years to complete. Using Monte Carlo simulation, you calculate the implied volatility of the logarithmic returns on the projected future cash flows to be 25 percent. The risk-free rate on a riskless asset for the next 5 years is found to be yielding 7.7 percent. The drug development effort's static valuation of future profitability using a DCF model (in other words, the present value of the future cash flows discounted at an appropriate market risk-adjusted discount rate) is found to be $1 billion. Do the exercises, answering the questions posed:

1. Solve the simultaneous compound option analytically and using the software. Recalculate the option value by changing the first cost to $800, second cost to $600, 7 percent risk-free rate, and 30 percent volatility. Finally, verify the results using the software (use 5 and 500 steps for comparison).

2. Swap the implementation costs such that the first cost is $500 and the second cost is $900. Is the resulting option value similar or different? Why?

3. What happens when part of the cost of the first option is allocated to the second option? For example, make the first cost $450 and the second cost $950. Does the result change? Explain.

4. Show how the *American Long-Term Call Option Approximation* model can be used to benchmark the results from a simultaneous compound option.

5. Show how the *American Sequential Compound Option* model can also be used to calculate or at least approximate the simultaneous compound option result. Use the software's *4D Multiple Sequential Compound Option* model to verify the results.

Analytical Solutions

This section shows the step-by-step calculation involved in obtaining the compound option value. For simplicity, assume that the maturity is 3 years rather than 5 years. Solve the simultaneous compound option by first completing the calculations on stepping time and step sizes.

Stepping Time	
Up Step-Size (up)	
Down Step-Size (down)	
Risk-neutral Probability (prob)	

Then complete the underlying asset lattice. The only required computation here is the up and down step sizes calculated previously.

Underlying Asset Lattice

Asset × up³
$1000 × 1.3499³ = $2459.6

Asset × up²
$1000 × 1.3499² = $1822.1

Asset × up
$1000 × 1.3499 = $1349.9

Asset
$1000.0

Asset × down × up
$1000 × 0.7408 × 1.3499 = 1000.0

Asset × down
$1000 × 0.7408 = $740.8

The second step involves the calculation of the intermediate equity lattice seen below. We see that the sample terminal node (denoted N) reveals a value of $1,559.6, which can be obtained through the value maximization of executing the option or not, thereby letting the option expire worthless. The value of the option is

$$\$\boxed{} - \$\boxed{} = \$\boxed{} \text{ million}$$

The profit-maximizing value is determined using

$$\text{MAX}[\boxed{};\boxed{}]$$

which yields $\boxed{} million.

Moving on to the intermediate nodes, we see that node O is calculated as $119.6 million. At this particular node, the value of executing the option is

$$\$\boxed{} - \$\boxed{} = -\$\boxed{} \text{ million}$$

Keep in mind that the value $740.8 comes from the lattice of the underlying asset at the same node as seen previously. The value of continuing is simply the discounted weighted average of potential future option values using the risk-neutral probability. As the risk adjustment is performed on the probabilities of future option cash flows, the discounting can be done using the risk-free rate. That is, for the value of keeping the option alive and open, we have

$$[(P)(\$\boxed{}) + (1 - P)(\$\boxed{})]\exp[(-\boxed{})(\boxed{})] = \$119.6 \text{ million}$$

which is the maximum of the two values. This calculation assumes a 7.7 percent risk-free rate rf, and a time-step δt of 1. Using this backward induction technique, this first equity lattice is back-calculated to the starting point to obtain the value of $\$\boxed{}$ million.

Equity Valuation Lattice

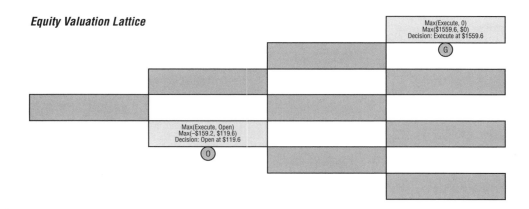

The third step is to calculate the option valuation lattice as shown below. The valuation of this lattice depends on the intermediate equity lattice seen previously. For instance, in the terminal node P, we see the value of the option as $1,059.6, which is nothing but the maximization between zero and the option value. The option value at that node is calculated as

$$\$\boxed{} - \$\boxed{} = \$\boxed{} \text{ million}$$

In node Q, similarly, we see that the value of the option is $0, which is obtained through

$$\text{MAX}[\$\boxed{}; \$\boxed{}]$$

Using backward induction, the value of the compound option is calculated as $\$\boxed{}$ million (rounded). Notice how this compares to a static decision value of $1,000 − $900 = $100 million for the first investment.

Option Valuation Lattice

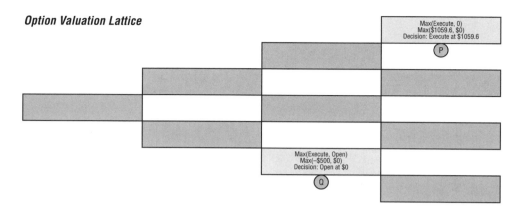

Exercise: Simultaneous Compound Option

Open the Excel file *Workbook Exercise (Simultaneous Option).xls* from the enclosed CD-ROM. Use the input parameters below and solve this modified simultaneous option by completing the lattices.

Creating and Solving a Simultaneous Option

Assumptions	
Asset Value ($)	$1,000.00
First Cost ($)	$800.00
Second Cost ($)	$600.00
Maturity (Years)	5.00
Risk-free Rate (%)	7.00%
Dividends (%)	0.00%
Volatility (%)	30.00%
Lattice Steps	5

Intermediate Calculations	
Stepping-Time (dt)	
Up Step-Size (up)	
Down Step-Size (down)	
Risk-neutral Probability (prob)	

Results	
Lattice Results	

Underlying Asset Lattice

First Option Valuation Lattice

Decision Lattice (First Option)

Second Option Valuation Lattice

Decision Lattice (Second Option)

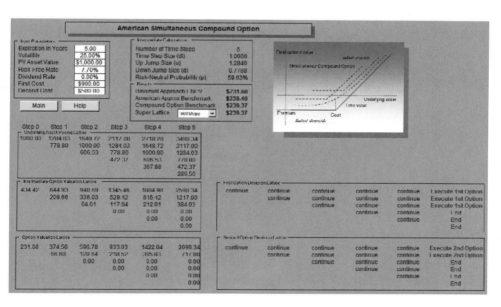

Software Solutions

1. Solve the simultaneous compound option using the software.

The resulting real option analysis value is $231.68 for 5 steps and $239.37 for 500 steps.

2. Swap the implementation costs such that the first cost is $500 and the second cost is $900. Is the resulting option value similar or different? Why?

The result remains unchanged because in a simultaneous compound option, both costs occur at the same time. As long as the total costs for both options remain the same, the value of the option will remain unchanged.

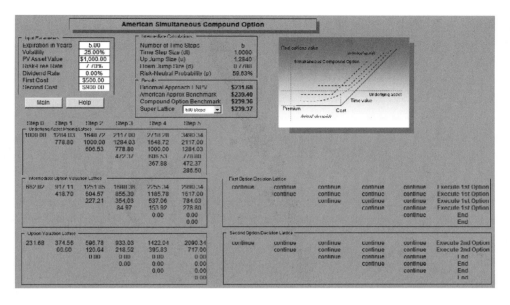

3. What happens when part of the cost of the first option is allocated to the second option? For example, make the first cost $450 and the second cost $950. Does the result change? Explain.

Again, the resulting option value remains unchanged because the total cost of the simultaneous compound option remains the same.

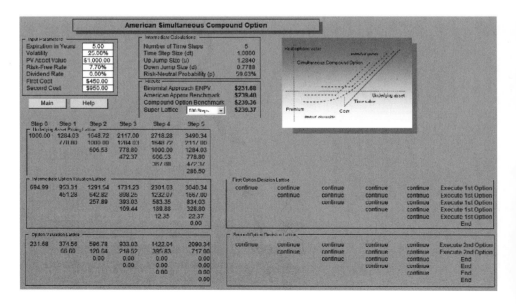

4. Show how an *American Long-Term Call Option Approximation* can be used to benchmark the results from a simultaneous compound option.

To use the American Long-Term Call Option Approximation *model, set the implementation cost to equal $1,400 or the sum of the two option costs ($900 and $500). This is a good approach to benchmarking the results. The 500-step simultaneous compound option value of $239.37 approaches the American closed-form call option approximation result of $239.40. As will be seen in question 5, the results from a simultaneous compound option with 1,000 steps approaches the closed-form value.*

American Long-Term Call Option Approximation

Inputs		Upside	Downside
Asset Value	$1,000.00	67.4501	-60.7701
Implementation Cost	$1,400.00	-37.1656	43.8387
Time to Maturity	5.00	25.6129	-26.3046
Risk-Free Rate	7.70%	15.7248	-15.3339
Dividend Rate	0.00%	0.0000	0.0000
Volatility	25.00%	20.7775	-20.9245
Closed Form Approx.	$239.40		
Binomial Approach 500 Steps ▼	$239.37	Reset to Original	

▲▼ +/-10% Sensitivity

Show Lattice   Show 5 Steps ▼

Main   Help

5. Show how the *American Sequential Compound Option* model can also be used to calculate or at least approximate the simultaneous compound option result. Use the software's *4D Multiple Sequential Compound Option* model.

Using the 4D Multiple Sequential Compound Option *model, a 100-step analysis yields $238.45 and $239.41 for 1,000 steps. The latter result approaches the American closed-form option approximation of $239.40.*

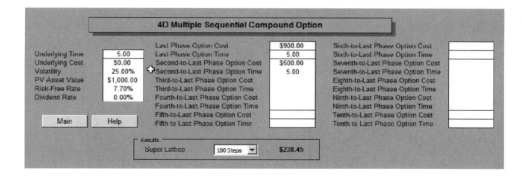

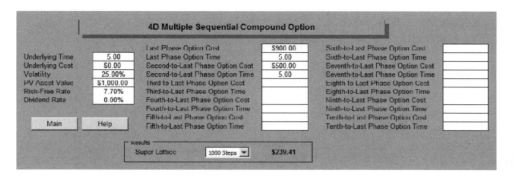

CLOSED-FORM COMPOUND OPTIONS

Compound options can also be analyzed using closed-form models rather than binomial lattices. In theory, the results obtained from binomial lattices have to approach closed-form models. As additional practice, do these exercises, answering the questions that are posed:

1. Using the *American Simultaneous Compound Option* model in the software, obtain the option value of an asset worth $1,000, 50 percent volatility, 5 years to maturity, and an assumed 5 percent risk-free rate. Further assume that the costs of the first and second options are both $500. Show the value obtained using a 5-step lattice and a 100-step super lattice analysis.

2. Compare the answers in the first exercise by using the *Compound Options on Options* closed-form model. Note that to approximate and benchmark a simultaneous compound option, you must set the time to maturity for the option on option as 4.9999 years and set the time to ma-

turity of the underlying asset as 5.0000 years, because the *Compound Options on Options* model only directly calculates sequential compound options, not simultaneous compound options.

3. Compare the answers using the *4D Multiple Sequential Compound Option* model with 1,000 steps.
4. Now, suppose the compound option occurs in sequence and not simultaneously. That is, assume that the underlying time is now 4 years and the option time is 2 years. All other input parameters are identical.
   a. Use the *American Sequential Compound Option* model to calculate the new option value (use 5 steps and 1,000 steps in the binomial lattice).
   b. Confirm your results using the *Compound Options on Options* model.
   c. Confirm your results again using the *4D Multiple Sequential Compound Option* model.

Software Solutions

1. Using the *American Simultaneous Compound Option* model in the software, obtain the option value of an asset worth $1,000, 50 percent volatility, 5 years to maturity, and an assumed 5 percent risk-free rate. Further, assume that the costs of the first and second options are both $500. Show the value obtained using a 5-step lattice and a 100-step super lattice analysis.

The 5-step lattice shows a value of $510, as compared to $495 when using 100 steps. The closed-form compound option benchmark also yields a value of $495.

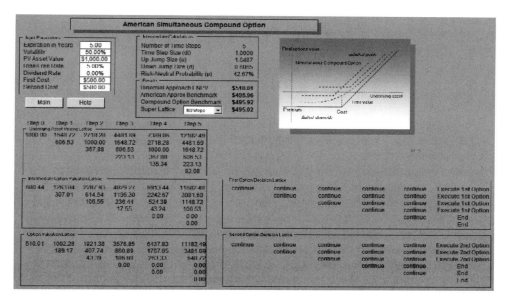

2. Compare the answers in the first exercise by using the *Compound Options on Options* closed-form model. Note that to approximate and benchmark a simultaneous compound option, you must set the time to maturity for the option on option as 4.9999 years and set the time to maturity of the underlying asset as 5.0000 years, because the *Compound Options on Options* model only directly calculates sequential compound options, not simultaneous compound options.

As shown earlier, the closed-form compound option shows a value of $495.

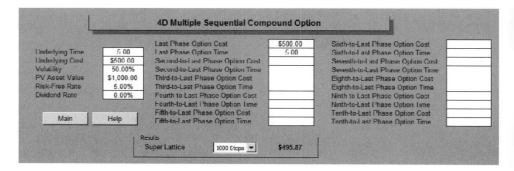

3. Compare the answers using the *4D Multiple Sequential Compound Option* model with 1,000 steps.

The 4D Multiple Sequential Compound Option *model simply extends the sequential compound option to include up to 10 phases. Therefore, with 2 phases, the resulting option value of $495 is identical to those previously calculated.*

4. Now, suppose the compound option occurs in sequence and not simultaneously, that is, assume that the underlying time is now 4 years and the option time is 2 years. All other input parameters are identical.

a. Use the *American Sequential Compound Option* model to calculate the new option value (use 5 steps and 1,000 steps in the binomial lattice).

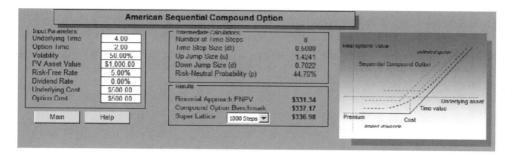

b. Confirm your results using the *Compound Options on Options* model.

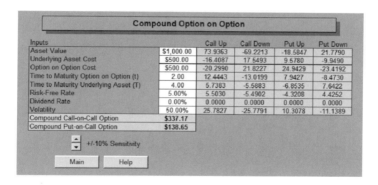

c. Confirm your results again using the *4D Multiple Sequential Compound Option* model.

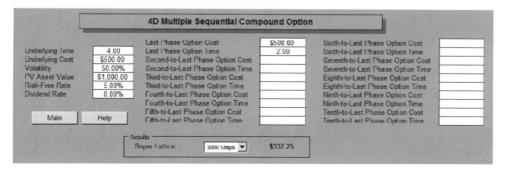

SEQUENTIAL COMPOUND OPTION

A sequential compound option exists when a project has multiple phases and later phases depend on the success of previous phases. Suppose a project has two phases, of which the first has a 1-year expiration that costs $500 million. The second phase's expiration is 3 years and costs $700 million. Using Monte Carlo simulation, the implied volatility of the logarithmic returns on the projected future cash flows is calculated to be 20 percent. The risk-free rate on a riskless asset for the next 3 years is found to be yielding 7.7 percent. The static valuation of future profitability using a DCF model—in other words, the present value of the future cash flows discounted at an appropriate market risk-adjusted discount rate—is found to be $1,000 million. Do these exercises, answering the questions that are posed:

1. Solve the sequential compound option analytically using a three-step lattice. Recalculate the option value by changing the asset value to $500, first cost to $300, second cost to $20, 7 percent risk-free rate, and 25 percent volatility. Finally, use the Real Options Analysis Toolkit software to solve the initial problem—use five steps instead of three steps and explain why there is a difference in results as well as why a five-step lattice is not the right approach.
2. Change the sequence of the costs, that is, set the first phase's cost to $700 and the second phase's cost to $500. For simplicity, keep five time-steps on the lattice. Compare your results to the initial problem. Explain what happens.

Analytical Solutions

The following figures show the results of your analysis using a binomial approach, using five time-steps. Solve the expansion option by first completing the calculations on stepping time and step sizes.

Stepping Time
Up Step-Size (up)
Down Step-Size (down)
Risk-neutral Probability (prob)

Then verify the underlying asset lattice. The only required computation here is the up and down step sizes calculated previously.

Underlying Asset Lattice

				Asset × up³ $1000 × 1.2214³ = $1822.1
			Asset × up² $1000 × 1.2214² = $1491.8	
	Asset × up $1000 × 1.2214 = $1221.4			Asset × up² × down¹ $1000 × 1.2214² × 0.8187 = $1221.4
Asset $1000		Asset × down × up $1000 × 0.8187 × 1.2214 = 1000.0		
	Asset × down $1000 × 0.8187 = $818.7			Asset × up¹ × down² $1000 × 1.2214¹ × 0.8187² = $818.7
		Asset × down² $1000 × 0.8187² = $670.3		
				Asset × down³ $1000 × 0.8187³ = $548.8

The next step is to calculate the intermediate equity lattice of the second option. The analysis requires the calculation of the longer-term option first and then the shorter-term option because the value of a compound option is based on another option. At node R, the value is $1,122.1 million because it is the maximum between zero and executing the option through

$$\$\boxed{} - \$\boxed{} = \$\boxed{} \text{ million}$$

The intermediate node S is $\boxed{}$ million, its being the maximum between executing the option

$$\$\boxed{} - \$\boxed{} = -\$\boxed{}\text{million}$$

and keeping the option open with

$$[(P)(\$\boxed{}) + (1 - P)(\$\boxed{})]\exp[(-\boxed{})(\boxed{})] = \$71.3 \text{ million}$$

which is the maximum value.

Equity Valuation Lattice

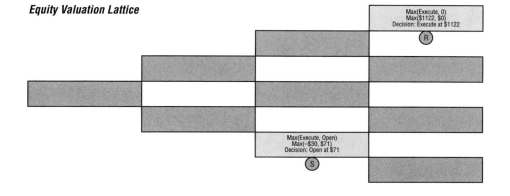

Next, the option valuation on the shorter-term option is performed. The analysis on this lattice depends on the lattice of the second, longer-term option as shown previously. For instance, node T has a value of $121.3 million, which is the maximum between zero and executing the option

$$ \$\boxed{} - \$\boxed{} = \$\boxed{} \text{ million} $$

Continuing with the calculation back to the starting value, the simultaneous option value is calculated to be $\$\boxed{}$.

Equity Valuation Lattice

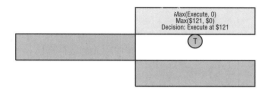

Exercise: Sequential Compound Option

Open the Excel file *Workbook Exercise (Sequential Option).xls* from the enclosed CD-ROM. Use the input assumptions below and solve this modified sequential option by completing the lattices.

Creating and Solving a Sequential Option

Assumptions

Asset Value ($)	$500.00
Underlying Cost ($)	$300.00
Option Cost ($)	$20.00
Maturity (Years)	5.00
Option Time (Years)	3.00
Risk-free Rate (%)	7.00%
Dividends (%)	0.00%
Volatility (%)	25.00%
Lattice Steps	5

Intermediate Calculations

Stepping-Time (dt)	
Up Step-Size (up)	
Down Step-Size (down)	
Risk-neutral Probability (prob)	

Results

Lattice Results	

Underlying Asset Lattice

Second Phase Option Valuation Lattice

Decision Lattice (Second Phase)

151

First Phase Option Valuation Lattice

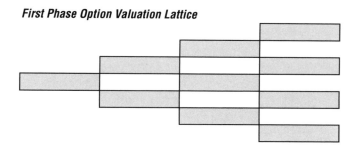

Decision Lattice (First Phase Option)

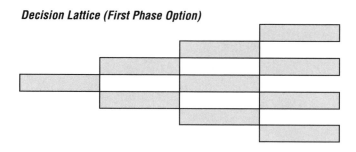

Combined Decision Lattice

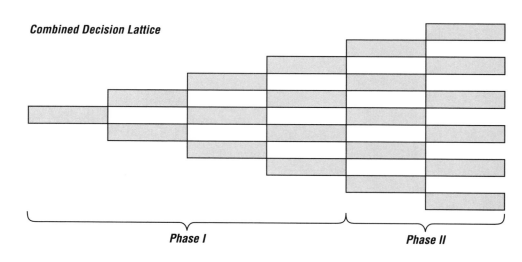

Software Solutions

1. Use the Real Options Analysis Toolkit software. Use five steps instead of three steps and explain why there is a difference in results as well as why a five-step lattice is not the right approach.

The value of the option is $87.05. Using a five-step lattice here is inappropriate as the stepping time (δt) is 0.6 and the first phase's time to execution of 1.0 years cannot fall precisely on a node. Instead, the model has to approximate this result by either rounding up or rounding down to the next appropriate step. Thus, the accuracy of the results will be compromised. Instead, use an n-*step lattice whose stepping time is perfectly divisible by both phases.*

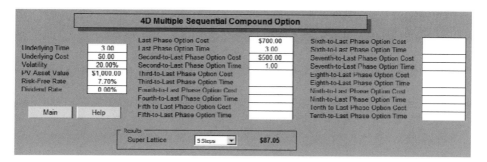

2. Change the sequence of the costs. That is, set the first phase's cost to $700 and the second phase's cost to $500. For simplicity, keep five time-steps on the lattice. Compare your results. Explain what happens.

The value of the option now becomes $78.17. This result is intuitive because the first phase costs more ($700), the hedging effect that phasing the options provides becomes less effective. For instance, the option value in the previous exercise was higher ($87.05) because the first phase only required a $500 implementation cost, thereby providing a larger hedge for the higher $700 future payout.

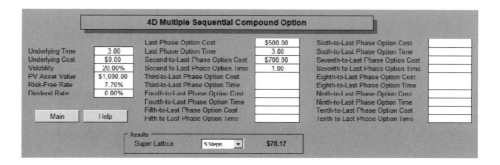

CHANGING COSTS

A modification to the option types we have thus far been discussing is the idea of changing costs (strikes); that is, implementation costs for projects may change over time. Putting off a project for a particular period may mean a higher cost. Keep in mind that changing strikes can be applied to any previous option types as well; in other words, one can mix and match different option types. Suppose implementation of a project in the first year costs $80 million but increases to $90 million in the second year due to expected increases in the cost of raw materials and input costs. Using Monte Carlo simulation, you calculate the implied volatility of the logarithmic returns on the projected future cash flows to be 50 percent. The risk-free rate on a riskless asset for the next 2 years is found to be yielding 7 percent. The static valuation of future profitability using a DCF model (in other words, the present value of the future cash flows discounted at an appropriate market risk-adjusted discount rate) is found to be $100 million. Do these exercises, answering the questions that are posed:

1. Solve the changing costs option analytically. Recalculate the option value by changing the asset value to $400, cost to $250 growing at 10 percent annually, 8 percent risk-free rate, 35 percent volatility, and 2 percent dividends. Finally, calculate the initial changing cost option using the Real Options Analysis Toolkit software by changing the maturity to 5 years instead of 2 years.
2. Rerun the analysis after changing the first year's costs to $90 million and the second year's costs to $80 million. Explain the results. Are they intuitive? Explain the differences if Monte Carlo simulation is used instead to capture changing or uncertain costs.

Analytical Solutions

Solve the changing cost option by first completing the calculations on stepping time and step sizes.

Stepping Time
Up Step-Size (up)
Down Step-Size (down)
Risk-neutral Probability (prob)

Then complete the underlying asset lattice. The only required computation here is the up and down step sizes calculated previously.

Underlying Asset Lattice

	Asset × up $100 × 1.6487 = $164.9	
Asset $100.0		Asset × down × up $100 × 1.6487 × 0.6065 = 100.0
	Asset × down $100 × 0.6065 = $60.7	

The next graphic shows the stepwise calculations on an option with changing strike prices. The value of the call option on changing strikes is $[   ] million. Compare this to a naive static DCF model's NPV of $[   ] million for the first year and $[   ] million for the second year.

Option Valuation Lattice

Exercise: Changing Costs Option

Open the Excel file *Workbook Exercise (Changing Costs).xls* from the enclosed CD-ROM. Use the input assumptions below and solve this modified changing costs option by completing the lattices.

Creating and Solving a Changing Cost Option

Assumptions

Asset Value ($)	$400.00
Implementation Cost ($)	$250.00
Maturity (Years)	5.00
Risk-free Rate (%)	8.00%
Dividends (%)	2.00%
Volatility (%)	35.00%
Lattice Steps	5
Cost Growth Rate (%)	10.00%

Intermediate Calculations

Stepping-Time (dt)	
Up Step-Size (up)	
Down Step-Size (down)	
Risk-neutral Probability (prob)	

Results

Lattice Results	

Underlying Asset Lattice

Implementation Costs

Option Valuation Lattice

Decision Lattice

Software Solutions

1. Solve the changing costs option using the software. However, change the maturity to 5 years instead of 2 years for the software. Use the binomial lattice of five steps. *The calculated option value is $56.51.*

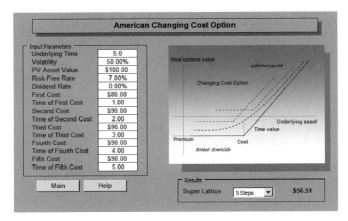

2. Rerun the analysis after changing the first year's cost to $90 and the second through fifth years' costs to $80. Explain the results. Are they intuitive?

The new option value is $59.34. The results are somewhat counterintuitive because the higher cost up front actually increases the value of the option. The reason this increase occurs is that the lower costs in the future ($80) occur for more years (years 2 through 5). This lower averaging effect reduces the total cost on the option, and increases the value of the overall option. Monte Carlo is used if cost is fixed but uncertain. A changing cost option is used when the cost changes. Monte Carlo can be used on both fixed cost or changing cost options.

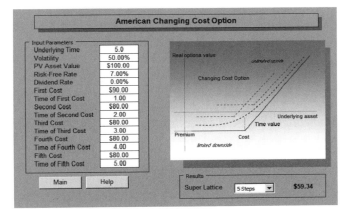

CHANGING VOLATILITY

Instead of changing strike costs over time, in certain cases volatility on cash-flow returns may differ over time. Assume a 2-year option in which volatility is 20 percent in the first year and 30 percent in the second year. In this circumstance, the up and down factors are different over the two time periods. Thus, the binomial lattice will no longer be recombining. Assume an asset value of $100, implementation costs of $110, and a risk-free rate of 10 percent. (Note that changing volatility options can also be solved analytically using nonrecombining trees—see the section on Nonrecombining Lattices later in this chapter.)

1. Solve the problem analytically. Then solve the changing volatility option using recombining lattices in the exercise. Finally, verify the original results using the Real Options Analysis Toolkit software (use five steps).
2. Change the first volatility to 30 percent and the second to 20 percent. What happens?

Analytical Solutions

Instead of changing strike costs over time, in certain cases, volatility on cash-flow returns may differ over time. The calculations can be seen in the following figures, for a 2-year option where volatility is 20 percent in the first year and 30 percent in the second year. In this case, the up and down factors are different over the two time periods. Thus, the binomial lattice will no longer be recombining. Solve the changing volatility option by first completing the calculations on stepping time and step sizes.

	First Phase	Second Phase
Stepping Time		
Up Step-Size (up)		
Down Step-Size (down)		
Risk-neutral Probability (prob)		

Then verify the underlying asset lattice. The only required computation here is the up and down step sizes calculated previously.

Underlying Asset Lattice

		Asset × up (1) × up (2) $100 × 1.2214 × 1.3499 = 164.8
	Asset × up (1) $100 × 1.2214 = $122.1	
		Asset × up (1) × down (2) $100 × 1.2214 × 0.7408 = 90.5
Asset $100.0		
		Asset × down (1) × up (2) $100 × 0.8187 × 1.3499 = 110.5
	Asset × down (1) $100 × 0.8187 = $81.87	
		Asset × down (1) × down (2) $100 × 0.8187 × 0.7408 = 60.6

Next, calculate and complete the option valuation lattice. Similar calculations are performed for an option with changing volatilities as for other option types. However, remember that the risk-neutral probability (p) changes over time when volatility changes. Using this backward induction technique, this option valuation lattice is back-calculated to the starting point to obtain the value of $[   ] million, as compared to the static net present value of $[   ] million.

Option Valuation Lattice

Exercise: Changing Volatility Option

Open the Excel file *Workbook Exercise (Volatility Recombining).xls* from the enclosed CD-ROM. Use the input assumptions below and solve this changing volatility option by completing the lattices.

Creating and Solving a Changing Volatility Option

Assumptions	
Asset Value ($)	$100.00
Implementation Cost ($)	$90.00
Maturity (Years)	5.00
Risk-free Rate (%)	7.00%
Dividends (%)	0.00%
Volatility (%)	30.00%
Lattice Steps	5
New Volatility (%	45.00%
New Volatility Step	3

Intermediate Calculations	
Stepping-Time (dt)	
Up Step-Size (up)	
Down Step-Size (down)	
Risk-neutral Probability (prob)	

Results	
Lattice Results	

Underlying Asset Lattice

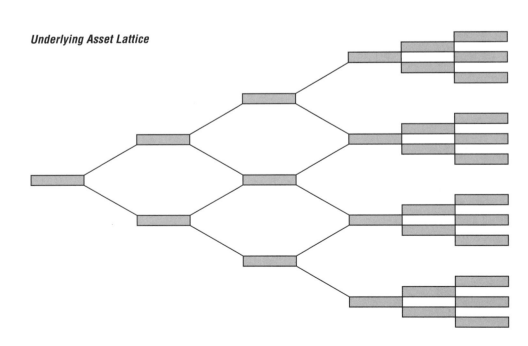

Option Valuation Lattice

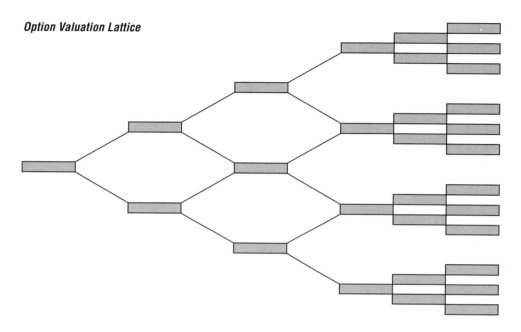

Software Solutions

1. Solve the problem using the software with five steps. *The option value is $20.32.*

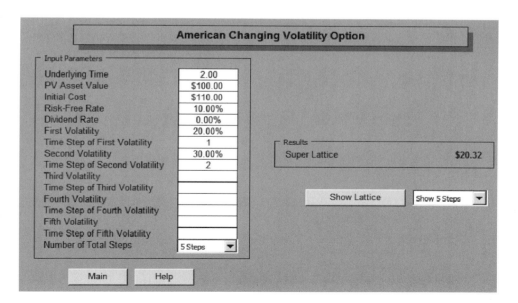

2. Change the first volatility to 30 percent and the second to 20 percent. What happens? *The value of the option decreases.*

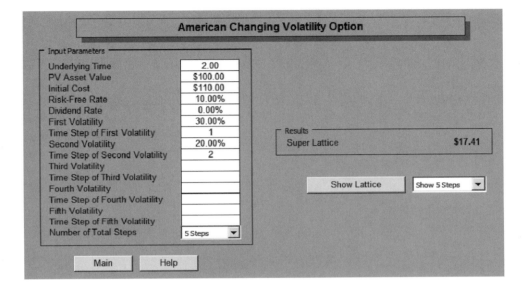

OPTION TO CONTRACT AND ABANDON

1. Solve the following Contraction and Abandonment option: Asset value of $100, 5-year economic life, 5 percent annualized risk-free rate of return, 25 percent annualized volatility, 25 percent contraction with a $25 savings, and a $70 abandonment salvage value.
2. Show and explain what happens when the salvage value of abandonment far exceeds any chances of a contraction. For example, set the salvage value at $200.
3. In contrast, set the salvage value back to $70 and increase the contraction savings to $100. What happens to the value of the project?
4. Solve just the contraction option in isolation, that is, set the contraction savings to $25 and explain what happens. Change the savings to $100 and explain the change in results. What can you infer from dominant option strategies?
5. Solve just the abandonment option in isolation, that is, set the salvage value to $70, and explain what happens. Change the salvage value to $200, and explain the change in results. What can you infer from dominant option strategies?

Software Solutions

1. Solve the following Contraction and Abandonment option: Asset value of $100, 5-year economic life, 5 percent annualized risk-free rate of return, 25 percent annualized volatility, 25 percent contraction with a $25 savings, and a $70 abandonment salvage value.

The value of the project is $104.31, where $100 comes from the NPV and $4.31 comes from the real options value. By having a safety net to contract and abandon during a downturn, the value of the project is higher than the NPV.

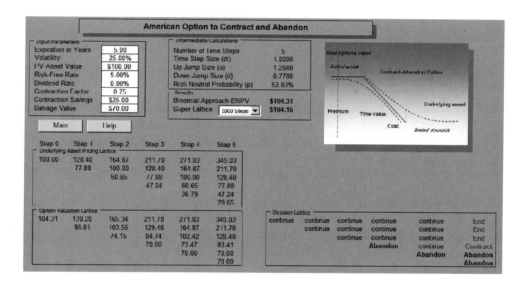

2. Show and explain what happens when the salvage value of abandonment far exceeds any chances of a contraction. For example, set the salvage value at $200.

With an asset value of $100 and a salvage value of $200, it is optimal to abandon more frequently. Thus, the abandonment option is the dominant strategy in this example. Therefore, the value of the project is $200. Care should be taken when interpreting the quasi-decision lattice because the first node shows abandonment, which implies that the dominant strategy is to abandon immediately. All other nodes should also imply abandonment. However, these abandonment decisions are options, not obligations. Although it is optional to abandon, management may not do so, thus keeping the option open for the future.

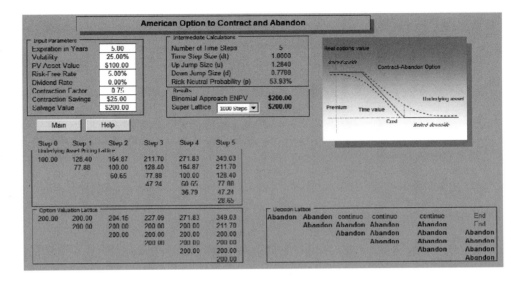

3. In contrast, set the salvage value back to $70, and increase the contraction savings to $100. What happens to the value of the project?

The dominant strategy now is the contraction option. Thus, it is optimal to exercise the contraction option more often. Therefore, the value of the project approaches the contraction option value of $175 (a 75 percent contraction factor on $100 asset value yields $75, plus the contraction savings of $100).

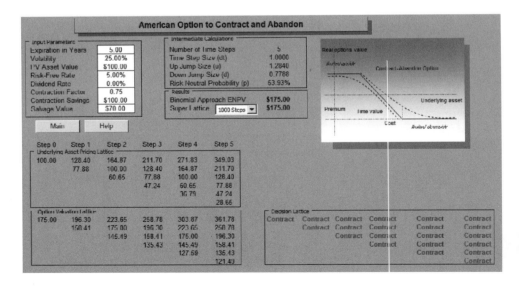

4. Solve just the contraction option in isolation, that is, set the contraction savings to $25 and explain what happens. Change the savings to $100 and explain the change in results. What can you infer from dominant option strategies?

Using $25 for savings, the resulting contraction option value of $103.35 is less than the combined contraction and abandonment option value of $104.31.

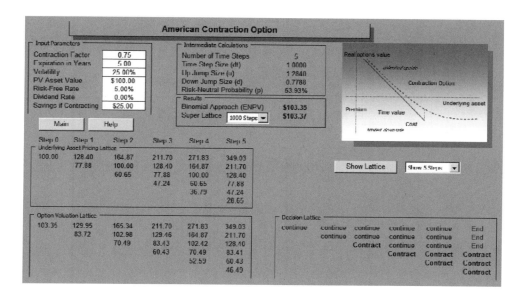

When savings is increased to $100 for the contraction option, this option becomes the dominant strategy. That is, for a $100 asset value, it is highly profitable to contract existing operations by 25 percent to obtain an additional $100 savings at all times. The value of the contraction option is the 75 percent reduced capacity ($75) plus the additional savings ($100), yielding $175. This result is important because the contraction and abandonment option value approaches a contraction option when it is the dominant strategy.

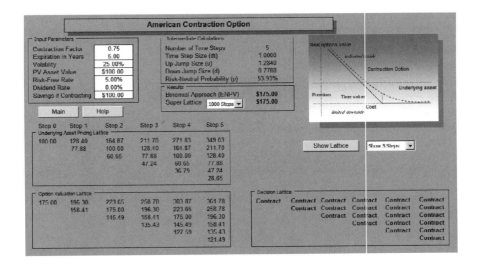

5. Solve just the abandonment option in isolation, that is, set the salvage value to $70, and explain what happens. Change the salvage value to $200, and explain the change in results. What can you infer from dominant option strategies?

The $103.21 option result is less than the combined contraction and abandonment option analysis value. This result is to be expected because the combined option analysis should yield a higher strategic option value as compared to the individual abandonment option.

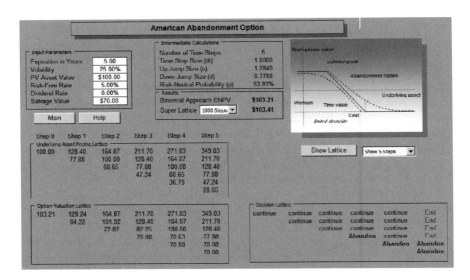

When the salvage value is increased to $200, the abandonment option becomes the dominant strategy. Therefore, it becomes more optimal to abandon earlier. In this case, the lattice nodes indicating where abandoning is optimal may be irrelevant because the project will almost always be abandoned. The value of the project becomes $200, the value of the abandonment salvage value. The decision lattice is correct (the first node says abandon but future nodes say continue) as abandonment nodes are options, not obligations. It may be optimal to abandon early, but management may not do so, leaving the ability to do other things in the future.

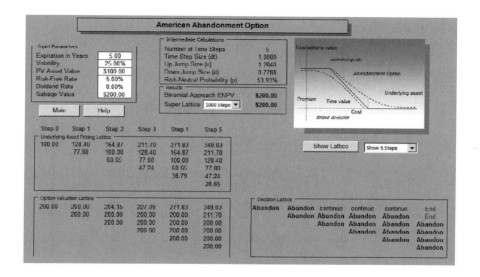

BASIC BLACK-SCHOLES WITH DIVIDENDS

The Black-Scholes equation is applicable for analyzing European-type options, that is, options that can be executed only at maturity and not before. The original Black-Scholes model cannot solve an option problem when there are dividend payments. However, extensions of the Black-Scholes model, collectively called the Generalized Black-Scholes models, can accommodate a continuous dividend payout for a European Option.

Do the exercises below, answering the questions that are posed, assuming that a European call option's asset value and strike cost are $100, subject to 25 percent volatility. The maturity on this option is 5 years, and the corresponding risk-free rate on a similar asset maturity is 5 percent.

1. Using the software, calculate the European call option.
2. Compare your results using 5, 10, 50, 100, 300, 500, 1,000, and 5,000 steps in the super lattice routine. Explain what happens when the number of steps gets higher.
3. Now assume that a continuous dividend payout yielding 3 percent exists. What happens to the value of the option?
4. Show that the value of an American option is identical to the European option when no dividends are paid; that is, it is never optimal to execute an American call option early when no dividend payouts exist.
5. Show that as a 3 percent dividend yield exists, the value of the American call option exceeds the value of a European option. Why is this so?

Software Solutions

1. Using the software, calculate the European call option.

The value of the European option is $33.16 using a five-step binomial approach and $32.50 using the Black-Scholes model.

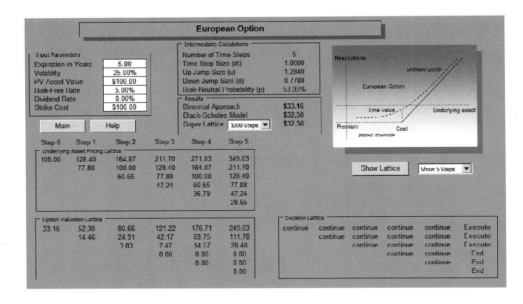

2. Compare your results using 5, 10, 50, 100, 300, 500, 1,000, and 5,000 steps in the super lattice routine. Explain what happens when the number of steps gets higher.

The value of the binomial lattice calculated option value approaches the closed-form Black-Scholes model value of $32.50 as the number of steps is increased.

Super Lattice 5 Steps = $33.1635
Super Lattice 10 Steps = $31.9863
Super Lattice 50 Steps = $32.3992
Super Lattice 100 Steps = $32.4515
Super Lattice 300 Steps = $32.4864
Super Lattice 500 Steps = $32.4934
Super Lattice 1,000 Steps = $32.4987
Super Lattice 5,000 Steps = $32.5092

The following graph charts the progression of number of steps (x-axis) and the resulting option value (y-axis) from a binomial lattice. The dotted horizontal line shows the value obtained from a Black-Scholes model. Notice that as the number of steps gets larger, the values obtained from binomial lattices approach the closed-form Black-Scholes model. However, initially, values from binomial lattices may fluctuate wildly around the closed-form results, thus sometimes overestimating and sometimes underestimating the true value of the option. Care should be taken when interpreting the binomial results if too few steps are used.

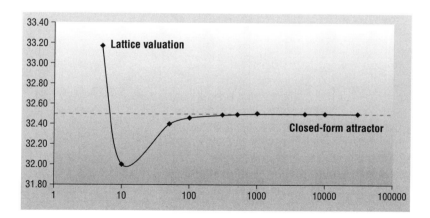

3. Now assume that a continuous dividend payout yielding 3 percent exists. What happens to the value of the option?

A continuous dividend payout erodes the underlying asset's par value over time. Therefore, the value of the option decreases.

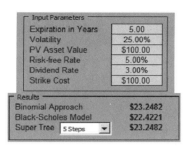

4. Show that the value of an American option is identical to the European option when no dividends are paid; that is, it is never optimal to execute an American call option early when no dividend payouts exist.

The value of the American Long-Term Call Option Approximation *yields an identical value ($32.50) to that in the Black-Scholes model.*

American Long-Term Call Option Approximation

Inputs		Upside	Downside
Asset Value	$100.00	7.9170	-7.3670
Implementation Cost	$100.00	-4.1454	4.6925
Time to Maturity	5.00	1.9176	-2.0044
Risk-Free Rate	5.00%	1.1063	-1.0996
Dividend Rate	0.00%	0.0000	0.0000
Volatility	25.00%	1.7213	-1.7001
Closed Form Approx.	$32.50		
Binomial Approach 1000 Steps ▼	$32.50	Reset to Original	

▲▼ +/-10% Sensitivity   Show Lattice   Show 5 Steps ▼

Main   Help

5. Show that as a 3 percent dividend yield exists, the value of the American call option exceeds the value of a European option. Why is this so?

The value of an American option exceeds the value of a European option because the former can be executed at any time up to its maturity. When no dividends exist, it is never optimal to execute an American call option early, because it is always more valuable to wait until the last possible moment to execute the option. Therefore, the value of an American option reverts to the value of a European option. However, when dividend payments exist, that is, when the value of the underlying asset erodes through the passage of time, it becomes optimal to execute the option earlier, prior to termination. Therefore, the value of the added ability to execute the op-

tion early, as in an American option, is worth more. Using the American Long-Term Call Option Approximation *model, the value of the American call option is $22.64 (closed-form) and $22.77 (1,000-step binomial).*

American Long-Term Call Option Approximation			
Inputs		Upside	Downside
Asset Value	$100.00	6.2260	-5.6271
Implementation Cost	$100.00	-3.3925	3.9914
Time to Maturity	5.00	0.9193	-0.9963
Risk-Free Rate	5.00%	0.8486	-0.8106
Dividend Rate	3.00%	-0.7455	0.8006
Volatility	25.00%	1.7954	-1.7942
Closed Form Approx.	$22.64		
Binomial Approach 1000 Steps	$22.77	Reset to Original	

+/-10% Sensitivity   Show Lattice   Show 5 Steps

Main   Help

BARRIER OPTIONS

Barrier options are combinations of call and put options such that they become in-the-money or out-of-the-money when the asset value breaches an artificial barrier.

Standard single upper-barrier options can be call-up-and-in, call-up-and-out, put-up-and-in, and put-up-and-out. Standard single lower-barrier options can be call-down-and-in, call-down-and-out, put-down-and-in, and put-down-and-out. Double barrier options are combinations of standard single upper- and lower-barrier options. Barrier options can be solved using the Custom Lattice module in the software by applying conditional *IF, AND, OR* nested statements within the traditional *MAX* function in Excel. However, for simplicity, the examples here use the closed-form model instead.

1. Using the *Double Barrier Option* model, change each input parameter, and explain the effects on the up-and-in and down-and-in call option, up-and-in and down-and-in put option, up-and-out and down-and-out call option, and up-and-out and down-and-out put option. Explain your observations when the barrier levels change or when volatility increases.
2. Replicate the analysis using a *Standard Lower-Barrier Option* model.
3. Replicate the analysis using a *Standard Upper-Barrier Option* model.

Exercise: Barrier Option

Open the Excel file *Workbook Exercise (Barrier Option).xls* from the enclosed CD-ROM. Using the input assumptions below, calculate the up-and-in call option using binomial lattices. Verify that the result is $93.82 using a five-step lattice, as compared to $94.79 using the closed-form model in the software.

Creating and Solving a Barrier Option (Up and In Call)

Assumptions

Asset Value ($)	$200.00
Implementation Cost ($)	$150.00
Maturity (Years)	5.00
Risk-free Rate (%)	5.00%
Dividends (%)	0.00%
Volatility (%)	30.00%
Lattice Steps	5
Barrier ($)	$220.00

Intermediate Calculations

Stepping-Time (dt)	
Up Step-Size (up)	
Down Step-Size (down)	
Risk-neutral Probability (prob)	

Results

Lattice Results	

Underlying Asset Lattice

Option Valuation Lattice

Decision Lattice

Software Solutions

1. Using the *Double Barrier Option* model, change each input parameter and explain the effects on the up-and-in and down-and-in call option, up-and-in and down-and-in put option, up-and-out and down-and-out call option, and up-and-out and down-and-out put option (see Table 6.1). Explain your observations when the barrier levels change or when volatility increases.

A higher lower-barrier value implies that it is easier to breach with the same level of asset fluctuation. Therefore, the down-and-in options will be worth more because the chances of these options being kicked into-the-money has increased, while the down-and-out options will be worth less

TABLE 6.1 Correlations Between Input Parameters and Each of the Option Values

Input Parameters	Call Up-and-In, Down-and-In	Put Up-and-In, Down-and-In	Call Up-and-Out, Down-and-Out	Put Up-and-Out, Down-and-Out
Asset Value	+	−	−	−
Implementation Cost	−	+	−	+
Lower Barrier	+	+	−	−
Upper Barrier	−	−	+	+
Time to Maturity	+	+	−	−
Risk-free Rate	+	−	−	−
Dividend Rate	−	−	−	−
Volatility	+	+	−	−

because they are more prone to be kicked out-of-the-money. In contrast, a higher upper-barrier value means that it is more difficult to breach this upper barrier. Thus, the up-and-in options will be worth less, and the up-and-out options will be worth more, because the former will have a lesser chance of coming into-the-money while the latter options will have a higher chance of staying in-the-money. Higher volatilities with unchanged levels of barriers imply a higher chance of breaching both upper and lower barriers, which means that up-and-in as well as down-and-in options are worth more, because they will be more frequently kicked into-the-money. In contrast, up-and-out as well as down-and-out options are worth less because they will be more frequently kicked out-of-the-money.

Double-Barrier Option								
Inputs								
Asset Value	$100.00	$110.00	$100.00	$100.00	$100.00	$100.00	$100.00	$100.00	$100.00
Implementation Cost	$100.00	$100.00	$110.00	$100.00	$100.00	$100.00	$100.00	$100.00	$100.00
Lower Barrier	$50.00	$50.00	$50.00	$60.00	$50.00	$50.00	$50.00	$50.00	$50.00
Upper Barrier	$150.00	$150.00	$150.00	$150.00	$160.00	$150.00	$150.00	$150.00	$150.00
Time to Maturity	5.00	5.00	5.00	5.00	5.00	6.00	5.00	5.00	5.00
Risk-Free Rate	5.00%	5.00%	5.00%	5.00%	5.00%	5.00%	6.00%	6.00%	5.00%
Carrying Cost	5.00%	5.00%	5.00%	5.00%	5.00%	5.00%	6.00%	5.00%	5.00%
Volatility	50.00%	50.00%	50.00%	50.00%	50.00%	50.00%	50.00%	50.00%	60.00%
Call Up-In, Down-In	$49.57	$57.53	$46.84	$49.59	$49.54	$54.01	$51.01	$47.16	$55.97
Put Up-In, Down-In	$27.39	$25.35	$32.39	$27.47	$27.33	$28.07	$25.02	$26.05	$33.85
Call Up-Out, Down-Out	$0.02	$0.02	$0.01	$0.00	$0.06	$0.01	$0.02	$0.02	$0.00
Put Up-Out, Down-Out	$0.09	$0.08	$0.13	$0.01	$0.15	$0.03	$0.09	$0.09	$0.01

2. Replicate the analysis using a *Standard Lower-Barrier Option* model.

Standard Lower-Barrier Option								
Inputs								
Asset Value	$100.00	$110.00	$100.00	$100.00	$100.00	$100.00	$100.00	$100.00	$100.00
Implementation Cost	$90.00	$90.00	$100.00	$90.00	$90.00	$90.00	$90.00	$90.00	$90.00
Artificial Barrier	$85.00	$85.00	$85.00	$95.00	$85.00	$85.00	$85.00	$85.00	$85.00
Cash Rebate	$0.00	$0.00	$0.00	$0.00	$10.00	$0.00	$0.00	$0.00	$0.00
Time to Maturity	1.00	1.00	1.00	1.00	1.00	2.00	1.00	1.00	1.00
Risk-Free Rate	5.00%	5.00%	5.00%	5.00%	5.00%	5.00%	6.00%	5.00%	5.00%
Dividend Rate	0.00%	0.00%	0.00%	0.00%	0.00%	0.00%	0.00%	2.00%	0.00%
Volatility	20.00%	20.00%	20.00%	20.00%	20.00%	20.00%	20.00%	20.00%	30.00%
Down-and-In Call Option	$1.36	$0.44	$0.50	$8.85	$7.38	$3.77	$1.36	$1.31	$4.11
Down-and-Out Call Option	$15.34	$24.92	$9.95	$7.85	$18.93	$18.27	$15.99	$13.81	$15.59
Down-and-In Put Option	$2.28	$0.95	$4.92	$2.31	$8.31	$3.46	$2.08	$2.69	$5.30
Down-and-Out Put Option	$0.03	$0.02	$0.66	$0.00	$3.61	$0.01	$0.03	$0.03	$0.01

3. Replicate the analysis using a *Standard Upper-Barrier Option* model.

Standard Upper-Barrier Option									
Inputs									
Asset Value	$100.00	$110.00	$100.00	$100.00	$100.00	$100.00	$100.00	$100.00	$100.00
Implementation Cost	$90.00	$90.00	$100.00	$90.00	$90.00	$90.00	$90.00	$90.00	$90.00
Artificial Barrier	$120.00	$120.00	$120.00	$130.00	$120.00	$120.00	$120.00	$120.00	$120.00
Cash Rebate	$20.00	$20.00	$20.00	$20.00	$30.00	$20.00	$20.00	$20.00	$20.00
Time to Maturity	2.00	2.00	2.00	2.00	2.00	3.00	2.00	2.00	2.00
Risk-Free Rate	5.00%	5.00%	5.00%	5.00%	5.00%	5.00%	6.00%	5.00%	5.00%
Dividend Rate	0.00%	0.00%	0.00%	0.00%	0.00%	0.00%	0.00%	1.00%	0.00%
Volatility	30.00%	30.00%	30.00%	30.00%	30.00%	30.00%	30.00%	30.00%	40.00%
Up-and-In Call Option	$31.57	$36.73	$26.93	$32.95	$34.52	$35.83	$32.22	$30.33	$35.55
Up-and-Out Call Option	$13.68	$16.87	$13.27	$12.02	$20.23	$14.46	$13.85	$13.41	$14.36
Up-and-In Put Option	$7.81	$5.75	$9.27	$9.13	$10.76	$7.71	$7.32	$8.16	$9.62
Up-and-Out Put Option	$18.87	$19.29	$21.41	$17.28	$25.43	$20.05	$18.57	$19.00	$21.73

STOCHASTIC TIMING OPTIONS

Stochastic timing options are very powerful tools in real options analysis. Please refer to my previous book, *Real Options Analysis*, for a detailed discussion of the specifics. Briefly, a timing option provides the holder the option to defer making an investment decision until a later time without much restriction; that is, competitive or market effects (market share erosion, first to market, strategic positioning, etc.) have negligible effect on the value of the project. Assuming that this situation holds true, then shifting a project for execution in the future depends on only two factors: (1) the rate of growth of the asset over time; and (2) the discount rate or rate of erosion of the time value of money. For instance, putting off a project to the future provides a higher return due to the growth rate in asset over time, but at the same time, returns are eroded because value obtained in the future is less valuable than value obtained today by virtue of time value. A highly simplified example includes when to cut down a tree for its lumber. If the tree's growth rate is substantial, the longer we wait, the more wood can be obtained. However, the higher the discount rate, the cost of money, or opportunity cost, the sooner the tree should be cut down. Therefore, what is the optimal time to wait before cutting down the tree?

Table 6.2 illustrates an example of stochastic timing options, where if the asset value at Time 0 is equivalent to the implementation cost $100, the discount rate is assumed to be 25 percent, and the corresponding risk-free rate is 5.5 percent, the calculated optimal time to execution is 4.52 years. Notice that the period 4.52 years provides the maximum NPV. Hence, this

TABLE 6.2   Optimal Timing Option with Maximum
Calculated NPV

Time	NPV ($)	
1.00	4.40	
2.00	7.05	
3.00	8.47	
4.00	9.05	
4.52	*9.12*	This is the maximum NPV
5.00	9.07	
6.00	8.72	
7.00	8.16	
8.00	7.48	

Notes: Assumptions are Asset Value at time 0 is $100; Fixed
Implementation Cost is $100; Discount Rate 25%; Growth Rate of
Underlying Asset 5.5%; Calculated Optimal Time to Execution 4.52.

maximum NPV of $9.12 is the option value of waiting, as compared to
$100 – $100 = $0 NPV if the project is executed immediately. The analysis
is manually verified by shifting the asset value out to the corresponding
times of execution. The maximum value is obtained at 4.52 years. The same
results can be obtained using the software's *Stochastic Timing Option*
model.

Complete these exercises:

1. Solve the stochastic timing option using the software.
2. Create a table indicating different growth rates and discount rates. Show
   what happens to the profitability index as measured by the optimal trigger values and optimal timing.

Software Solutions

1. Solve the stochastic timing option using the software.

Stochastic Timing Option			
Strategy	A	B	C
Project's Total Marginal Revenues	$100.00	$100.00	$100.00
Project's Total Marginal Operating Costs	$0.00	$0.00	$0.00
Project's Total Marginal Capital Implementation Costs	$100.00	$100.00	$100.00
Projected Time to Implementation in Years	0.00	0.00	0.00
Growth Rate	5.50%	3.00%	5.00%
Discount Rate	25.00%	25.00%	40.00%
Strategic Option Value	$9.12	$4.70	$4.91
Synopsis	Has Option Value	Has Option Value	Has Option Value
Optimal Trigger Value on Marginal Revenues	$128.21	$113.64	$114.29
Optimal Time to Execution	4.52 Years	4.26 Years	2.67 Years
Optimal Execution Decision	Optimal to Wait	Optimal to Wait	Optimal to Wait
Net Present Value	$0.00	$0.00	$0.00
Present Value Free Cash Flow	$100.00	$100.00	$100.00

2. Create a table indicating different growth rates and discount rates. Show what happens to the profitability index as measured by the optimal trigger values and optimal timing.

Tables 6.3 and 6.4 show the optimal timing to execute an option given the respective growth and discount rates. Notice in Table 6.3 that as discount rates increase, holding the growth rate constant, it is more optimal to execute the option earlier, because the time value of money of opportunity cost losses in revenues surpasses the growth rate in asset value over longer periods of time. In contrast, when holding the discount rate constant and increasing the growth rate, it is clear that waiting is more optimal than immediate execution, because the growth rate in asset value appreciation far surpasses the discount rate's opportunity cost of lost revenues. For example,

TABLE 6.3   Optimal Timing for Different Growth and Discount Rates

Discount Rate (%)	Growth Rates				
	1.00%	2.00%	3.00%	4.00%	5.00%
10	*10.54*	11.16	11.89	12.77	13.86
15	6.90	7.16	7.44	7.75	8.11
20	5.13	5.27	5.42	5.58	5.75
25	4.08	4.17	*4.26*	4.36	4.46
30	3.39	3.45	3.51	3.58	3.65
35	2.90	2.94	2.99	3.03	3.08
40	2.53	2.56	2.60	2.63	*2.67*

Note: Investment Cost is $100 and Asset Value is $100.

TABLE 6.4   Profitability Indexes for Different Growth and Discount Rates

Discount Rate (%)	Growth Rates				
	1.00%	2.00%	3.00%	4.00%	5.00%
10	*1.111*	1.250	1.429	1.667	2.000
15	1.071	1.154	1.250	1.364	1.500
20	1.053	1.111	1.176	1.250	1.333
25	1.042	1.087	*1.136*	1.190	1.250
30	1.034	1.071	1.111	1.154	1.200
35	1.029	1.061	1.094	1.129	1.167
40	1.026	1.053	1.081	1.111	*1.143*

Note: Investment Cost is $100 and Asset Value is $100.

in Table 6.4, assuming a 10 percent discount rate and a 1 percent growth rate, if a project's asset value exceeds the implementation cost by a ratio of 1.111, or if the net profit exceeds the implementation cost by 11.1 percent, it is optimal to execute the project immediately; otherwise, it is optimal to wait.

SWITCHING OPTION

A switching option looks at the flexibility of being able to switch resources, assets, or technology. This ability to switch technology provides added value to a project as a risk-hedging mechanism, in case the value of another technology or project becomes more profitable in the future, subject to a switching cost.

1. Calculate the value of switching technologies, assuming that the first technology is worth $100, but the second is worth only $90. Assume a 5-year maturity, 10 percent switching costs, and a negligible 0.001 percent risk-free rate. The first asset has a volatility of 20 percent, while the second has 35 percent volatility. Further, assume a cross-correlation coefficient of –0.2. How does the switching option compare with a static NPV?
2. Change the correlation coefficient to +0.2. What happens to the value of the switching option? Explain.
3. Run a series of switching-option calculations. Change the input parameters and explain what happens to the value of the switching option:
   a. Second asset's volatility
   b. Present value of the first asset
   c. Present value of the second asset
   d. Cost multiplier
   e. Time to expiration

Software Solutions

1. Calculate the value of switching technologies, assuming that the first technology is worth $100, but the second is worth only $90. Assume a 5-year maturity, 10 percent switching costs, and a negligible 0.001 percent risk-free rate. The first asset has a volatility of 20 percent, while the second has 35 percent volatility. Further, assume a cross-correlation coefficient of –0.2. How does the switching option compare with a static NPV?

The calculated value is $28.17. The real option value is $48.17 (after accounting for the –$20 NPV). Although it costs $10 to switch (10 percent on $100) from the first, profitable asset ($100), to the second, less profitable asset ($90), there is strategic value because the volatility on the second asset is higher. There is a chance that the second asset's value may overtake the first asset's value. In addition, due to the negative correlation coefficient, the ability to switch to the second asset provides a risk-diversification effect for the first asset, making the flexibility to switch valuable. Compare this to an NPV of –$20 if switching immediately ($10 loss switching from $100 to $90 plus the added $10 switching cost).

Switching Option

Inputs		Upside	Downside
PV First Asset	$100.00	-2.5165	2.8710
PV Second Asset	$90.00	5.6700	-5.3159
First Asset Volatility	20.00%	0.9729	-0.9345
Second Asset Volatility	35.00%	2.4152	-2.4052
Correlation Between Assets	-0.20	0.2464	-0.2486
Cost Multiplier	0.10	-0.2425	0.2454
Time to Maturity	5.00	1.6354	-1.7364
Risk-Free Rate	0.00%		
Portfolio Volatility	43.65%		
Switching Option	$28.17		
Static NPV	($20.00)		

+/-10% Sensitivity

Main   Help

2. Change the correlation coefficient to +0.2. What happens to the value of the switching option? Explain.

A positive correlation provides less risk diversification and therefore reduces the value of the switching option. The ability to switch use is important if both assets move inversely with each other. That is, when the existing asset value decreases, the option holder will switch use to the second asset whose value is increasing, due to the negative correlation.

Switching Option			
Inputs		**Upside**	**Downside**
PV First Asset	$100.00	-2.6159	3.0491
PV Second Asset	$90.00	5.2984	-4.8661
First Asset Volatility	20.00%	0.5978	-0.5235
Second Asset Volatility	35.00%	2.3665	-2.3110
Correlation Between Assets	0.20	-0.3041	0.3006
Cost Multiplier	0.10	-0.2545	0.2581
Time to Maturity	5.00	1.4137	-1.4944
Risk-Free Rate	0.00%		
Portfolio Volatility	**36.67%**		
Switching Option	**$22.71**		
Static NPV	**($20.00)**		

+/-10% Sensitivity

Main   Help

3. Run a series of switching option calculations. Change the input parameters and explain what happens to the value of the switching option:

    a. Second asset's volatility
    b. Present value of the first asset
    c. Present value of the second asset
    d. Cost multiplier
    e. Time to expiration

Panels A through E in Table 6.5 illustrate the relationships between the value of a switching option from an old technology to a new technology and its corresponding input parameters. For example, in Panel A, where the present values of both technologies are currently on par with each other and the volatility is very close to 0 percent (with this negligible uncertainty, the value of the option is close to $0, similar to the static NPV of $0 because there is no point in being able to switch technology if the values of both technologies are identical). In contrast, when volatility increases slightly in the second technology, the value of being able to switch to this second technology increases. The rest of the examples are fairly self-explanatory.

TABLE 6.5 Switching Options with Corresponding Input Parameters

PANEL A: The higher the volatility of the new technology, the greater the value of the ability to switch technology

PV First Asset	100.00	100.00	100.00	100.00	100.00	100.00
PV Second Asset	100.00	100.00	100.00	100.00	100.00	100.00
First Asset Volatility	0%	1%	1%	1%	1%	1%
Second Asset Volatility	*0%*	*1%*	*2%*	*3%*	*4%*	*5%*
Correlation between Assets	0.00	0.00	0.00	0.00	0.00	0.00
Cost Multiplier	0.00	0.00	0.00	0.00	0.00	0.00
Time to Maturity	1.00	1.00	1.00	1.00	1.00	1.00
Risk-free Rate	0%	0%	0%	0%	0%	0%
Portfolio Volatility	0.00	0.01	0.02	0.03	0.04	0.05
Switching Option Value	**0.01**	**0.56**	**0.89**	**1.26**	**1.64**	**2.03**
Static NPV	0.00	0.00	0.00	0.00	0.00	0.00

PANEL B: The higher the value of the original technology, the lower the value of the ability to switch technology

PV First Asset	*100.00*	*110.00*	*120.00*	*130.00*	*140.00*	*150.00*
PV Second Asset	100.00	100.00	100.00	100.00	100.00	100.00
First Asset Volatility	10%	10%	10%	10%	10%	10%
Second Asset Volatility	10%	10%	10%	10%	10%	10%
Correlation between Assets	0.00	0.00	0.00	0.00	0.00	0.00
Cost Multiplier	0.00	0.00	0.00	0.00	0.00	0.00
Time to Maturity	1.00	1.00	1.00	1.00	1.00	1.00
Risk-free Rate	0%	0%	0%	0%	0%	0%
Portfolio Volatility	0.14	0.14	0.14	0.14	0.14	0.14
Switching Option Value	**5.64**	**2.21**	**0.72**	**0.20**	**0.05**	**0.01**
Static NPV	0.00	−10.00	−20.00	−30.00	−40.00	−50.00

PANEL C: The higher the value of the new technology, the higher the value of the ability to switch technology

PV First Asset	100.00	100.00	100.00	100.00	100.00	100.00
PV Second Asset	*100.00*	*110.00*	*120.00*	*130.00*	*140.00*	*150.00*
First Asset Volatility	10%	10%	10%	10%	10%	10%
Second Asset Volatility	10%	10%	10%	10%	10%	10%
Correlation between Assets	0.00	0.00	0.00	0.00	0.00	0.00
Cost Multiplier	0.00	0.00	0.00	0.00	0.00	0.00
Time to Maturity	1.00	1.00	1.00	1.00	1.00	1.00
Risk-free Rate	0%	0%	0%	0%	0%	0%
Portfolio Volatility	0.14	0.14	0.14	0.14	0.14	0.14
Switching Option Value	**5.64**	**12.21**	**20.72**	**30.20**	**40.05**	**50.01**
Static NPV	0.00	10.00	20.00	30.00	40.00	50.00

PANEL D: The higher the switching cost, the lower the value of the ability to switch technology

PV First Asset	100.00	100.00	100.00	100.00	100.00	100.00
PV Second Asset	100.00	100.00	100.00	100.00	100.00	100.00
First Asset Volatility	10%	10%	10%	10%	10%	10%
Second Asset Volatility	10%	10%	10%	10%	10%	10%
Correlation between Assets	0.00	0.00	0.00	0.00	0.00	0.00
Cost Multiplier	*0.00*	*0.10*	*0.20*	*0.30*	*0.40*	*0.50*
Time to Maturity	1.00	1.00	1.00	1.00	1.00	1.00
Risk-free Rate	0%	0%	0%	0%	0%	0%
Portfolio Volatility	0.14	0.14	0.14	0.14	0.14	0.14
Switching Option Value	5.64	2.21	0.72	0.20	0.05	0.01
Static NPV	0.00	−10.00	−20.00	−30.00	−40.00	−50.00

PANEL E: The longer the ability to switch, the higher the value of the ability to switch technology

PV First Asset	100.00	100.00	100.00	100.00	100.00	100.00
PV Second Asset	100.00	100.00	100.00	100.00	100.00	100.00
First Asset Volatility	10%	10%	10%	10%	10%	10%
Second Asset Volatility	10%	10%	10%	10%	10%	10%
Correlation between Assets	0.00	0.00	0.00	0.00	0.00	0.00
Cost Multiplier	0.00	0.00	0.00	0.00	0.00	0.00
Time to Maturity	*1.00*	*2.00*	*3.00*	*4.00*	*5.00*	*6.00*
Risk-free Rate	0%	0%	0%	0%	0%	0%
Portfolio Volatility	0.14	0.14	0.14	0.14	0.14	0.14
Switching Option Value	5.64	7.97	9.75	11.25	12.56	13.75
Static NPV	0.00	0.00	0.00	0.00	0.00	0.00

CLOSED-FORM EQUATIONS
AND BINOMIAL CONVERGENCE

A very interesting stability and convergence test can be performed on binomial lattices. In calculating the value of a European call option, the Black-Scholes model can be used. In addition, a binomial lattice also can be used to estimate the option value. Because the binomial lattice in the limit approaches the closed-form Black-Scholes model for a simple European call option, the higher the number of steps, the closer the results. In addition, because a binomial lattice is simply a discrete simulation of closed-form continuous models, how consistent, reliable, and stable are the results? This is a valid question because simulations do not always provide exact results as, by definition, simulations provide randomly assigned inputs and the outputs that may change from trial to trial.

To answer the question of stability, the Black-Scholes model is used, together with binomial lattices using 5, 50, 100, and 500 steps. Each model is then simulated 10,000 times using Crystal Ball Monte Carlo simulation software. Table 6.6 shows that the binomial lattice is indeed highly consistent, reliable, and stable, and that results from a binomial lattice are replicable.

TABLE 6.6 Convergence and Stability of Binomial Results

	Mean	Standard Deviation	10th Percentile	90th Percentile
Black-Scholes	32.41	7.89	22.86	43.17
5-Step Lattice	33.47	8.15	23.54	44.30
50-Step Lattice	32.68	8.04	23.02	43.53
100-Step Lattice	32.68	8.04	22.96	43.57
500-Step Lattice	32.67	8.04	22.95	43.56

Forecast: Black-Scholes Model with Dividends

Summary:
   Certainty Level is 90.00%
   Certainty Range is from 20.82 to 46.16
   Display Range is from 13.33 to 53.12
   Entire Range is from 10.15 to 63.04
   After 1,000 Trials, the Std. Error of the Mean is 0.25

Statistics:	Value
Trials	1000
Mean	32.41
Median	31.48
Mode	—
Standard Deviation	7.89
Variance	62.27
Skewness	0.51
Kurtosis	3.46
Coeff. of Variability	0.24
Range Minimum	10.15
Range Maximum	63.04
Range Width	52.89
Mean Std. Error	0.25

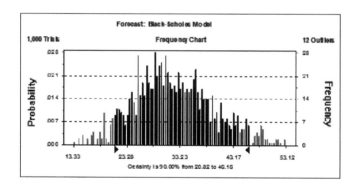

Forecast: Black-Scholes Model (cont'd)

Percentiles:

Percentile	Value
0%	10.15
10%	22.86
20%	25.81
30%	27.88
40%	29.74
50%	31.48
60%	33.66
70%	35.97
80%	38.56
90%	43.17
100%	63.04

Forecast: American Binomial Call (5 Steps)

Summary:
  Certainty Level is 90.00%
  Certainty Range is from 21.19 to 47.59
  Display Range is from 12.42 to 54.86
  Entire Range is from 9.99 to 64.05
  After 1,000 Trials, the Std. Error of the Mean is 0.26

Statistics:	*Value*
Trials	1000
Mean	33.47
Median	32.65
Mode	—
Standard Deviation	8.15
Variance	66.48
Skewness	0.40
Kurtosis	3.33
Coeff. of Variability	0.24
Range Minimum	9.99
Range Maximum	64.05
Range Width	54.06
Mean Std. Error	0.26

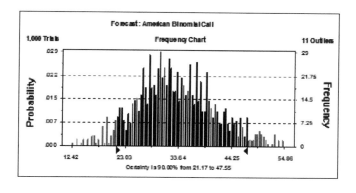

Forecast: American Binomial Call (cont'd)

Percentiles:

Percentile	*Value*
0%	9.99
10%	23.54
20%	26.62
30%	28.89
40%	30.88
50%	32.65
60%	34.95
70%	37.29
80%	39.89
90%	44.30
100%	64.05

Forecast: American Binomial Call (50 Steps)

Summary:
    Certainty Level is 90.00%
    Certainty Range is from 20.97 to 46.75
    Display Range is from 11.38 to 53.99
    Entire Range is from 10.14 to 63.98
    After 1,000 Trials, the Std. Error of the Mean is 0.25

Statistics:	*Value*
Trials	1000
Mean	32.68
Median	31.67
Mode	—
Standard Deviation	8.04
Variance	64.68
Skewness	0.53
Kurtosis	3.48
Coeff. of Variability	0.25
Range Minimum	10.14
Range Maximum	63.98
Range Width	53.84
Mean Std. Error	0.25

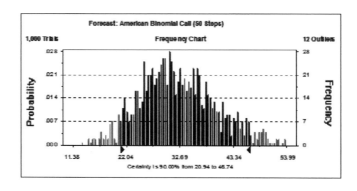

Forecast: American Binomial Call (50 Steps) (cont'd)

Percentiles:

Percentile	*Value*
0%	10.14
10%	23.02
20%	25.93
30%	28.06
40%	29.97
50%	31.67
60%	33.96
70%	36.26
80%	38.87
90%	43.53
100%	63.98

Forecast: American Binomial Call (100 Steps)

Summary:
Certainty Level is 90.00%
Certainty Range is from 20.90 to 46.67
Display Range is from 11.38 to 53.98
Entire Range is from 10.12 to 64.15
After 1,000 Trials, the Std. Error of the Mean is 0.25

Statistics:	Value
Trials	1000
Mean	32.68
Median	31.69
Mode	—
Standard Deviation	8.04
Variance	64.66
Skewness	0.53
Kurtosis	3.48
Coeff. of Variability	0.25
Range Minimum	10.12
Range Maximum	64.15
Range Width	54.03
Mean Std. Error	0.25

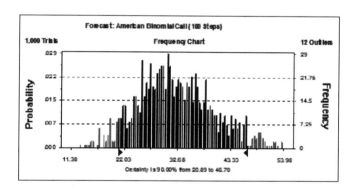

Forecast: American Binomial Call (100 Steps) (cont'd)

Percentiles:

Percentile	Value
0%	10.12
10%	22.96
20%	25.94
30%	28.04
40%	29.97
50%	31.69
60%	33.96
70%	36.30
80%	38.88
90%	43.57
100%	64.15

Forecast: American Binomial Call (500 Steps)

Summary:
Certainty Level is 90.00%
Certainty Range is from 20.89 to 46.67
Display Range is from 11.38 to 53.97
Entire Range is from 10.17 to 64.10
After 1,000 Trials, the Std. Error of the Mean is 0.25

Statistics:	Value
Trials	1000
Mean	32.67
Median	31.68
Mode	—
Standard Deviation	8.04
Variance	64.85
Skewness	0.53
Kurtosis	3.48
Coeff. of Variability	0.25
Range Minimum	10.17
Range Maximum	64.10
Range Width	53.93
Mean Std. Error	0.25

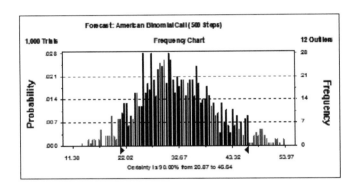

Forecast: American Binomial Call (500 Steps) (cont'd)

Percentiles:

Percentile	Value
0%	10.17
10%	22.95
20%	25.94
30%	28.03
40%	29.95
50%	31.68
60%	33.98
70%	36.31
80%	38.91
90%	43.56
100%	64.10

NONRECOMBINING LATTICES

This graphic illustrates a 5-step nonrecombining lattice for solving an American call option. Each node branches into two pathways that do not meet with other branches along the way (i.e., they do not recombine). The lattice shown here is the first lattice of the underlying asset.

Underlying Asset Lattice

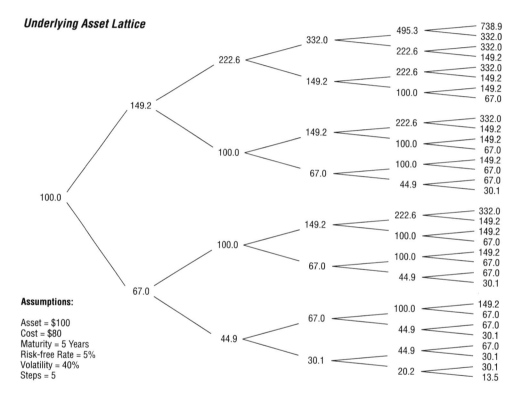

Assumptions:

Asset = $100
Cost = $80
Maturity = 5 Years
Risk-free Rate = 5%
Volatility = 40%
Steps = 5

The lattice shown next is the valuation lattice of the American call option, obtained using the backward-induction approach and applying a risk-neutral probability analysis.

Valuation Lattice

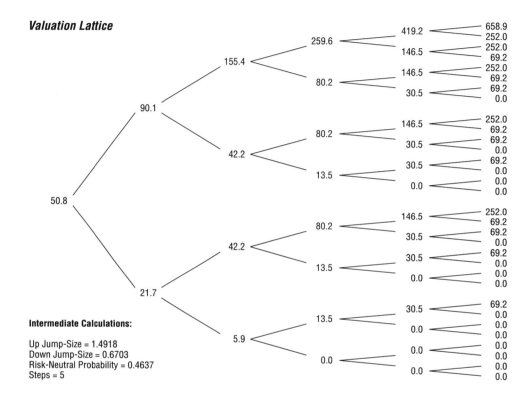

Intermediate Calculations:

Up Jump-Size = 1.4918
Down Jump-Size = 0.6703
Risk-Neutral Probability = 0.4637
Steps = 5

The problem also can be solved using a recombining lattice as shown here. Notice the similar values along the nonrecombining and recombining lattices. In the recombining lattice, the amount of computational work is significantly reduced because identical values for a particular time period are collapsed and summarized as unique nodes.

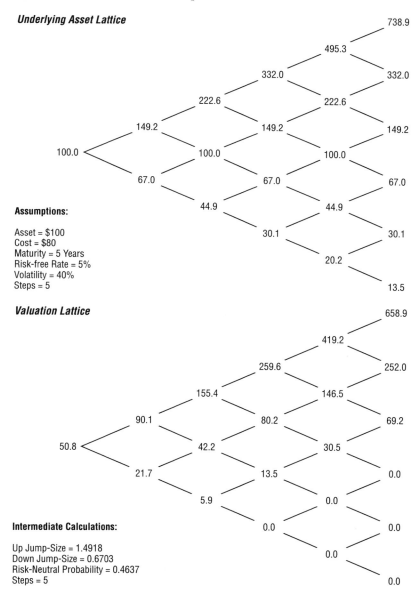

Underlying Asset Lattice

Assumptions:

Asset = $100
Cost = $80
Maturity = 5 Years
Risk-free Rate = 5%
Volatility = 40%
Steps = 5

Valuation Lattice

Intermediate Calculations:

Up Jump-Size = 1.4918
Down Jump-Size = 0.6703
Risk-Neutral Probability = 0.4637
Steps = 5

Notice the similar results obtained using the recombining and nonrecombining lattice approaches.

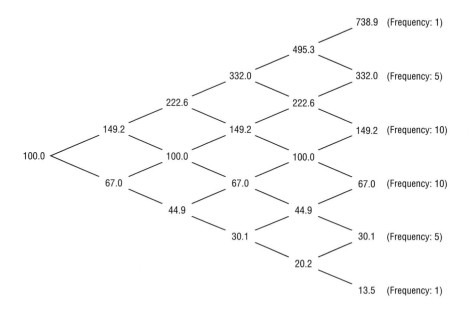

However, there is a caveat in comparing the recombining and nonre-combining lattices. For instance, the six terminal nodes on a recombining tree are unique occurrences and a summary of the 32 terminal nodes on the nonrecombining tree. Therefore, it is incorrect to assume that there is a one-sixth probability of occurrence for each of the values 738, 332, 149, 67, 30, and 13. In reality, the distribution of the terminal nodes looks somewhat normal, with different outcome probabilities as seen in the chart. Depending on the input parameters, the distribution of the terminal nodes may change slightly (higher volatility means a higher frequency of occurrence in the extreme values).

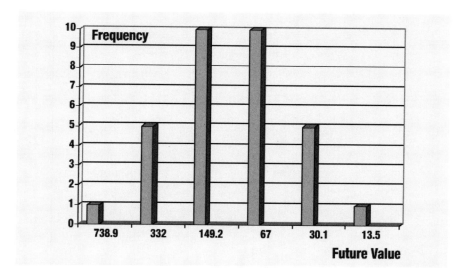

Although recombining lattices are easier to calculate and arrive at identical answers to nonrecombining lattices, there are conditions when nonrecombining lattices are required for the analysis. These conditions include when there are multiple sources of uncertainty or when volatility changes over time, as in the next example.

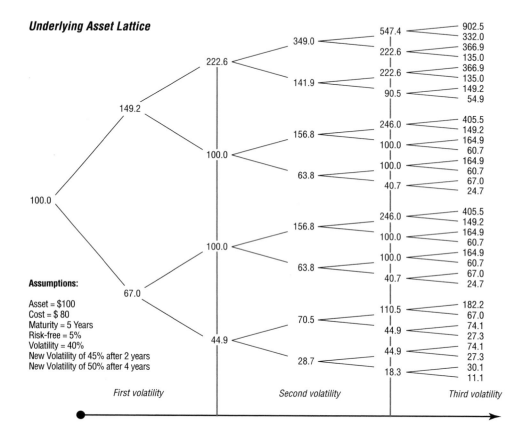

Underlying Asset Lattice

Assumptions:

Asset = $100
Cost = $ 80
Maturity = 5 Years
Risk-free = 5%
Volatility = 40%
New Volatility of 45% after 2 years
New Volatility of 50% after 4 years

First volatility   *Second volatility*   *Third volatility*

The next valuation lattice is on an American call option with changing volatilities using the risk-neutral probability approach.

Valuation Lattice

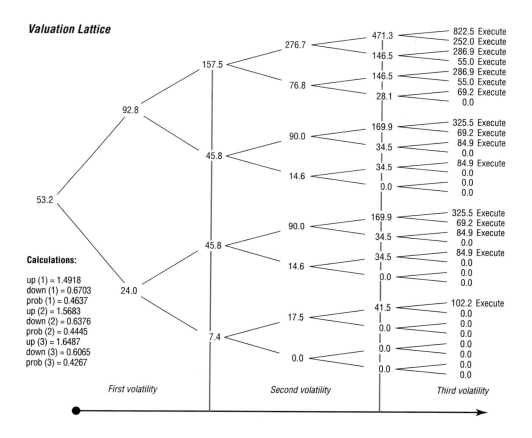

Calculations:

up (1) = 1.4918
down (1) = 0.6703
prob (1) = 0.4637
up (2) = 1.5683
down (2) = 0.6376
prob (2) = 0.4445
up (3) = 1.6487
down (3) = 0.6065
prob (3) = 0.4267

First volatility   *Second volatility*   *Third volatility*

Although nonrecombining lattices are better suited for solving options with changing volatilities, recombining lattices also can be modified to handle this condition, thereby cutting down on analytical time and effort. The results obtained are identical no matter which approach is used. The modified recombining lattice below makes use of the fact that although volatility changes three times within the 5-year maturity period, volatility remains constant within particular time periods. For instance, the 40 percent volatility applies from Time 0 to Time 2, and the 45 percent volatility holds for Time 2 to Time 4. Within these time periods, volatility remains constant; hence, the lattice bifurcations are recombining. The entire lattice analysis below can be segregated into three stages of recombining lattices. At the end of a constant volatility period, each resulting node becomes the starting point of a new recombining lattice.

Underlying Asset Lattice

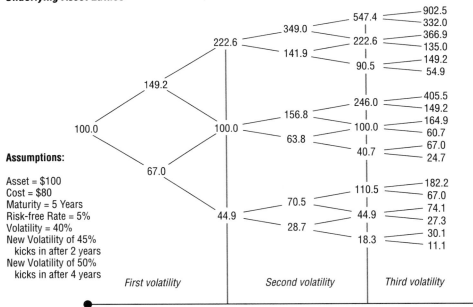

Assumptions:

Asset = $100
Cost = $80
Maturity = 5 Years
Risk-free Rate = 5%
Volatility = 40%
New Volatility of 45%
  kicks in after 2 years
New Volatility of 50%
  kicks in after 4 years

This valuation lattice is the modified recombining valuation lattice approach for the changing volatility option analysis. Notice that the resulting option value of $53.2 is identical to the result obtained using the nonrecombining lattice.

Valuation Lattice

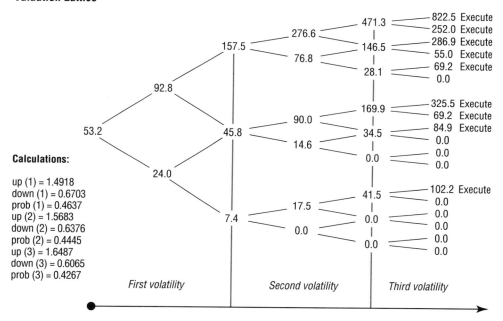

Calculations:

up (1) = 1.4918
down (1) = 0.6703
prob (1) = 0.4637
up (2) = 1.5683
down (2) = 0.6376
prob (2) = 0.4445
up (3) = 1.6487
down (3) = 0.6065
prob (3) = 0.4267

Exercise: Changing Volatility Option (Nonrecombining Lattices)

Open the Excel file *Workbook Exercise (Volatility Nonrecombining).xls* from the enclosed CD-ROM. Using the nonrecombining lattices below, solve the changing volatility option.

Creating and Solving a Changing Volatility Option

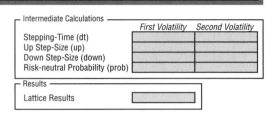

Assumptions

Asset Value ($)	$100.00
Implementation Cost ($)	$90.00
Maturity (Years)	5.00
Risk-free Rate (%)	7.00%
Dividends (%)	0.00%
Volatility (%)	30.00%
Lattice Steps	5
New Volatility (%)	45.00%
New Volatility Step	3

Intermediate Calculations

	First Volatility	Second Volatility
Stepping-Time (dt)		
Up Step-Size (up)		
Down Step-Size (down)		
Risk-neutral Probability (prob)		

Results

Lattice Results

Underlying Asset Lattice

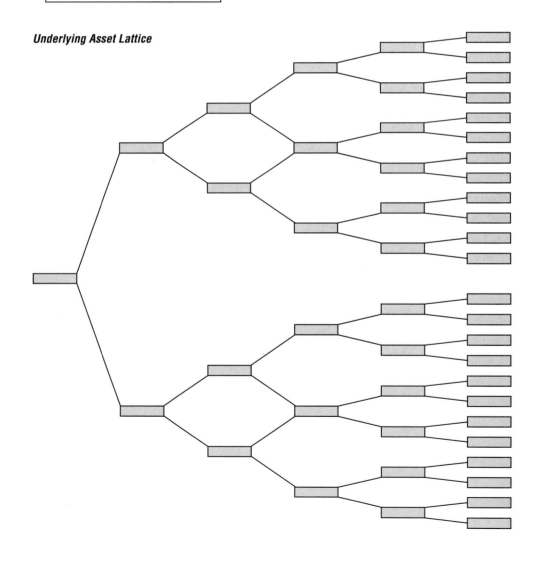

Option Valuation Lattice

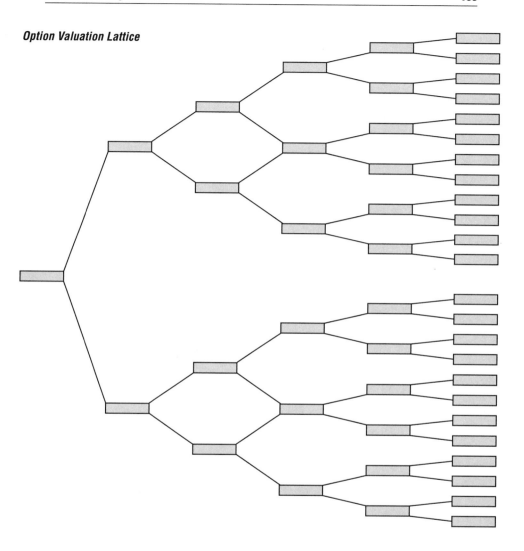

CHAPTER 7

Extended Problems

Combining Forecasting, DCF Modeling, Real Options, and Optimization

The Excel file *Workbook Exercise (Step by Step Analysis).xls* from the enclosed CD-ROM is provided for you to follow along with the current example. This example assumes that you are now sufficiently proficient in the use of Crystal Ball, OptQuest, Real Options Analysis Toolkit, and have a good understanding of binomial lattices. This example is meant only as a guide to the steps taken in a comprehensive decision-analysis methodology. Certain simplified assumptions are made to facilitate the computation and illustration.

Suppose a biotechnology firm is looking at valuing a patent for a biochemical compound developed by university researchers. Further, suppose that the biochemical compound is currently highly unstable and requires significant amounts of testing. However, the firm believes that further research is warranted and if results indicate that the compound can be stabilized, the potential financial ramifications are very significant. The complete research takes up to 10 years with the most intensive research done in the first 5 years, costing the firm $200 million each year for the first 5 years. However, due to the current Federal Drug Administration (FDA) guidelines, the drug can be marketed for consumption under strict controlled dissemination within the first 5 years. To do so would mean additional funding for human trials and subsequent FDA approval. The cost to obtain FDA approval is approximately half of the total research costs. Therefore, the firm has a sequential compound option to first research the efficacy of the drug for short-term development while continuing with long-term investigation of its full effects. The firm has to decide what the value of this biochemical compound is, and what the value is of being able to research and develop the drug's long-run full potential at the same time to capitalize on obtaining revenues in the short run with the limited version. In addition, the firm needs to identify the optimal royalty rate to pay to the university researchers for licensing their technology. These royalty rates must fall within contractual terms under obligation with the university, and must fall in line with management's expectations as well as be competitive. These royalty rates must be accounted for within a real options paradigm where the value of the project is greater than its net present value (NPV) as management has the flexibility not to execute on the short-run limited version of the drug should the long-term research results and market acceptance indicate that it is unprofitable. In addition, the firm wants the analysis to account for competitive effects, cannibalization by other comparable products under development, market saturation effects, and other uncertainties while accounting and controlling for the risks such that the project will still be profitable above a certain management-set threshold.

The first step is to collect historical data on revenues of the comparable product. Suppose the only available historical data on revenues are quarterly data starting from 1997 through 2002 of a highly similar product that was developed by the firm. Using these historical data, the analyst performs time-series analysis using Crystal Ball's Predictor (Figure 7.1).

	D	E	F	G
5				
6	Periodicity:		Quarterly	
7	Seasonality:		4	
8				
9	**Historical Data**		Forecast	
10	Date	Revenues	Date	Revenues
11	Q1 1997	30		
12	Q2 1997	35		
13	Q3 1997	42		
14	Q4 1997	49		
15	Q1 1998	50		
16	Q2 1998	57		
17	Q3 1998	63		
18	Q4 1998	72		
19	Q1 1999	80		
20	Q2 1999	85		
21	Q3 1999	92		
22	Q4 1999	112		
23	Q1 2000	120		
24	Q2 2000	135		
25	Q3 2000	144		
26	Q4 2000	156		
27	Q1 2001	153		
28	Q2 2001	166		
29	Q3 2001	178		
30	Q4 2001	180		
31	Q1 2002	178		
32	Q2 2002	185		
33	Q3 2002	190		
34	Q4 2002	200		

FIGURE 7.1   Sample historical data in Microsoft Excel.

The following step shows the selection of the historical data range using Crystal Ball's Predictor (Figure 7.2). Assuming the historical data exhibits seasonality, a quarterly seasonality correction is performed in the next step as shown in Figure 7.3. Predictor automatically chooses the best fitting time-series model from a series of eight different approaches as shown in Figure 7.4.

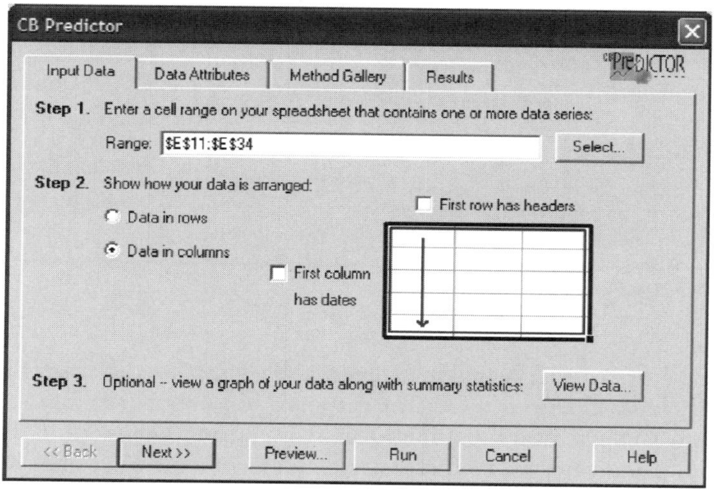

FIGURE 7.2   Crystal Ball's Predictor step 1 through 3: input data.

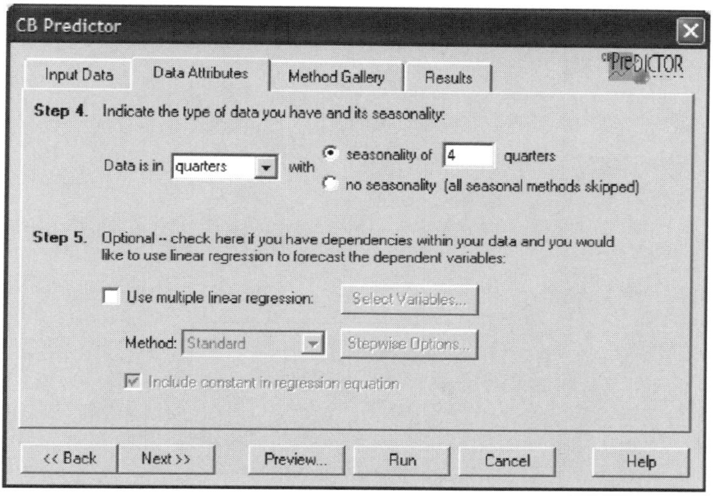

FIGURE 7.3   Crystal Ball's Predictor step 4 and 5: data attributes.

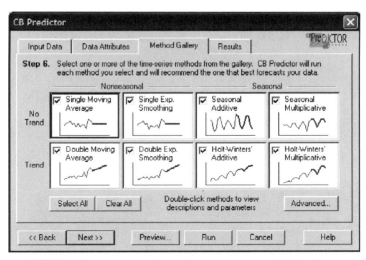

FIGURE 7.4   Crystal Ball's Predictor step 6: method gallery.

Then, a forecast is created for 20 periods (Figure 7.5): For each of the 20 quarterly forecast periods, Predictor automatically creates the revenue point forecasts with the relevant distributional assumptions (Figure 7.6). The highlighted cells indicate where forecast revenues with distributional assumptions are attached. These point forecasts are based on the best fitting line in the gallery of time-series approaches. The graph shown in Figure 7.7 illus-

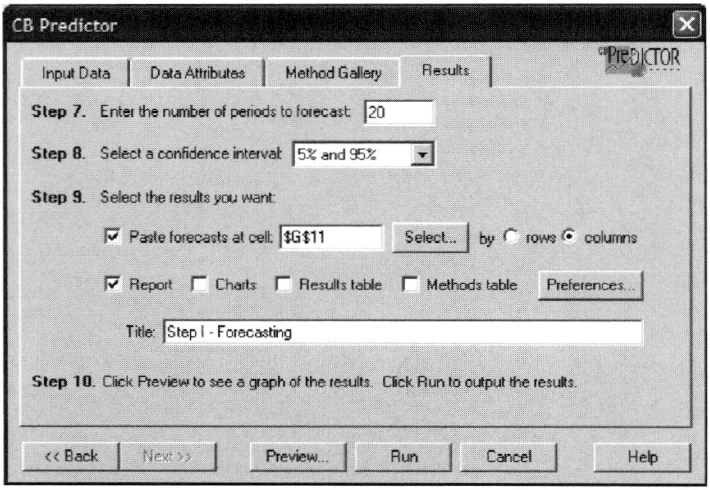

FIGURE 7.5   Crystal Ball's Predictor step 7 through 10: results.

	D	E	F	G
5				
6	Periodicity:		Quarterly	
7	Seasonality:		4	
8				
9	**Historical Data**		**Forecast**	
10	Date	Revenues	Date	Revenues
11	Q1 1997	30	Q1 2003	202.27
12	Q2 1997	35	Q2 2003	210.25
13	Q3 1997	42	Q3 2003	217.26
14	Q4 1997	49	Q4 2003	230.30
15	Q1 1998	50	Q1 2004	231.80
16	Q2 1998	57	Q2 2004	239.86
17	Q3 1998	63	Q3 2004	246.81
18	Q4 1998	72	Q4 2004	260.60
19	Q1 1999	80	Q1 2005	261.33
20	Q2 1999	85	Q2 2005	269.47
21	Q3 1999	92	Q3 2005	276.37
22	Q4 1999	112	Q4 2005	290.90
23	Q1 2000	120	Q1 2006	290.85
24	Q2 2000	135	Q2 2006	299.08
25	Q3 2000	144	Q3 2006	305.93
26	Q4 2000	156	Q4 2006	321.20
27	Q1 2001	153	Q1 2007	320.38
28	Q2 2001	166	Q2 2007	328.69
29	Q3 2001	178	Q3 2007	335.48
30	Q4 2001	180	Q4 2007	351.50
31	Q1 2002	178		
32	Q2 2002	185		
33	Q3 2002	190		
34	Q4 2002	200		

FIGURE 7.6 Forecast results with distributional assumptions in Excel.

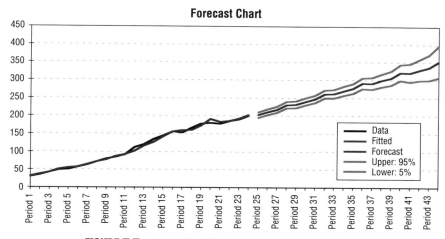

FIGURE 7.7 Crystal Ball's Predictor's forecast charts.

trates this fitting of historical data, as well as the forecast out to the future, complete with a 5th percentile and 95th percentile confidence interval. Table 7.1 lists the point forecast for each succeeding quarter, with its corresponding 5th percentile and 95th percentile.

The second step is to create a discounted cash flow (DCF) model using the forecast revenues as shown in Figure 7.8. The following illustrates a simple DCF model. As the revenues are based on the forecast values with distributional assumptions, the resulting NPV will have Monte Carlo simulation performed as well. In addition, other stochastic variable inputs affecting the DCF model can also be accounted for. As an example, several adjustments to revenues such as competitive effects, cannibalization by other product substitutes, and market saturation effects are stochastic and unknown in the future. However, management can decide what the potential ranges of effects may be over time. These stochastic variables are linked to the DCF model and the resulting stream of net cash flows will be stochastic. Using the logarithmic cash-flow-returns approach, the asset's volatility is estimated at 11.67 percent. The calculated volatility is also a distribution of values as the inputs into the DCF model are distributions of values.

TABLE 7.1   Crystal Ball Predictor Forecast Results

Date	Lower: 5%	Forecast	Upper: 95%
Q1 2003	194.53	202.27	210.02
Q2 2003	202.15	210.25	218.35
Q3 2003	208.78	217.26	225.74
Q4 2003	221.39	230.30	239.21
Q1 2004	222.42	231.80	241.17
Q2 2004	229.96	239.86	249.76
Q3 2004	236.34	246.81	257.29
Q4 2004	249.47	260.60	271.73
Q1 2005	249.45	261.33	273.20
Q2 2005	256.75	269.47	282.19
Q3 2005	262.67	276.37	290.07
Q4 2005	276.06	290.90	305.74
Q1 2006	274.66	290.85	307.04
Q2 2006	281.27	299.08	316.89
Q3 2006	286.13	305.93	325.72
Q4 2006	298.93	321.20	343.47
Q1 2007	294.93	320.38	345.82
Q2 2007	299.00	328.69	358.38
Q3 2007	299.86	335.48	371.11
Q4 2007	306.97	351.50	396.03

Step II: DCF

Input Parameters

Discount Rate (Cash Flow)	15.00%
Discount Rate (Impl. Cost)	5.00%
Tax Rate	10.00%

Results

Present Value (Cash Flow)	$1,265.09
Present Value (Impl. Cost)	($865.90)
Net Present Value	$399.20

Year	2003	2004	2005	2006	2007
Revenue	$860.08	$979.07	$1,098.06	$1,217.06	$1,336.05
Adjustment to Revenue	$51.60	$97.91	$197.65	$316.43	$467.62
Cost of Revenue	$86.01	$97.91	$109.81	$121.71	$133.60
Royalties Paid	$43.00	$48.95	$164.71	$182.56	$200.41
Gross Profit	$679.46	$734.30	$625.90	$596.36	$534.42
Operating Expenses	$135.89	$146.86	$125.18	$119.27	$106.88
Depreciation Expense	$10.00	$10.00	$10.00	$10.00	$10.00
Interest Expense	$100.00	$100.00	$100.00	$100.00	$100.00
Income Before Taxes	$433.57	$477.44	$390.72	$367.09	$317.54
Taxes	$43.36	$47.74	$39.07	$36.71	$31.75
Income After Taxes	$390.21	$429.70	$351.65	$330.38	$285.78
Non-Cash Expenses	$4.30	$4.90	$16.47	$18.26	$20.04
Cash Flow	$394.51	$434.59	$368.12	$348.63	$305.82
Implementation Cost	($200.00)	($200.00)	($200.00)	($200.00)	($200.00)

FIGURE 7.8   Second step in the analysis: creating a DCF model.

Notice that another variable of interest is the royalty rate paid to the patent holders. These rates are subject to negotiation and as such are decision variables. These decision variables are to be used in a later step of stochastic optimization (Figure 7.9).

The next step is to input the results from the DCF and simulation analyses into the real options paradigm (Figure 7.10). The resulting present value of future cash flows now becomes the starting asset value in the real options analysis. The present value of implementation costs now becomes the implementation cost of the underlying option. The volatility of the simulated cash-flow stream now becomes the input volatility to the analysis. The other

Adjustment to Revenue:	2003	2004	2005	2006	2007
Competitive Effects	1.00%	2.00%	3.00%	4.00%	5.00%
Cannibalization Effects	5.00%	8.00%	10.00%	12.00%	15.00%
Market Saturation	0.00%	0.00%	5.00%	10.00%	15.00%

Adjustment to Revenue:	2003	2004	2005	2006	2007
Royalty Rate	5.00%	5.00%	15.00%	15.00%	15.00%
Minimum Rate	5.00%	5.00%	10.00%	10.00%	10.00%
Maximum Rate	10.00%	10.00%	15.00%	15.00%	20.00%
Maximum Total Rate	50.00%		Minimum Total Rate		20.00%

Volatility Measure:					
Logarithmic Returns		0.0968	-0.1660	-0.0544	-0.1310
Volatility	11.67%				

FIGURE 7.9   Simulation assumptions, forecasts, and decision variables.

Step III: Real Options Analysis

Input Assumptions

Present Value of Future Cash Flows (asset)	$1,265.09
Implementation Cost (cost)	$865.90
Volatility (volatility)	11.67%
Maturity (maturity)	10
Risk-Free Rate (rf)	5.00%
Binomial Lattice Steps (steps)	10
Second Phase Implementation Cost (cost 2)	$432.95
Time to Second Phase (time2)	5

Intermediate Calculations

Time Step (dt)	1.00
Up Jump (up)	1.1237
Down Jump (down)	0.8899
Risk-Neutral Probability (prob)	0.6901

Results

Binomial Lattice Result	429.48

FIGURE 7.10 Step three in the analysis: applying real options analysis.

input parameters are based on the initial set of assumptions. Then, a binomial approach is applied to value the sequential compound option. The resulting underlying asset lattice, equity lattice, and valuation lattice are shown in Figure 7.11.

The next step is to run a stochastic optimization analysis. That is, given the uncertain environment of multiple interacting stochastic variables, you

Underlying Asset Lattice

1265.09	1421.64	1597.56	1795.25	2017.41	2267.05	2547.58	2862.83	3217.09	3615.19	4062.55
	1125.79	1265.09	1421.64	1597.56	1795.25	2017.41	2267.05	2547.58	2862.83	3217.09
		1001.82	1125.79	1265.09	1421.64	1597.56	1795.25	2017.41	2267.05	2547.58
			891.50	1001.82	1125.79	1265.09	1421.64	1597.56	1795.25	2017.41
				793.33	891.50	1001.82	1125.79	1265.09	1421.64	1597.56
					705.97	793.33	891.50	1001.82	1125.79	1265.09
						628.23	705.97	793.33	891.50	1001.82
							559.05	705.97	793.33	793.33
								628.23	705.97	628.23
									559.05	497.49
									442.71	393.96

Equity Lattice

740.69	869.83	1017.22	1185.08	1375.94	1592.69	1838.65	2117.55	2433.60	2791.53	3196.66
	575.64	685.50	811.72	956.14	1120.89	1308.47	1521.77	1764.09	2039.17	2351.20
		426.23	517.85	624.42	747.45	888.63	1049.97	1233.91	1443.38	1681.69
			292.73	366.21	453.75	556.71	676.36	814.07	971.59	1151.51
				177.51	231.86	299.56	382.36	481.60	597.98	731.67
					85.86	119.46	164.72	224.63	302.12	399.20
						25.24	38.45	58.57	89.22	135.92
							0.00	0.00	0.00	0.00
								0.00	0.00	0.00
									0.00	0.00
										0.00

Valuation Lattice

429.48	536.65	663.76	812.44	984.19	1180.86	1405.70
	261.86	342.38	442.50	564.39	709.06	875.52
		125.90	176.06	244.26	335.61	455.68
			35.01	53.33	81.24	123.76
				0.00	0.00	0.00
					0.00	0.00
						0.00

FIGURE 7.11 Resulting underlying asset lattice, equity lattice, and valuation lattice.

know that the asset value of the project is highly volatile. Given this uncertainty, what is the optimal level of royalty rates that should be paid over time such that the best outcome can be guaranteed at a certain probability, subject to satisfying some constraints? By contractual agreement, the firm must pay a royalty rate between 5 percent and 10 percent for the first 2 years, between 10 percent and 15 percent for the following 2 years, and between 10 percent and 20 percent in year 5. This result is seen through the first step in the optimization process using OptQuest (Figure 7.12).

Next, by internal management-set constraints, the total amount of royalties paid for the next 5 years should fall between 20 percent and 50 percent (Figure 7.13). Next, the optimization is set to maximize the mean of the total project expanded net present value (ENPV), including the strategic options value, at the same time satisfying the requirement that at least 90 percent of the time, the project should yield at least $400 million in NPV (Figure 7.14). The stochastic optimization is run for 10 minutes to produce an initial answer (Figure 7.15).

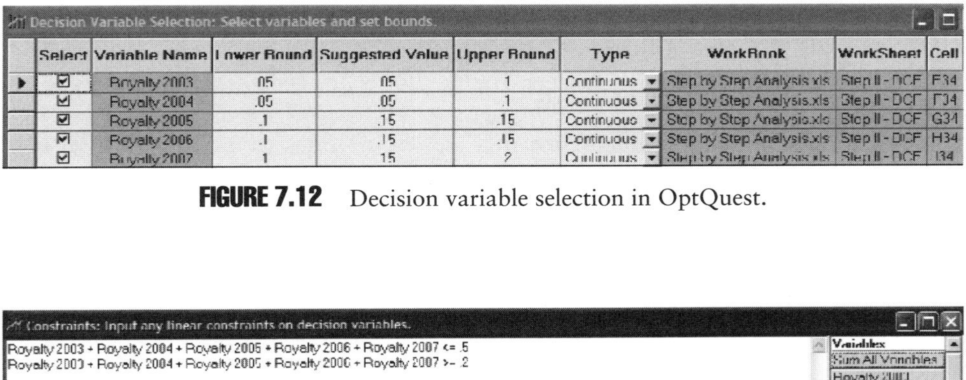

Decision Variable Selection: Select variables and set bounds.

Select	Variable Name	Lower Bound	Suggested Value	Upper Bound	Type	WorkBook	WorkSheet	Cell
☑	Royalty 2003	.05	.05	.1	Continuous	Step by Step Analysis.xls	Step II - DCF	F34
☑	Royalty 2004	.05	.05	.1	Continuous	Step by Step Analysis.xls	Step II - DCF	F34
☑	Royalty 2005	.1	.15	.15	Continuous	Step by Step Analysis.xls	Step II - DCF	G34
☑	Royalty 2006	.1	.15	.15	Continuous	Step by Step Analysis.xls	Step II - DCF	H34
☑	Royalty 2007	.1	.15	.2	Continuous	Step by Step Analysis.xls	Step II - DCF	I34

FIGURE 7.12 Decision variable selection in OptQuest.

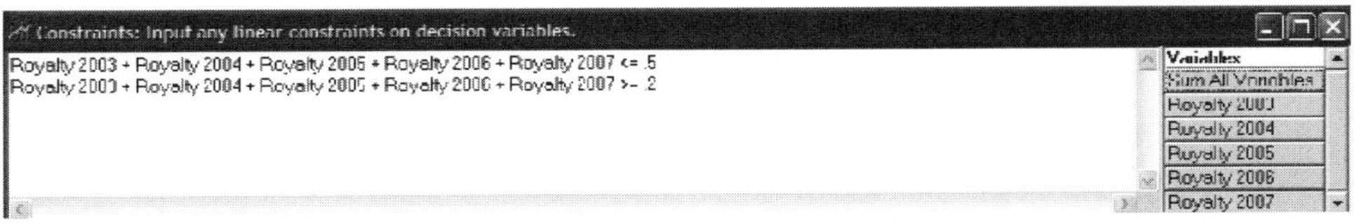

FIGURE 7.13 Setting up constraints in OptQuest.

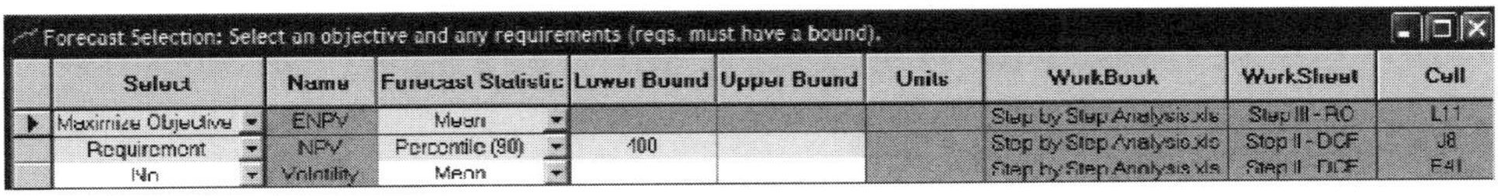

Forecast Selection: Select an objective and any requirements (reqs. must have a bound).

Select	Name	Forecast Statistic	Lower Bound	Upper Bound	Units	WorkBook	WorkSheet	Cell
Maximize Objective	ENPV	Mean				Step by Step Analysis.xls	Step III - RO	L11
Requirement	NPV	Percentile (90)	400			Step by Step Analysis.xls	Step II - DCF	J8
No	Volatility	Mean				Step by Step Analysis.xls	Step II - DCF	F41

FIGURE 7.14 Setting up the objective in OptQuest.

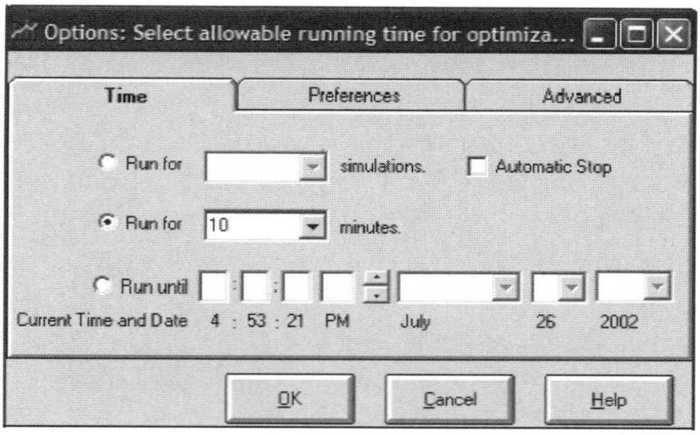

FIGURE 7.15   OptQuest's stochastic optimization preferences.

Based on running 1,000 simulation trials for each optimization set, the results indicate that the optimal decision is to provide a 5 percent royalty rate for the first 2 years, see what happens, then increase the royalty rate to 10 percent for the third and fourth years, before going to 20 percent the final year (Figure 7.16). Based on these royalty rates, the project will yield at least $400 million in NPV while maximizing the overall strategic profitability of the project and at the same time still satisfying management and other legal contractual obligations.

Finally, based on the performance graph, it would seem that these royalty rates are the most efficient and optimal, and that slight variations from these rates will yield fairly insignificant increases in value (Figure 7.17).

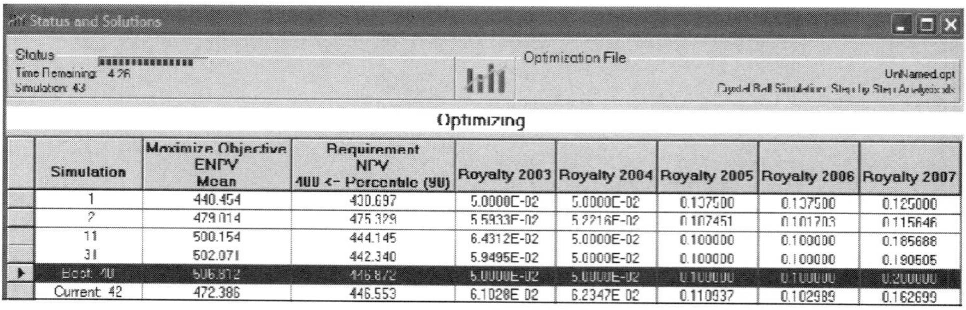

Simulation	Maximize Objective ENPV Mean	Requirement NPV 400 <- Percentile (90)	Royalty 2003	Royalty 2004	Royalty 2005	Royalty 2006	Royalty 2007
1	440.454	430.697	5.0000E-02	5.0000E-02	0.137500	0.137500	0.125000
2	479.014	475.329	5.5933E-02	5.2216E-02	0.107451	0.101703	0.115646
11	500.154	444.145	6.4312E-02	5.0000E-02	0.100000	0.100000	0.185688
31	502.071	442.340	5.9495E-02	5.0000E-02	0.100000	0.100000	0.190505
Best 40	506.912	446.872	5.0000E-02	5.0000E-02	0.100000	0.100000	0.200000
Current 42	472.386	446.553	6.1028E-02	6.2347E-02	0.110937	0.102989	0.162699

FIGURE 7.16   OptQuest's status and solutions screen.

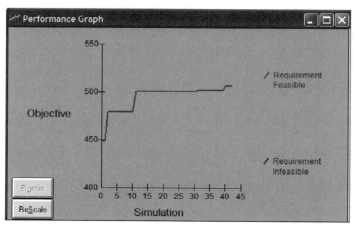

FIGURE 7.17   Resulting performance graph.

CHAPTER 8

Exercise Solutions

Solutions for DCF Model

Discounted Cash Flow Analysis

Discount Rate   20%

Discrete Discounting

Year	2002	2003	2004	2005	2006	2007
Revenues		$100	$200	$300	$400	$500
Operating Expenses		$10	$20	$30	$40	$50
Net Income		$90	$180	$270	$360	$450
Investment Costs	($450)					
Free Cash Flow	($450)	$90	$180	$270	$360	$450
Present Value of Cash Flow	($450)	$75	$125	$156	$174	$181
Net Present Value	**$261**					

Continuous Discounting

Year	2002	2003	2004	2005	2006	2007
Revenues		$100	$200	$300	$400	$500
Operating Expenses		$10	$20	$30	$40	$50
Net Income		$90	$180	$270	$360	$450
Investment Costs	($450)					
Free Cash Flow	($450)	$90	$180	$270	$360	$450
Present Value of Cash Flow	($450)	$74	$121	$148	$162	$166
Net Present Value	**$220**					

Solutions for Simulation I (Simulating a DCF Model)

Monte Carlo Simulation

Input Parameters

Discount Rate (Cash Flow)	15.00%
Discount Rate (Impl. Cost)	7.00%
Tax Rate	40.00%

Results

Present Value (Cash Flow)	$334.72
Present Value (Impl. Cost)	$234.94
Net Present Value	$99.79

	2002	2003	2004	2005	2006
Revenue	$100.00	$200.00	$300.00	$400.00	$500.00
Cost of Revenue	$25.00	$50.00	$75.00	$100.00	$125.00
Gross Profit	$75.00	$150.00	$225.00	$300.00	$375.00
Operating Expenses	$10.00	$20.00	$30.00	$40.00	$50.00
Depreciation Expense	$5.00	$10.00	$15.00	$20.00	$25.00
Interest Expense	$5.00	$10.00	$15.00	$20.00	$25.00
Income Before Taxes	$55.00	$110.00	$165.00	$220.00	$275.00
Taxes	$22.00	$44.00	$66.00	$88.00	$110.00
Income After Taxes	$33.00	$66.00	$99.00	$132.00	$165.00
Non-Cash Expenses	$10.00	$10.00	$10.00	$10.00	$10.00
Cash Flow	$43.00	$76.00	$109.00	$142.00	$175.00
Implementation Cost	$20.00	$40.00	$60.00	$80.00	$100.00

Solutions for Simulation II (Simulating a Stock Price Path)

Simulated Stock Price Path

Stock returns annualized volatility	Annualized mean growth of returns	Starting stock price at time 0	Calculated periodic volatility
100.00%	8.00%	$100.00	13.87%

Simulate	Date	Value
	01-Jan-01	$100.00
−0.8962	08-Jan-01	$87.73
0.6556	15-Jan-01	$95.84
0.8031	22-Jan-01	$106.66
−0.3144	29-Jan-01	$102.17
0.7859	05-Feb-01	$113.46
−0.8904	12-Feb-01	$99.63
−1.1061	19-Feb-01	$84.50
−0.0203	26-Feb-01	$84.39
−0.4653	05-Mar-01	$79.08
−0.4988	12-Mar-01	$73.73
−0.2829	19-Mar-01	$70.95
2.2697	26-Mar-01	$93.39
−1.0476	02-Apr-01	$79.96
1.0232	09-Apr-01	$91.43
0.1844	16-Apr-01	$93.91
−0.8955	23-Apr-01	$82.29
0.3269	30-Apr-01	$86.26
−1.5852	7-May-01	$67.43
0.4027	14-May-01	$71.30
1.3701	21-May-01	$84.95

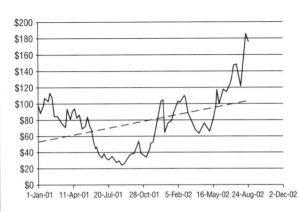

Solutions for Volatility Estimates

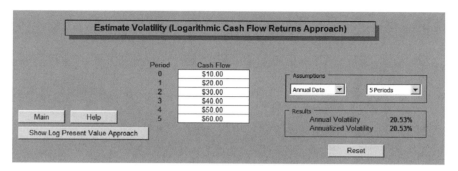

Solutions for Creating and Solving Lattices

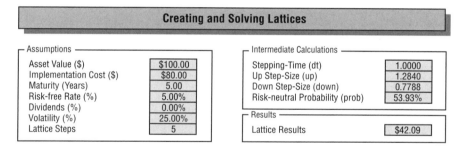

Creating and Solving Lattices

Assumptions

Asset Value ($)	$100.00
Implementation Cost ($)	$80.00
Maturity (Years)	5.00
Risk-free Rate (%)	5.00%
Dividends (%)	0.00%
Volatility (%)	25.00%
Lattice Steps	5

Intermediate Calculations

Stepping-Time (dt)	1.0000
Up Step-Size (up)	1.2840
Down Step-Size (down)	0.7788
Risk-neutral Probability (prob)	53.93%

Results

Lattice Results	$42.09

Underlying Asset Lattice

					349.03
				271.83	
			211.70		211.70
		164.87		164.87	
	128.40		128.40		128.40
100.00		100.00		100.00	
	77.88		77.88		77.88
		60.65		60.65	
			47.24		47.24
				36.79	
					28.65

Option Valuation Lattice

					269.03
				195.73	
			139.31		131.70
		96.19		88.77	
	64.48		56.42		48.40
42.09		34.53		24.83	
	20.58		12.74		0.00
		6.53		0.00	
			0.00		0.00
				0.00	
					0.00

Solutions for Granularity in Lattice

Granularity in Lattices

Assumptions

Asset Value ($)	$100.00
Implementation Cost ($)	$90.00
Maturity (Years)	5.00
Risk-free Rate (%)	5.00%
Dividends (%)	0.00%
Volatility (%)	20.00%
Small Lattice Steps	5
Large Lattice Steps	10

Intermediate Calculations

Stepping-Time (dt)	1.0000	0.5000
Up Step-Size (up)	1.2214	1.1519
Down Step-Size (down)	0.8187	0.8881
Risk-neutral Probability (prob)	57.75%	55.39%

Underlying Asset Lattice

					271.83	
				222.55		
			182.21		182.21	
		149.18		149.18		
	122.14		122.14		122.14	
100.00		100.00		100.00		
	81.87		81.87		81.86	
		67.03		67.03		
			54.88		54.88	
				44.93		
					36.79	

Underlying Asset Lattice (10 Steps)

										411.33
									357.08	
								309.99		309.99
							269.11		269.11	
						233.62		233.62		233.62
					202.81		202.81		202.81	
				176.07		176.07		176.07		176.07
			152.85		152.85		152.85		152.85	
		132.85		132.69		132.69		132.69		132.69
	115.19		115.19		115.19		115.19		115.19	
100.00		100.00		100.00		100.00		100.00		100.00
	86.81		86.81		86.81		86.81		86.81	
		75.36		75.36		75.36		75.36		75.36
		65.43		65.43		65.43		65.43		
			56.80		56.80		56.80		56.80	
				49.31		49.31		49.31		
				42.80		42.80		42.80		42.80
					37.16		37.16			
						32.26		32.26		32.26
							28.00			
								24.31		

Solutions for European Option

European Option Calculations

Assumptions

Asset Value ($)	$100.00
Implementation Cost ($)	$100.00
Maturity (Years)	1.00
Risk-free Rate (%)	5.00%
Dividends (%)	0.00%
Volatility (%)	25.00%
Lattice Steps	5

Intermediate Calculations

Stepping-Time (dt)	0.20000
Up Step-Size (up)	1.1183
Down Step-Size (down)	0.8942
Risk-neutral Probability (prob)	51.69%

Results

Lattice Results	$12.79
Black-Scholes Results	$12.34

Underlying Asset

					174.90
				156.39	
			139.85		139.85
		125.06		125.06	
	111.83		111.83		111.83
100.00		100.00		100.00	
	89.42		89.42		89.42
		79.96		79.96	
			71.50		71.50
				63.94	
					57.18

Option Valuation

					74.90
				57.39	
			41.83		39.85
		29.17		26.05	
	19.61		16.23		11.83
12.79		9.79		6.05	
	5.77		3.10		0.00
		1.59		0.00	
			0.00		0.00
				0.00	
					0.00

Decision Lattice

					Execute
				Continue	
			Continue		Execute
		Continue		Continue	
	Continue		Continue		Execute
Continue		Continue		Continue	
	Continue		Continue		End
		Continue		Continue	
			Continue		End
				Continue	
					End

Solutions for American Option

American Option Calculations

Assumptions

Asset Value ($)	$100.00
Implementation Cost ($)	$80.00
Maturity (Years)	3.00
Risk-free Rate (%)	5.00%
Dividends (%)	12.00%
Volatility (%)	35.00%
Lattice Steps	5

Intermediate Calculations

Stepping-Time (dt)	0.6000
Up Step-Size (up)	1.3114
Down Step-Size (down)	0.7625
Risk-neutral Probability (prob)	35.77%

Results

Lattice Results	$23.47

Underlying Asset

					387.98
				295.78	
			225.54		225.54
		171.98		171.98	
	131.14		131.14		131.14
100.00		100.00		100.00	
	76.25		76.25		76.25
		58.15		58.15	
			44.34		44.34
				33.81	
					25.78

Option Valuation

					307.89
				215.78	
			145.54		145.54
		91.98		91.98	
	51.14		51.14		51.14
23.47		22.08		20.00	
	9.17		6.94		0.00
		2.41		0.00	
			0.00		0.00
				0.00	
					0.00

Decision Lattice

					Execute
				Execute	
			Execute		Execute
		Execute		Execute	
	Execute		Execute		Execute
Continue		Continue		Execute	
	Continue		Continue		End
		Continue		Continue	
			Continue		End
				Continue	
					End

Solutions for Risk-Neutral Probability Approach Versus Market-Replicating Portfolio

Part I: Risk-Neutral Probability Approach

Stepping Time = 1.00
Up Jump-Size (up) = 1.1052
Down Jump-Size (down) = 0.9048
Risk-Neutral Probability = 0.7309

Option Valuation Lattice

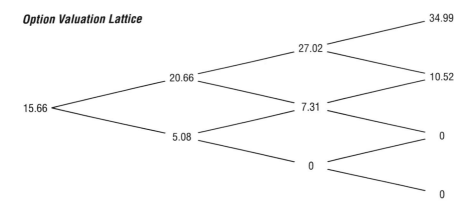

Part II: Market-Replicating Portfolio Approach

Step 1: Get the call values at the terminal nodes.

$$C_{3UU} = 34.99$$
$$C_{3UD} = 10.52$$
$$C_{3DU} = 0.00$$
$$C_{3DD} = 0.00$$

Step 2: Get the hedge ratios for the terminal branches.

$$h_{2U} = 1.0000$$
$$h_{2M} = 0.5250$$
$$h_{2D} = 0.0000$$

Step 3: Get the debt load for the terminal branches.

$$D_{2U} = 100.0000$$
$$D_{2M} = 47.5030$$
$$D_{2L} = 0.0000$$

Step 4: Get the call values one node back, $t = 2$.

$$C_{2U} = 27.0171$$
$$C_{2M} = 7.3137$$
$$C_{2D} = 0.0000$$

Step 5: Get the hedge ratios for the one branch back, $t = 1$.

$$h_{1U} = 0.8899$$
$$h_{1D} = 0.4034$$

Step 6: Get the debt load for one branch back, $t = 1$.

$$D_{1U} = 81.6753$$
$$D_{1D} = 33.0263$$

Step 7: Get the call values one node back.

$$C_{1U} = 20.6598$$
$$C_{1D} = 5.0840$$

Step 8: Get the hedge ratios for two branches back, $t = 0$.

$$h_0 = 0.7772$$

Step 9: Get the debt load for two branches back, $t = 0$.

$$D_0 = 65.2363$$

Step 10: Get the call value at $t = 0$, the option value of this analysis.

$$C_0 = 15.66$$

Solutions for State-Pricing Approach

European Option Calculations — State Pricing Approach

Assumptions

Asset Value ($)	$100.00
Implementation Cost ($)	$100.00
Maturity (Years)	5.00
Risk-free Rate (%)	5.00%
Dividends (%)	0.00%
Volatility (%)	25.00%
Lattice Steps	5

Intermediate Calculations

Stepping-Time (dt)	1.0000
Up Step-Size (up)	1.2840
Down Step-Size (down)	0.7788
Up Jump Increment	28.40%
Down Jump Increment	−22.12%
Up State Price	0.5106
Down State Price	0.4406

Results

Lattice Results	$32.71
Black-Scholes Results	$32.50

Underlying Asset Lattice

					349.03
				271.83	
			211.70		211.70
		164.87		164.87	
	128.40		128.40		128.40
100.00		100.00		100.00	
	77.88		77.88		77.88
		60.65		60.65	
			47.24		47.24
				36.79	
					28.65

State Prices Lattice

					249.03
				176.38	
			120.70		111.70
		80.10		69.55	
	51.76		41.90		28.40
32.71		24.66		14.50	
	14.26		7.41		0.00
		3.78		0.00	
			0.00		0.00
				0.00	
					0.00

Decision Lattice

					Execute
				Continue	
			Continue		Execute
		Continue		Continue	
	Continue		Continue		Execute
Continue		Continue		Continue	
	Continue		Continue		End
		Continue		Continue	
			Continue		End
				Continue	
					End

Solutions for Trinomial Lattices

American Option Calculations (Trinomial Lattice)

Assumptions

Asset Value ($)	$100.00
Implementation Cost ($)	$100.00
Maturity (Years)	3.00
Risk-free Rate (%)	5.00%
Dividends (%)	0.00%
Volatility (%)	35.00%
Lattice Steps	3

Intermediate Calculations

Stepping-Time (dt)	1.0000
Up Step-Size (up)	1.8335
Down Step-Size (down)	0.5454
High Branch Probability (P_H)	0.1574
Middle Branch Probability (P_M)	0.6667
Low Branch Probability (P_L)	0.1759

Results

Lattice Results	$27.80

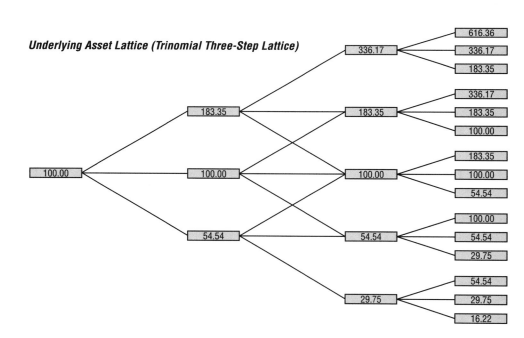

Underlying Asset Lattice (Trinomial Three-Step Lattice)

Option Valuation Lattice (Trinomial Three-Step Lattice)

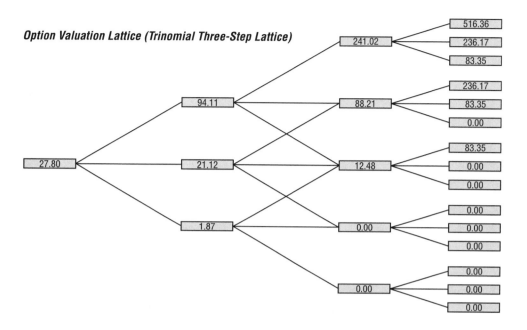

```
┌─ Intermediate Calculations ──────────────────────┐
│                                                   │
│  Steps (N)                          │ 3.0000 │    │
│  Stepping-Time (dt)                 │ 1.0000 │    │
│  Up Step-Size (up)                  │ 1.4191 │    │
│  Down Step-Size (down)              │ 0.7047 │    │
│  Risk-neutral Probability (prob)    │ 0.4852 │    │
│                                                   │
└───────────────────────────────────────────────────┘
```

Underlying Asset Lattice (Binomial Three-Step Lattice)

			285.77
		201.38	
	141.91		141.91
100.00		100.00	
	70.47		70.47
		49.66	
			34.99

Option Valuation Lattice (Binomial Three-Step Lattice)

			185.77
		106.25	
	58.51		41.91
31.37		19.34	
	8.93		0.00
		0.00	
			0.00

┌─ Intermediate Calculations ─────────────────────┐

Steps (N)	4.0000
Stepping-Time (dt)	0.7500
Up Step-Size (up)	1.3541
Down Step-Size (down)	0.7385
Risk-neutral Probability (prob)	0.4869

└──┘

Underlying Asset Lattice
(Binomial Four-Step Lattice)

				336.17
			248.27	
		183.35		183.35
	135.41		135.41	
100.00		100.00		100.00
	73.85		73.85	
		54.54		54.54
			40.28	
				29.75

Option Valuation Lattice
(Binomial Four-Step Lattice)

				236.17
			151.85	
		90.57		83.35
	51.53		39.09	
28.42		18.33		0.00
	8.60		0.00	
		0.00		0.00
			0.00	
				0.00

Solutions for Abandonment Option

Creating and Solving an Abandonment Option

Assumptions

Asset Value ($)	$150.00
Maturity (Years)	5.00
Risk-free Rate (%)	5.00%
Dividends (%)	2.00%
Volatility (%)	30.00%
Lattice Steps	5
Salvage Value ($)	$100.00
Growth Rate (%)	3.00%

Intermediate Calculations

Stepping-Time (dt)	1.0000
Up Step-Size (up)	1.3499
Down Step-Size (down)	0.7408
Risk-neutral Probability (prob)	47.56%

Results

Lattice Results	$148.12

Underlying Asset

					672.25
				499.02	
			368.94		368.94
		273.32		273.32	
	202.48		202.48		202.48
150.00		150.00		150.00	
	111.12		111.12		111.12
		82.32		82.32	
			60.99		60.99
				45.18	
					33.47

Salvage Values

100.00	103.00	106.09	109.27	112.55	115.93

Option Valuation

					672.25
				488.16	
			354.47		368.94
		258.00		267.91	
	191.68		195.74		202.48
148.12		150.28		149.43	
	123.10		123.74		115.93
		110.49		112.55	
			109.27		115.93
				112.55	
					115.93

Decision Lattice

					End
				Continue	
			Continue		End
		Continue		Continue	
	Continue		Continue		End
Continue		Continue		Continue	
	Continue		Continue		Abandon
		Continue		Abandon	
			Abandon		Abandon
				Abandon	
					Abandon

Solutions for Expansion Option (American Expansion Option)

Creating and Solving an Expansion Option I

Assumptions ─

Asset Value ($)	$400.00
Implementation Cost ($)	$250.00
Maturity (Years)	5.00
Risk-free Rate (%)	7.00%
Dividends (%)	0.00%
Volatility (%)	35.00%
Lattice Steps	5
Expansion Factor	2.00

Intermediate Calculations ─

Stepping-Time (dt)	1.0000
Up Step-Size (up)	1.4191
Down Step-Size (down)	0.7047
Risk-neutral Probability (prob)	51.49%

Results ─

Lattice Results	$638.30

This exercise assumes a static expansion factor.

Underlying Asset Lattice

					2301.84
				1622.08	
			1143.06		1143.06
		805.50		805.50	
	567.63		567.63		567.63
400.00		400.00		400.00	
	281.88		281.88		281.88
		198.63		198.63	
			139.98		139.98
				98.64	
					69.51

Option Valuation Lattice

					4353.68
				3011.06	
			2068.78		2036.12
		1408.36		1377.90	
	950.91		917.91		885.25
638.30		607.54		566.90	
	401.91		368.92		313.75
		243.75		213.94	
			147.32		139.98
				98.64	
					69.51

Solutions for Expansion Option (Growing Expansion Rate)

Creating and Solving an Expansion Option II

Assumptions

Asset Value ($)	$400.00
Implementation Cost ($)	$250.00
Maturity (Years)	5.00
Risk-free Rate (%)	8.00%
Dividends (%)	2.00%
Volatility (%)	35.00%
Lattice Steps	5
Expansion Factor	1.50
Expansion Growth Rate	10.00%

Intermediate Calculations

Stepping-Time (dt)	1.0000
Up Step-Size (up)	1.4191
Down Step-Size (down)	0.7047
Risk-neutral Probability (prob)	49.99%

Results

Lattice Results	$715.38

This exercise assumes a dynamic expansion factor.

Underlying Asset Lattice

					2301.84
				1622.08	
			1143.06		1143.06
		805.50		805.50	
	567.63		567.63		567.63
400.00		400.00		400.00	
	281.88		281.88		281.88
		198.63		198.63	
			139.98		139.98
				98.64	
					69.51

Expansion Factors

1.5	1.65	1.82	2.00	2.20	2.42

Option Valuation Lattice

					5310.71
				3610.19	
			2440.05		2511.37
		1635.92		1676.59	
	1086.64		1104.45		1121.25
715.38		718.47		716.39	
	463.35		452.25		430.94
		285.45		263.50	
			166.24		139.98
				96.69	
					69.51

Solutions for Expansion Option (Competitive Risks)

Creating and Solving an Expansion Option III

Assumptions

	Your Firm	Competition
Asset Value ($)	$400.00	$400.00
Implementation Cost ($)	$250.00	
Maturity (Years)	5.00	
Risk-free Rate (%)	7.00%	
Dividends (%)	0.00%	
Volatility (%)	35.00%	25.00%
Lattice Steps	5	

Intermediate Calculations

	Your Firm	Competition
Stepping-Time (dt)	1.0000	
Up Step-Size (up)	1.4191	1.2840
Down Step-Size (down)	0.7047	0.7788
Risk-neutral Probability (prob)	51.49%	

Results

Lattice Results $577.01

This exercise assumes a dynamic expansion factor that depends on a competitive firm growing at different rates.

Firm's Underlying Asset Lattice

					2301.84
				1622.08	
			1143.06		1143.06
		805.50		805.50	
	567.63		567.63		567.63
400.00		400.00		400.00	
	281.88		281.88		281.88
		198.63		198.63	
			139.98		139.98
				98.64	
					69.51

Competitor's Underlying Asset Lattice

					1396.14
				1087.31	
			846.80		846.80
		659.49		659.49	
	513.61		513.61		513.61
400.00		400.00		400.00	
	311.52		311.52		311.52
		242.61		242.61	
			188.95		188.95
				147.15	
					114.60

Expansion Factors

					1.61
				1.67	
			1.74		1.74
		1.82		1.82	
	1.90		1.90		1.90
2.00		2.00		2.00	
	2.11		2.11		2.11
		2.22		2.22	
			2.35		2.35
				2.49	
					2.65

Option Valuation Lattice

					3447.98
				2459.39	
			1739.86		1739.86
		1214.99		1214.99	
	839.96		834.04		831.24
577.01		567.46		554.38	
	384.16		369.35		343.40
		247.04		228.17	
			154.15		139.98
				98.64	
					69.51

Decision Lattice

					Expand
				Expand	
			Expand		Expand
		Expand		Expand	
	Continue		Continue		Expand
Continue		Continue		Continue	
	Continue		Continue		Expand
		Continue		Continue	
			Continue		End
				Continue	
					End

Solutions for Contraction Option

Creating and Solving a Contraction Option

┌─ Assumptions ──────────────────────────────┐

Asset Value ($)	$1000.00
Maturity (Years)	5.00
Risk-free Rate (%)	5.00%
Dividends (%)	2.00%
Volatility (%)	50.00%
Lattice Steps	5
Savings ($)	$400.00
Contraction Factor	0.50
Contraction Growth Rate (%)	−5.00%

┌─ Intermediate Calculations ──────────────┐

Stepping-Time (dt)	1.0000
Up Step-Size (up)	1.6487
Down Step-Size (down)	0.6065
Risk-neutral Probability (prob)	40.68%

┌─ Results ─────────────────┐

Lattice Results	$1,004.85

This exercise assumes a dynamic contraction factor.

Underlying Asset Lattice

					12182.49
				7389.06	
			4481.69		4481.69
		2718.28		2718.28	
	1648.72		1648.72		1648.72
1000.00		1000.00		1000.00	
	606.53		606.53		606.53
		367.88		367.88	
			223.13		223.13
				135.34	
					82.08

Contraction Factors

0.50	0.48	0.45	0.43	0.41	0.39

Option Valuation Lattice

					12182.49
				7242.74	
			4305.96		4481.69
		2565.04		2664.46	
	1561.83		1593.03		1648.72
1004.85		1008.95		996.07	
	709.79		695.67		634.66
		566.01		549.82	
			495.65		486.33
				455.12	
					431.76

Solutions for Chooser (Contract, Expand, and Abandon) Option

Creating and Solving a Chooser Option

Assumptions

Asset Value ($)	$100.00
Maturity (Years)	5.00
Risk-free Rate (%)	7.00%
Dividends (%)	2.00%
Volatility (%)	25.00%
Lattice Steps	5
Expansion Factor	2.50
Expansion Cost ($)	$120.00
Contraction Factor	0.90
Contraction Savings ($)	$50.00
Salvage Value ($)	$100.00

Intermediate Calculations

Stepping-Time (dt)	1.0000
Up Step-Size (up)	1.2840
Down Step-Size (down)	0.7788
Risk-neutral Probability (prob)	53.93%

Results

Lattice Results	$163.15

Underlying Asset

					349.03
				271.83	
			211.70		211.70
		164.97		164.97	
	128.40		128.40		128.40
100.00		100.00		100.00	
	77.88		77.88		77.88
		60.65		60.65	
			47.24		47.24
				36.79	
					28.65

Option Valuation

					752.59
				559.57	
			409.25		409.25
		297.07		292.18	
	217.73		212.50		201.01
163.15		159.12		152.66	
	124.94		121.69		120.09
		104.59		104.59	
			100.00		100.00
				100.00	
					100.00

Decision Lattice

					Expand
				Expand	
			Expand		Expand
		Continue		Expand	
	Continue		Continue		Expand
Continue		Continue		Continue	
	Continue		Continue		Contract
		Contract		Contract	
			Salvage		Salvage
				Salvage	
					Salvage

Solutions for Simultaneous Compound Option

Creating and Solving a Simultaneous Option

Assumptions

Asset Value ($)	$1000.00
First Cost ($)	$800.00
Second Cost ($)	$600.00
Maturity (Years)	5.00
Risk-free Rate (%)	7.00%
Dividends (%)	0.00%
Volatility (%)	30.00%
Lattice Steps	5

Intermediate Calculations

Stepping-Time (dt)	1.0000
Up Step-Size (up)	1.3499
Down Step-Size (down)	0.7408
Risk-neutral Probability (prob)	54.46%

Results

Lattice Results	$253.61

Underlying Asset Lattice

					4481.69
				3320.12	
			2459.60		2459.60
		1822.12		1822.12	
	1349.86		1349.86		1349.86
1000.00		1000.00		1000.00	
	740.82		740.82		740.82
		548.81		548.81	
			406.57		406.57
				301.19	
					223.13

First Option Valuation Lattice

					3681.69
				2574.20	
			1764.12		1659.60
		1178.18		1076.20	
	767.22		665.04		549.86
488.36		397.18		279.21	
	232.62		141.78		0.00
		72.00		0.00	
			0.00		0.00
				0.00	
					0.00

Second Option Valuation Lattice

					3081.69
				2014.77	
			1251.54		1059.60
		751.53		538.06	
	440.53		273.22		0.00
253.61		138.74		0.00	
	70.45		0.00		0.00
		0.00		0.00	
			0.00		0.00
				0.00	
					0.00

Decision Lattice (First Option)

					Execute
				Continue	
			Continue		Execute
		Continue		Continue	
	Continue		Continue		Execute
Continue		Continue		Continue	
	Continue		Continue		End
		Continue		Continue	
			Continue		End
				Continue	
					End

Decision Lattice (Second Option)

					Execute
				Continue	
			Continue		Execute
		Continue		Continue	
	Continue		Continue		End
Continue		Continue		Continue	
	Continue		Continue		End
		Continue		Continue	
			Continue		End
				Continue	
					End

Solutions for Sequential Compound Option

Creating and Solving a Sequential Option

Assumptions

Asset Value ($)	$500.00
Underlying Cost ($)	$300.00
Option Cost ($)	$20.00
Maturity (Years)	5.00
Option Time (Years)	3.00
Risk-free Rate (%)	7.00%
Dividends (%)	0.00%
Volatility (%)	25.00%
Lattice Steps	5

Intermediate Calculations

Stepping-Time (dt)	1.0000
Up Step-Size (up)	1.2840
Down Step-Size (down)	0.7788
Risk-neutral Probability (prob)	58.13%

Results

Lattice Results	$277.82

Underlying Asset Lattice

					1745.17
				1359.14	
			1058.50		1058.50
		824.36		824.36	
	642.01		642.01		642.01
500.00		500.00		500.00	
	389.40		389.40		389.40
		303.27		303.27	
			236.18		236.18
				183.94	
					143.25

Second Phase Option Valuation Lattice

					1445.17
				1079.42	
			797.69		758.50
		581.19		544.64	
	416.76		381.21		342.01
294.03		260.62		220.28	
	174.53		138.32		89.40
		85.23		48.46	
			26.27		0.00
				0.00	
					0.00

First Phase Option Valuation Lattice

			777.69
		562.54	
	399.37		361.21
277.82		241.97	
	157.15		118.32
		66.58	
			6.27

Decision Lattice (Second Phase)

					Execute
				Continue	
			Continue		Execute
		Continue		Continue	
	Continue		Continue		Execute
Continue		Continue		Continue	
	Continue		Continue		Execute
		Continue		Continue	
			Continue		End
				Continue	
					End

Decision Lattice (First Phase)

			Execute
		Continue	
	Continue		Execute
Continue		Continue	
	Continue		Execute
		Continue	
			Execute

Solutions for Changing Costs Option

Creating and Solving a Changing Cost Option

Assumptions	
Asset Value ($)	$400.00
Implementation Cost ($)	$250.00
Maturity (Years)	5.00
Risk-free Rate (%)	8.00%
Dividends (%)	2.00%
Volatility (%)	35.00%
Lattice Steps	5
Cost Growth Rate (%)	10.00%

Intermediate Calculations	
Stepping-Time (dt)	1.0000
Up Step-Size (up)	1.4191
Down Step-Size (down)	0.7047
Risk-neutral Probability (prob)	49.99%

Results	
Lattice Results	$165.36

Underlying Asset Lattice

					2301.84
				1622.08	
			1143.06		1143.06
		805.50		805.50	
	567.63		567.63		567.63
400.00		400.00		400.00	
	281.88		281.88		281.88
		198.63		198.63	
			139.98		139.98
				98.64	
					69.51

Implementation Costs

250.00	275.00	302.50	332.75	366.03	402.63

Option Valuation Lattice

					1899.21
				1256.05	
			810.31		740.43
		503.00		439.48	
	292.63		237.97		165.00
165.36		126.05		76.15	
	65.66		35.14		0.00
		16.22		0.00	
			0.00		0.00
				0.00	
					0.00

Solutions for Changing Volatility Option

Creating and Solving a Changing Volatility Option

Assumptions

Asset Value ($)	$100.00
Implementation Cost ($)	$90.00
Maturity (Years)	5.00
Risk-free Rate (%)	7.00%
Dividends (%)	0.00%
Volatility (%)	30.00%
Lattice Steps	5
New Volatility (%)	45.00%
New Volatility Step	3

Intermediate Calculations

	First Volatility	Second Volatility
Stepping-Time (dt)	1.0000	1.0000
Up Step-Size (up)	1.3499	1.5683
Down Step-Size (down)	0.7408	0.6376
Risk-neutral Probability (prob)	54.46%	46.73%

Results

Lattice Results	$48.40

Underlying Asset Lattice

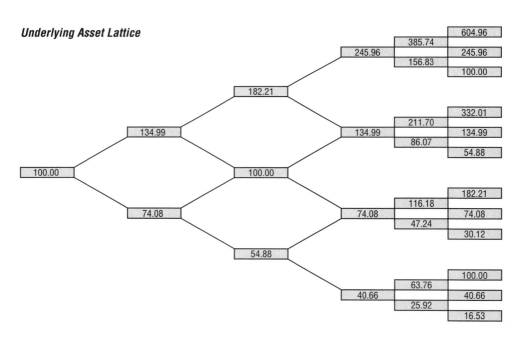

Option Valuation Lattice

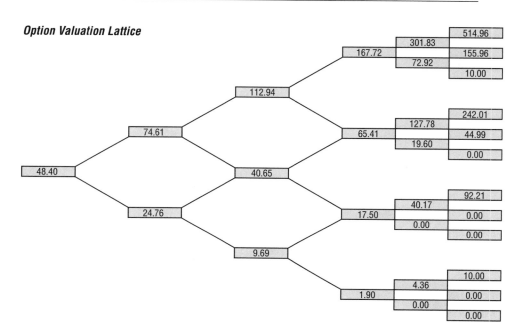

Solutions for Barrier Option

Creating and Solving a Barrier Option (Up and In Call)

Assumptions

Asset Value ($)	$200.00
Implementation Cost ($)	$150.00
Maturity (Years)	5.00
Risk-free Rate (%)	5.00%
Dividends (%)	0.00%
Volatility (%)	30.00%
Lattice Steps	5
Barrier ($)	$220.00

Intermediate Calculations

Stepping-Time (dt)	1.0000
Up Step-Size (up)	1.3499
Down Step-Size (down)	0.7408
Risk-neutral Probability (prob)	50.97%

Results

Lattice Results	$93.82

Underlying Asset Lattice

					896.34
				664.02	
			491.92		491.92
		364.42		364.42	
	269.97		269.97		269.97
200.00		200.00		200.00	
	148.16		148.16		148.16
		109.76		109.76	
			81.31		81.31
				60.24	
					44.63

Option Valuation Lattice

					746.34
				521.34	
			356.20		341.92
		235.50		221.74	
	150.77		134.65		119.97
93.82		78.44		58.17	
	44.41		28.21		0.00
		13.68		0.00	
			0.00		0.00
				0.00	
					0.00

Solutions for Changing Volatility Option (Nonrecombining Lattices)

Creating and Solving a Changing Volatility Option (Nonrecombining)

Assumptions

Asset Value ($)	$100.00
Implementation Cost ($)	$90.00
Maturity (Years)	5.00
Risk-free Rate (%)	7.00%
Dividends (%)	0.00%
Volatility (%)	30.00%
Lattice Steps	5
New Volatility (%)	45.00%
New Volatility Step	3

Intermediate Calculations

	First Volatility	Second Volatility
Stepping-Time (dt)	1.0000	1.0000
Up Step-Size (up)	1.3499	1.5683
Down Step-Size (down)	0.7408	0.6376
Risk-neutral Probability (prob)	54.46%	46.73%

Results

Lattice Results	$48.40

Underlying Asset Lattice

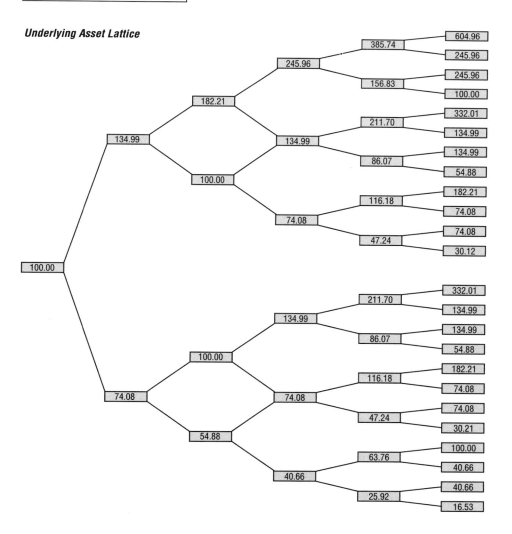

Option Valuation Lattice

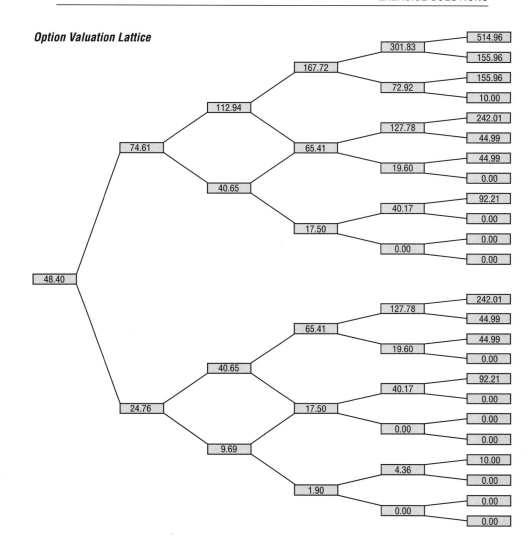

CHAPTER 9

Real Options Analysis Toolkit
Software Function
Description for Excel

These functions are available for use only in the full version of the Real Options Analysis Toolkit software. Once installed, simply click on *Start*, select *Programs* and *Real Options Analysis Toolkit*. Then select *Functions*. The software will be loaded into Excel, and the following models are accessible through Excel by typing them directly in a spreadsheet or by clicking on the Paste Equation Wizard and selecting the Financial/All categories. Scroll down to the RO section for a listing of all the functions.

1. American 3D Binomial Two-Asset Call Option with Dual Strike Prices. This European option is exercisable at termination, where the value of the option depends on two correlated assets with different implementation strike costs, calculated using a combination of multiple binomial lattices.

    Function: RO3DBinomialAmericanCallDualStrike(1st Asset, 2nd Asset, 1st Quantity, 2nd Quantity, 1st Cost, 2nd Cost, Maturity Time, Riskfree, 1st Carrying Cost, 2nd Carrying Cost, 1st Volatility, 2nd Volatility, Correlation, Steps)

2. American 3D Binomial Two-Asset Call Option on the Maximum. This European option is exercisable at termination, where the value of the option depends on the maximum of two correlated underlying assets' values, calculated using a combination of multiple binomial lattices.

    Function: RO3DBinomialAmericanCallMax(1st Asset, 2nd Asset, 1st Quantity, 2nd Quantity, 1st Cost, 2nd Cost, Maturity Time, Riskfree, 1st Carrying Cost, 2nd Carrying Cost, 1st Volatility, 2nd Volatility, Correlation, Steps)

3. American 3D Binomial Two-Asset Call Option on the Minimum. This European option is exercisable at termination, where the value of the option depends on the minimum of two correlated underlying assets' values, calculated using a combination of multiple binomial lattices.

Function: RO3DBinomialAmericanCallMin(1st Asset, 2nd Asset, 1st Quantity, 2nd Quantity, 1st Cost, 2nd Cost, Maturity Time, Riskfree, 1st Carrying Cost, 2nd Carrying Cost, 1st Volatility, 2nd Volatility, Correlation, Steps)

4. American 3D Binomial Two-Asset Portfolio Call Option. This European option is exercisable at termination, where the value of the option depends on the portfolio effect of two correlated underlying assets' values, calculated using a combination of multiple binomial lattices.

Function: RO3DBinomialAmericanCallPortfolio(1st Asset, 2nd Asset, 1st Quantity, 2nd Quantity, 1st Cost, 2nd Cost, Maturity Time, Riskfree, 1st Carrying Cost, 2nd Carrying Cost, 1st Volatility, 2nd Volatility, Correlation, Steps)

5. American Call Option Approximation with a Single Dividend Payment. This American call option is based on a closed-form approximation of a call that can be exercised at any time up to and including its expiration date, and has a single lump-sum dividend payment in the future prior to expiration.

Function: ROAmericanDividendCall(Asset, Cost, Dividend Time, Expiration Time, Riskfree, Volatility, Dividend)

6. American Long-Term Call Option Approximation with a Dividend Stream. This American call option is based on a closed-form approximation of a call, with a constant percent dividend stream and can be exercised at any time up to and including its expiration date.

Function: ROAmericanLongTermCall(Asset, Cost, Time, Riskfree, Carrying Cost, Volatility)

7. American Long-Term Put Option Approximation with a Dividend Stream. This American put option is based on a closed-form approximation of a put, with a constant percent dividend stream and can be exercised at any time up to and including its expiration date.

Function: ROAmericanLongTermPut(Asset, Cost, Time, Riskfree, Carrying Cost, Volatility)

8. Single Barrier Option: Down-and-In Call. This European single lower-barrier call option is exercisable only at expiration. The value of this call option becomes activated only when the asset value breaches a lower barrier.

Function: ROBarrierCallDownIn(Asset, Cost, Barrier, Cash Rebate, Time, Riskfree, Carrying Cost, Volatility)

9. Single Barrier Option: Down-and-Out Call.   This European single lower-barrier call option is exercisable only at expiration. This call option becomes activated only when the asset value does not breach a lower barrier.

Function: ROBarrierCallDownOut(Asset, Cost, Barrier, Cash Rebate, Time, Riskfree, Carrying Cost, Volatility)

10. Single Barrier Option: Up-and-In Call.   This European single upper-barrier call option is exercisable only at expiration. This call option becomes activated only when the asset value breaches an upper barrier.

Function: ROBarrierCallUpIn(Asset, Cost, Barrier, Cash Rebate, Time, Riskfree, Carrying Cost, Volatility)

11. Single Barrier Option: Up-and-Out Call.   This European single upper-barrier call option is exercisable only at expiration. This call option becomes activated only when the asset value does not breach an upper barrier.

Function: ROBarrierCallUpOut(Asset, Cost, Barrier, Cash Rebate, Time, Riskfree, Carrying Cost, Volatility)

12. Single Barrier Option: Down-and-In Put.   This European single lower-barrier put option is exercisable only at expiration. This put option becomes activated only when the asset value breaches a lower barrier.

Function: ROBarrierPutDownIn(Asset, Cost, Barrier, Cash Rebate, Time, Riskfree, Carrying Cost, Volatility)

13. Single Barrier Option: Down-and-Out Put.   This European single lower-barrier put option is exercisable only at expiration. This put option becomes activated only when the asset value does not breach a lower barrier.

Function: ROBarrierPutDownOut(Asset, Cost, Barrier, Cash Rebate, Time, Riskfree, Carrying Cost, Volatility)

14. Single Barrier Option: Up-and-In Put.   This European single upper-barrier put option is exercisable only at expiration. The value of this put option becomes in-the-money only when the asset value breaches an upper barrier.

Function: ROBarrierPutUpIn(Asset, Cost, Barrier, Cash Rebate, Time, Riskfree, Carrying Cost, Volatility)

15. Single Barrier Option: Up-and-Out Put.   This European single upper-barrier put option is exercisable only at expiration. This put option becomes activated only when the asset value does not breach an upper barrier.

Function: ROBarrierPutUpOut(Asset, Cost, Barrier, Cash Rebate, Time, Riskfree, Carrying Cost, Volatility)

16. Basic Chooser Option.   This option gives the holder the right to choose between a call or put. Both calls and puts are constrained by the same expiration date and strike price. Either option may be exercised prior to the expiration date.

Function: ROBasicChooser(Asset, Cost, Chooser Time 1, Maturity Time 2, Riskfree, Carrying Cost, Volatility)

17. American Call Option Using the Binomial (Super Lattice) Approach. This American option gives the holder the right to execute its existing operations at any time within a particular period.

Function: ROBinomialAmerican(Asset, Cost, Time, Riskfree, Volatility, Dividend, Steps)

18. American Abandonment Option Using the Binomial (Super Lattice) Approach. This American option gives the holder the right to abandon existing operations at any time within a particular period and receive the salvage value.

Function: ROBinomialAmericanAbandon(Salvage, Asset, Time, Riskfree, Volatility, Dividend, Steps)

19. American Call Option Using the Binomial (Super Lattice) Approach. This American call option gives the holder the right to execute a project at any time within a particular period at a set implementation cost, calculated using the binomial approach with consideration for dividend payments.

Function: ROBinomialAmericanCall(Asset, Cost, Time, Riskfree, Volatility, Dividend, Steps)

20. American Contraction and Abandonment Option Using the Binomial Approach. This American option gives the holder the right to either contract its existing operations by a contraction factor in order to create some savings, or to abandon entirely its existing operations at any time within a particular period and receive the salvage value.

Function: ROBinomialAmericanConAban(Salvage, Contraction, Savings, Asset, Time, Riskfree, Volatility, Dividend, Steps)

21. American Contraction and Expansion Option Using the Binomial (Super Lattice) Approach. This American option gives the holder the right to either contract its existing operations by a contraction factor in order to create some savings in a market downturn, or to expand its existing operations at an expansion factor at any time within a particular period by spending an appropriate implementation cost in a market upturn.

Function: ROBinomialAmericanConExp(Contraction, Savings, Expansion, Asset, Cost, Time, Riskfree, Volatility, Dividend, Steps)

22. American Contraction, Expansion, and Abandonment Option Using the Binomial (Super Lattice) Approach. This American option gives the holder the right to choose among contracting its existing operations by a contraction factor in order to create some savings, or to expand its existing operations at an expansion factor by spending an appropriate implementation cost, or to abandon its operations entirely and receive a salvage value at any time within a particular period.

Function: ROBinomialAmericanConExpAban(Salvage, Contraction, Savings, Expansion, Asset, Cost, Time, Riskfree, Volatility, Dividend, Steps)

23. American Contraction Option Using the Binomial (Super Lattice) Approach.   This American option gives the holder the right to contract its existing operations by a contraction factor in order to create some savings at any time within a particular period.

Function: ROBinomialAmericanContract(Contraction, Asset, Savings, Time, Riskfree, Volatility, Dividend, Steps)

24. American Expansion and Abandonment Option Using the Binomial (Super Lattice) Approach.   This American option gives the holder the right to choose between expanding its existing operations at an expansion factor by spending an appropriate implementation cost, or to abandon its operations entirely and receive a salvage value at any time within a particular period.

Function: ROBinomialAmericanExpAban(Salvage, Expansion, Asset, Cost, Time, Riskfree, Volatility, Dividend, Steps)

25. American Expansion Option Using the Binomial (Super Lattice) Approach.   This American option gives the holder the right to expand its existing operations at an expansion factor by spending an appropriate implementation cost at any time within a particular period.

Function: ROBinomialAmericanExpansion(Expansion, Asset, Cost, Time, Riskfree, Volatility, Dividend, Steps)

26. American Put Option Using the Binomial (Super Lattice) Approach.   This American put option approximation with dividends is exercisable at any time within a particular period, calculated using the binomial approach, with consideration for dividend payments.

Function: ROBinomialAmericanPut(Asset, Cost, Time, Riskfree, Volatility, Dividend, Steps)

27. American Sequential Compound Option Using the Binomial (Super Lattice) Approach.   This American option is the value of two option phases occurring in sequence, and is exercisable at any time within a particular period, where the execution of the second option depends on the successful implementation of the first option.

Function: ROBinomialAmericanSeqCompound(Asset, Underlying 1st Cost, Option 2nd Cost, Underlying 1st Time, Option 2nd Time, Riskfree, Volatility, Dividend, Steps)

28. American Simultaneous Compound Option Using the Binomial (Super Lattice) Approach. This American option is the value of two option phases occurring simultaneously, and is exercisable at any time within a particular period, where the execution of the second option depends on the successful implementation of the first option.

Function: ROBinomialAmericanSimCompound(Asset, Underlying Cost1, Option Cost2, Maturity Time, Riskfree, Volatility, Dividend, Steps)

29. Changing Cost Option Using the Binomial (Super Lattice) Approach. This is the value of an American option with different implementation costs at different times, where the option is executable at any time up to maturity.

Function: ROBinomialCost(Asset, Cost 1, Cost 2, Cost 3, Cost 4, Cost 5, Time 1, Time 2, Time 3, Time 4, Time 5, Volatility, Riskfree, Dividend, Steps)

30. Binomial Lattice Down Jump Step-Size. This calculation is used in obtaining the down jump step-size on a binomial lattice.

Function: ROBinomialDown(Volatility, Time, Steps)

31. European Call Option Using the Binomial (Super Lattice) Approach. This European call calculation is performed using a binomial approach and is exercisable only at termination.

Function: ROBinomialEuropeanCall(Asset, Cost, Time, Riskfree, Volatility, Dividend, Steps)

32. European Put Option Using the Binomial (Super Lattice) Approach. This European put calculation is performed using a binomial approach and is exercisable only at termination.

Function: ROBinomialEuropeanPut(Asset, Cost, Time, Riskfree, Volatility, Dividend, Steps)

33. Binomial Lattice Risk-Neutral Probability. This calculation is used in obtaining the risk-neutral probability on a binomial lattice.

Function: ROBinomialProb(Volatility, Time, Steps, Riskfree, Dividend)

34. Binomial Lattice Up Jump Step-Size. This calculation is used in obtaining the up jump step-size on a binomial lattice.

Function: ROBinomialUp(Volatility, Time, Steps)

35. Black-Scholes Call Option with No Dividends. This European call is calculated using the Black-Scholes model, with no dividend payments, and exercisable only at expiration.

Function: ROBlackScholesCall(Asset, Cost, Time, Riskfree, Volatility)

36. Black-Scholes Call Option with a Carrying Cost. This European call is calculated using the Generalized Black-Scholes model, with a carrying cost adjustment, and exercisable only at expiration. The carrying cost adjustment is simply the difference between the risk-free rate and the dividend payments, both in percent.

Function: ROBlackScholesCarryingCall(Asset, Cost, Time, Riskfree, Volatility, Carrying Cost)

37. Black-Scholes Put Option with a Carrying Cost. This European put is calculated using the Generalized Black-Scholes model, with a carrying cost adjustment, and exercisable only at expiration. The carrying cost adjustment is simply the difference between the risk-free rate and the dividend payments, both in percent.

Function: ROBlackScholesCarryingPut(Asset, Cost, Time, Riskfree, Volatility, Carrying Cost)

38. Black-Scholes Call Option with Dividends. This European call is calculated using the Generalized Black-Scholes model, with a dividend stream in percent and exercisable only at expiration.

Function: ROBlackScholesDividendCall(Asset, Cost, Time, Riskfree, Volatility, Dividend)

39. Black-Scholes Put Option with Dividends. This European put is calculated using the Generalized Black-Scholes model, with a dividend stream in percent, and exercisable only at expiration.

Function: ROBlackScholesDividendPut(Asset, Cost, Time, Riskfree, Volatility, Dividend)

40. Black-Scholes Put Option with No Dividends. This European put is calculated using the Black-Scholes model, with no dividend payments, and exercisable only at expiration.

Function: ROBlackScholesPut(Asset, Cost, Time, Riskfree, Volatility)

41. Complex Chooser Option. This European complex chooser option is exercisable only at expiration. This option gives the option holder the right to choose between a call or put at different times with different strike prices. The same expiration date applies to both puts and calls.

Function: ROComplexChooser(Asset, Call Cost, Put Cost, Chooser Time, Call End Time, Put End Time, Riskfree, Carrying Cost, Volatility)

42. Compound Call-on-Call Option. This European Compound option is exercisable only at expiration, where the value of the option depends on another underlying option. This is the continuous counterpart of the Binomial Sequential Compound Option.

Function: ROCompoundCallonCall(Asset, Underlying Cost 1, Option Cost 2, Option Time 1 , Underlying Time 2, Riskfree, Carrying Cost, Volatility)

43. Compound Put-on-Call Option.   This European Compound option is exercisable only at expiration, where the value of the option depends on another underlying option. This option is the continuous counterpart of the Binomial Sequential Compound Option.

Function: ROCompoundPutonCall(Asset, Underlying Cost 1, Option Cost 2, Option Time 1, Underlying Time 2, Riskfree, Carrying Cost, Volatility)

44. Simple Sequential Compound Option Using the Binomial (Super Lattice) Approach.   This American Compound option is exercisable at any time up to expiration, where the value of the option depends on a series of up to 10 other options, occurring in sequence. Each option phase has its own implementation cost occurring at different times.

Function: ROCorrSeqCompound(Asset, Cost 1...Cost 11, Time 1... Time 11, Riskfree, Volatility, Dividends, Steps)

45. Customized Complex Sequential Compound Option Using the Binomial (Super Lattice) Approach.   This Customized American sequential phased compound option is exercisable at any time up to expiration, where the value of the option depends on a series of up to four other phases, occurring in sequence. Each option phase has its own asset value, volatility, implementation cost, and different implementation times. In addition, at any phase, there is an option to execute the expanded phase, abandon, or contract. Please note that this function is not available in the Equation Wizard due to limitations in Excel, but is available by directly entering the function and its associated values in Excel.

Function: ROCustomLattice(Asset, Cost 1...Cost 4, Time 1...Time 4, Riskfree, Volatility, Dividends, Steps, Expansion Phase 1, Expansion Phase 2, Expansion Phase 3, Expansion Phase 4, Abandon Value Phase 1, Abandon Value Phase 2, Abandon Value Phase 3, Abandon Value Phase 4, Contraction Phase 1, Contraction Phase 2, Contraction Phase 3, Contraction Phase 4, Savings Phase 1, Savings Phase 2, Savings Phase 3, Savings Phase 4)

46. Double Barrier Option: Up-and-In, Down-and-In Call Option. This European double-barrier call option becomes activated and in-the-money when the asset value crosses above the upper barrier or below the lower barrier and is exercisable only at expiration.

Function: RODoubleBarrierUIDICall(Asset, Cost, Lower Barrier, Upper Barrier, Time, Riskfree, Carrying Cost, Volatility)

47. Double Barrier Option: Up-and-In, Down-and-In Put Option. This European double-barrier put option becomes activated and in-the-money when the asset value crosses above the upper barrier or below the lower barrier and is exercisable only at expiration.

Function: RODoubleBarrierUIDIPut(Asset, Cost, Lower Barrier, Upper Barrier, Time, Riskfree, Carrying Cost, Volatility)

48. Double Barrier Option: Up-and-Out, Down-and-Out Call Option. This European double-barrier call option becomes in-the-money and activated when the asset value does not breach the upper barrier or below the lower barrier and is exercisable only at expiration.

Function: RODoubleBarrierUODOCall(Asset, Cost, Lower Barrier, Upper Barrier, Time, Riskfree, Carrying Cost, Volatility)

49. Double Barrier Option: Up-and-Out, Down-and-Out Put Option. This European double-barrier put option becomes in-the-money and activated when the asset value does not breach the upper barrier or below the lower barrier and is exercisable only at expiration.

Function: RODoubleBarrierUODOPut(Asset, Cost, Lower Barrier, Upper Barrier, Time, Riskfree, Carrying Cost, Volatility)

50. Forward Start Call Option. This European call option starts only sometime in the future and is exercisable only at expiration.

Function: ROForwardStartCall(Asset, Alpha, Forward Time, Time to Maturity, Riskfree, Carrying Cost, Volatility)

51. Forward Start Put Option. This European put option starts only sometime in the future and is exercisable only at expiration.

Function: ROForwardStartPut(Asset, Alpha, Forward Time, Time to Maturity, Riskfree, Carrying Cost, Volatility)

52. Futures Call Option. This European call option depends on an underlying asset that resembles a futures contract and is exercisable only at expiration.

Function: ROFuturesCall(Futures, Cost, Time, Riskfree, Volatility)

53. Futures Put Option. This European put option depends on an underlying asset that resembles a futures contract and is exercisable only at expiration.

Function: ROFuturesPut(Futures, Cost, Time, Riskfree, Volatility)

54. Standard-Normal Cumulative Distribution. This is the standard-normal cumulative distribution of a Z-value, based on a normal distribution with a mean of zero and variance of one.

Function: RONormDist(Z) or ROPhiDist(Z)

55. Multiple Volatility Option Analysis. This American option applies different volatilities at different times.

Function: ROMultiVolatility(Asset, Cost, Time, Riskfree, Volatility, Dividend, Steps, Volatility 2, TimeStep 2, Volatility 3, TimeStep 3, Volatility 4, TimeStep 4, Volatility 5, TimeStep 5)

56. Standard Bivariate-Normal Cumulative Distribution. This is the standard Bivariate-Normal cumulative distribution of two correlated variables.

Function: ROOmegaDist(Variable 1, Variable 2, Correlation)

57. Stochastic Option Flexibility Parameter. This is the Flexibility Parameter calculated using stochastic methodologies, where the optimal exercise price is obtained by multiplying this parameter with the option's implementation cost.

Function: ROStochasticFlexibility(Interest Rate, Opportunity Cost, Volatility)

58. Stochastic Option Value. This is the stochastic valuation of an option based on its asset value, implementation cost, volatility, interest rate, and opportunity cost.

Function: ROStochasticOptionValue (Interest Rate, Opportunity Cost, Volatility, Implementation Cost, Asset Value)

59. Switching Option. This European switching option values two exchangeable assets, each with its own risk structure or volatility, but at the same time may be correlated to each other. There is a cost associated with switching, which is the cost multipler multipled by the value of the first asset.

Function: ROSwitching(Asset 1, Asset 2, Volatility 1, Volatility 2, Correlation, Cost Multiplier, Time, Riskfree)

60. Stochastic Timing Option—Option Value. This is the value of the timing option assuming the execution of the option falls exactly on the optimal time to execute.

Function: ROTimingOption(Revenue, Operating Expenses, Implementation Cost, Time, Growth Rate, Discount Rate)

61. Stochastic Timing Option—Optimal Timing. This model provides the optimal time to execute an option given a growth rate in the asset value and a discount rate.

Function: ROTimingTime(Revenue, Operating Expenses, Implementation Cost, Growth Rate, Discount Rate)

62. Stochastic Timing Option—Trigger Value. This is the optimal trigger value on a timing option, where if the net value of the asset exceeds this trigger, it is optimal to exercise the option immediately.

Function: ROTimingTrigger(Implementation Cost, Growth Rate, Discount Rate)

63. Two-Asset Correlation Call Option. This European call option is exercisable only at expiration, where the value of the option depends on two correlated underlying assets.

Function: ROTwoAssetCorrelationCall(Asset 1, Asset 2, Cost 1, Cost 2, Time, Dividend 1, Dividend 2, Riskfree, Volatility 1, Volatility 2, Correlation)

64. Two-Asset Correlation Put Option. This European put option is exercisable only at expiration, where the value of the option depends on two correlated underlying assets.

Function: ROTwoAssetCorrelationPut(Asset 1, Asset 2, Cost 1, Cost 2, Time, Dividend 1, Dividend 2, Riskfree, Volatility 1, Volatility 2, Correlation)

65. Call Sensitivity on Asset. This is the instantaneous sensitivity on asset value, that is, the change in option value given a unit change in asset value.

Function: ROSensitivityAsset(Asset, Cost, Time, Riskfree, Dividend, Volatility)

66. Call Sensitivity on Cost. This is the instantaneous sensitivity on cost, that is, the change in option value given a unit change in cost.

Function: ROSensitivityCost(Asset, Cost, Time, Riskfree, Dividend, Volatility)

67. Call Sensitivity on Risk-Free. This is the instantaneous sensitivity on risk-free rate, that is, the change in option value given a unit change in risk-free rate.

Function: ROSensitivityRiskfree(Asset, Cost, Time, Riskfree, Dividend, Volatility)

68. Call Sensitivity on Time. This is the instantaneous sensitivity on time, that is, the change in option value given a unit change in time.

Function: ROSensitivityTime(Asset, Cost, Time, Riskfree, Dividend, Volatility)

69. Call Sensitivity on Volatility. This is the instantaneous sensitivity on volatility, that is, the change in option value given a unit change in volatility.

Function: ROSensitivityVolatility(Asset, Cost, Time, Riskfree, Dividend, Volatility)

CHAPTER 10

Real Options Tables

REAL OPTIONS VALUE TABLES

Tables 10.1 through 10.7 provide the real options value of both American and European options as a percentage of asset value. The columns list the profitability ratio percentage, and the rows list the volatility of the underlying asset. The tables assume a constant 5 percent risk-free rate and no dividend outflows. In addition, tables for 1-, 3-, 5-, 7-, 10-, 15-, and 30-year maturation periods are available. These tables are useful as a first pass at certain projects to benchmark if a detailed real options analysis is warranted, providing the analyst a first look at what the strategic option value may be. Notice that as the profitability ratio or volatility increases, the value of the option increases.

Example

Suppose a real option exists that has a $110 million present value of free cash flows (S), $100 million in implementation costs (X), 33 percent volatility, 5 percent risk-free rate, and a 1-year maturity. Estimate the real options value of this simple option.

The calculated profitability ratio is $110/$100 = 1.1 or 10 percent in-the-money. Using the 1-year table, the options value as a percent of asset is 20.13 percent, for a 10 percent profitability ratio and 33 percent volatility, which means that for the $110 asset value, the option value is 20.13 percent of $110 or $22.15 million. In addition, if the asset value were $330 million, then the option value is 20.13 percent of $330 million or $66.44 million as long as the 10 percent profitability ratio remains the same (the implementation cost now becomes $300 million). The options value as a percentage of asset value does not change as long as the maturity, profitability ratio, and volatility remain constant for these tables.

TABLE 10.1 Real Options Value—1-Year Maturity

Maturity	1	Year(s)	Risk-Free Rate 5%							
Profitability Ratio (% in-the-money)										
Volatility	−99%	−90.00%	−80.00%	−70.00%	−60.00%	−50.00%	−40.00%	−30.00%	−20.00%	−10.00%	0.00%
1.00%	0.00%	0.00%	0.00%	0.00%	0.00%	0.00%	0.00%	0.00%	0.00%	0.00%	4.88%
3.00%	0.00%	0.00%	0.00%	0.00%	0.00%	0.00%	0.00%	0.00%	0.00%	0.04%	4.94%
5.00%	0.00%	0.00%	0.00%	0.00%	0.00%	0.00%	0.00%	0.00%	0.00%	0.35%	5.28%
7.00%	0.00%	0.00%	0.00%	0.00%	0.00%	0.00%	0.00%	0.00%	0.02%	0.88%	5.83%
9.00%	0.00%	0.00%	0.00%	0.00%	0.00%	0.00%	0.00%	0.00%	0.10%	1.52%	6.47%
11.00%	0.00%	0.00%	0.00%	0.00%	0.00%	0.00%	0.00%	0.01%	0.30%	2.22%	7.15%
13.00%	0.00%	0.00%	0.00%	0.00%	0.00%	0.00%	0.00%	0.05%	0.60%	2.96%	7.86%
15.00%	0.00%	0.00%	0.00%	0.00%	0.00%	0.00%	0.01%	0.13%	1.01%	3.72%	8.59%
17.00%	0.00%	0.00%	0.00%	0.00%	0.00%	0.00%	0.02%	0.28%	1.49%	4.49%	9.33%
19.00%	0.00%	0.00%	0.00%	0.00%	0.00%	0.00%	0.06%	0.50%	2.03%	5.26%	10.08%
21.00%	0.00%	0.00%	0.00%	0.00%	0.00%	0.01%	0.13%	0.78%	2.63%	6.05%	10.83%
23.00%	0.00%	0.00%	0.00%	0.00%	0.00%	0.02%	0.24%	1.13%	3.26%	6.84%	11.58%
25.00%	0.00%	0.00%	0.00%	0.00%	0.00%	0.05%	0.40%	1.54%	3.93%	7.63%	12.34%
27.00%	0.00%	0.00%	0.00%	0.00%	0.01%	0.11%	0.61%	2.00%	4.62%	8.43%	13.09%
29.00%	0.00%	0.00%	0.00%	0.00%	0.02%	0.18%	0.86%	2.50%	5.33%	9.22%	13.85%
31.00%	0.00%	0.00%	0.00%	0.00%	0.04%	0.29%	1.17%	3.05%	6.06%	10.02%	14.61%
33.00%	0.00%	0.00%	0.00%	0.00%	0.07%	0.44%	1.52%	3.63%	6.80%	10.82%	15.37%
35.00%	0.00%	0.00%	0.00%	0.01%	0.12%	0.62%	1.92%	4.24%	7.55%	11.62%	16.13%
37.00%	0.00%	0.00%	0.00%	0.02%	0.18%	0.84%	2.35%	4.88%	8.32%	12.42%	16.89%
39.00%	0.00%	0.00%	0.00%	0.03%	0.27%	1.10%	2.82%	5.54%	9.09%	13.21%	17.64%
41.00%	0.00%	0.00%	0.00%	0.05%	0.39%	1.39%	3.33%	6.22%	9.86%	14.01%	18.40%
43.00%	0.00%	0.00%	0.00%	0.08%	0.53%	1.73%	3.87%	6.91%	10.64%	14.80%	19.16%
45.00%	0.00%	0.00%	0.01%	0.13%	0.70%	2.10%	4.44%	7.62%	11.43%	15.60%	19.91%
47.00%	0.00%	0.00%	0.01%	0.19%	0.91%	2.50%	5.03%	8.35%	12.22%	16.39%	20.67%
49.00%	0.00%	0.00%	0.02%	0.26%	1.14%	2.93%	5.64%	9.09%	13.01%	17.18%	21.42%
51.00%	0.00%	0.00%	0.03%	0.36%	1.41%	3.40%	6.28%	9.83%	13.80%	17.97%	22.17%
53.00%	0.00%	0.00%	0.05%	0.48%	1.71%	3.90%	6.94%	10.59%	14.60%	18.76%	22.92%
55.00%	0.00%	0.00%	0.08%	0.62%	2.03%	4.42%	7.61%	11.35%	15.40%	19.55%	23.66%
57.00%	0.00%	0.00%	0.11%	0.78%	2.39%	4.96%	8.30%	12.12%	16.20%	20.33%	24.41%
59.00%	0.00%	0.00%	0.16%	0.97%	2.78%	5.54%	9.00%	12.90%	16.99%	21.12%	25.15%
61.00%	0.00%	0.00%	0.21%	1.18%	3.19%	6.13%	9.72%	13.68%	17.79%	21.90%	25.89%
63.00%	0.00%	0.01%	0.29%	1.42%	3.63%	6.74%	10.44%	14.46%	18.59%	22.68%	26.63%
65.00%	0.00%	0.01%	0.37%	1.69%	4.10%	7.37%	11.18%	15.25%	19.39%	23.45%	27.37%
67.00%	0.00%	0.02%	0.47%	1.98%	4.59%	8.02%	11.92%	16.04%	20.18%	24.23%	28.10%
69.00%	0.00%	0.03%	0.59%	2.30%	5.11%	8.68%	12.68%	16.83%	20.98%	25.00%	28.84%
71.00%	0.00%	0.04%	0.73%	2.64%	5.65%	9.36%	13.44%	17.63%	21.77%	25.77%	29.57%
73.00%	0.00%	0.06%	0.88%	3.01%	6.21%	10.05%	14.21%	18.42%	22.56%	26.53%	30.29%
75.00%	0.00%	0.08%	1.06%	3.40%	6.79%	10.76%	14.98%	19.22%	23.35%	27.30%	31.02%
77.00%	0.00%	0.11%	1.26%	3.82%	7.38%	11.47%	15.76%	20.02%	24.14%	28.06%	31.74%
79.00%	0.00%	0.15%	1.48%	4.26%	8.00%	12.20%	16.54%	20.82%	24.93%	28.82%	32.46%
81.00%	0.00%	0.19%	1.72%	4.72%	8.63%	12.94%	17.32%	21.61%	25.71%	29.57%	33.18%
83.00%	0.00%	0.24%	1.98%	5.21%	9.28%	13.68%	18.11%	22.41%	26.49%	30.33%	33.89%
85.00%	0.00%	0.30%	2.26%	5.72%	9.94%	14.43%	18.90%	23.21%	27.27%	31.07%	34.60%
87.00%	0.00%	0.38%	2.57%	6.24%	10.62%	15.19%	19.70%	24.00%	28.05%	31.82%	35.31%
89.00%	0.00%	0.46%	2.90%	6.79%	11.30%	15.95%	20.49%	24.80%	28.83%	32.56%	36.02%
91.00%	0.00%	0.56%	3.25%	7.35%	12.00%	16.72%	21.29%	25.59%	29.60%	33.30%	36.72%
93.00%	0.00%	0.67%	3.62%	7.93%	12.71%	17.50%	22.09%	26.38%	30.37%	34.04%	37.42%
95.00%	0.00%	0.79%	4.01%	8.53%	13.43%	18.28%	22.88%	27.17%	31.13%	34.77%	38.11%
97.00%	0.00%	0.93%	4.43%	9.15%	14.16%	19.06%	23.68%	27.96%	31.90%	35.50%	38.81%
99.00%	0.00%	1.09%	4.86%	9.78%	14.90%	19.85%	24.48%	28.75%	32.66%	36.23%	39.50%
101.00%	0.00%	1.26%	5.32%	10.42%	15.65%	20.64%	25.28%	29.53%	33.41%	36.95%	40.18%

Note: Risk-free rate is 5 percent.

TABLE 10.1 Continued

Volatility	10.00%	20.00%	30.00%	40.00%	50.00%	60.00%	70.00%	80.00%	90.00%	100.00%
1.00%	13.52%	20.73%	26.83%	32.06%	36.58%	40.55%	44.05%	47.15%	49.94%	52.44%
3.00%	13.52%	20.73%	26.83%	32.06%	36.58%	40.55%	44.05%	47.15%	49.94%	52.44%
5.00%	13.53%	20.73%	26.83%	32.06%	36.58%	40.55%	44.05%	47.15%	49.94%	52.44%
7.00%	13.57%	20.73%	26.83%	32.06%	36.58%	40.55%	44.05%	47.15%	49.94%	52.44%
9.00%	13.71%	20.74%	26.83%	32.06%	36.58%	40.55%	44.05%	47.15%	49.94%	52.44%
11.00%	13.97%	20.79%	26.83%	32.06%	36.58%	40.55%	44.05%	47.15%	49.94%	52.44%
13.00%	14.32%	20.90%	26.86%	32.06%	36.59%	40.55%	44.05%	47.15%	49.94%	52.44%
15.00%	14.76%	21.08%	26.92%	32.07%	36.59%	40.55%	44.05%	47.15%	49.94%	52.44%
17.00%	15.24%	21.33%	27.02%	32.11%	36.60%	40.55%	44.05%	47.15%	49.94%	52.44%
19.00%	15.78%	21.63%	27.17%	32.18%	36.63%	40.56%	44.05%	47.16%	49.94%	52.44%
21.00%	16.34%	21.99%	27.37%	32.28%	36.67%	40.58%	44.06%	47.16%	49.94%	52.44%
23.00%	16.94%	22.40%	27.62%	32.42%	36.75%	40.62%	44.08%	47.17%	49.94%	52.44%
25.00%	17.55%	22.84%	27.91%	32.60%	36.85%	40.68%	44.11%	47.18%	49.95%	52.45%
27.00%	18.18%	23.31%	28.23%	32.81%	36.99%	40.76%	44.16%	47.21%	49.97%	52.46%
29.00%	18.82%	23.81%	28.60%	33.06%	37.16%	40.87%	44.23%	47.26%	49.99%	52.47%
31.00%	19.47%	24.33%	28.99%	33.35%	37.35%	41.01%	44.32%	47.32%	50.03%	52.50%
33.00%	20.13%	24.87%	29.41%	33.66%	37.58%	41.17%	44.43%	47.39%	50.09%	52.53%
35.00%	20.80%	25.42%	29.85%	34.00%	37.84%	41.36%	44.57%	47.49%	50.16%	52.58%
37.00%	21.47%	25.99%	30.31%	34.36%	38.12%	41.57%	44.73%	47.61%	50.24%	52.65%
39.00%	22.15%	26.57%	30.79%	34.75%	38.42%	41.81%	44.91%	47.75%	50.35%	52.73%
41.00%	22.83%	27.16%	31.28%	35.15%	38.75%	42.07%	45.11%	47.91%	50.47%	52.82%
43.00%	23.52%	27.75%	31.79%	35.57%	39.09%	42.34%	45.34%	48.09%	50.62%	52.94%
45.00%	24.20%	28.36%	32.30%	36.01%	39.46%	42.64%	45.58%	48.29%	50.78%	53.06%
47.00%	24.89%	28.97%	32.83%	36.46%	39.83%	42.96%	45.84%	48.50%	50.95%	53.21%
49.00%	25.58%	29.58%	33.37%	36.92%	40.23%	43.29%	46.12%	48.74%	51.15%	53.37%
51.00%	26.27%	30.20%	33.91%	37.39%	40.63%	43.64%	46.42%	48.99%	51.36%	53.55%
53.00%	26.96%	30.82%	34.46%	37.88%	41.05%	44.00%	46.73%	49.25%	51.58%	53.74%
55.00%	27.65%	31.44%	35.02%	38.37%	41.48%	44.37%	47.05%	49.53%	51.82%	53.95%
57.00%	28.34%	32.07%	35.58%	38.87%	41.92%	44.76%	47.39%	49.82%	52.08%	54.16%
59.00%	29.03%	32.70%	36.15%	39.37%	42.37%	45.15%	47.73%	50.12%	52.34%	54.40%
61.00%	29.72%	33.33%	36.72%	39.88%	42.82%	45.56%	48.09%	50.44%	52.62%	54.64%
63.00%	30.40%	33.96%	37.29%	40.40%	43.29%	45.97%	48.46%	50.76%	52.91%	54.90%
65.00%	31.09%	34.59%	37.87%	40.92%	43.75%	46.39%	48.83%	51.10%	53.21%	55.16%
67.00%	31.78%	35.22%	38.44%	41.44%	44.23%	46.82%	49.22%	51.44%	53.51%	55.44%
69.00%	32.46%	35.86%	39.02%	41.97%	44.71%	47.25%	49.61%	51.80%	53.83%	55.73%
71.00%	33.14%	36.49%	39.61%	42.50%	45.19%	47.69%	50.01%	52.16%	54.16%	56.02%
73.00%	33.83%	37.12%	40.19%	43.04%	45.68%	48.13%	50.41%	52.52%	54.49%	56.32%
75.00%	34.50%	37.75%	40.77%	43.57%	46.17%	48.58%	50.82%	52.90%	54.83%	56.63%
77.00%	35.18%	38.38%	41.35%	44.11%	46.66%	49.03%	51.23%	53.28%	55.18%	56.95%
79.00%	35.86%	39.01%	41.94%	44.65%	47.16%	49.49%	51.65%	53.66%	55.53%	57.27%
81.00%	36.53%	39.64%	42.52%	45.19%	47.66%	49.95%	52.08%	54.05%	55.89%	57.60%
83.00%	37.20%	40.27%	43.11%	45.73%	48.16%	50.41%	52.50%	54.45%	56.25%	57.94%
85.00%	37.87%	40.89%	43.69%	46.27%	48.66%	50.88%	52.93%	54.84%	56.62%	58.28%
87.00%	38.54%	41.52%	44.27%	46.81%	49.17%	51.34%	53.37%	55.25%	56.99%	58.63%
89.00%	39.20%	42.14%	44.85%	47.36%	49.67%	51.81%	53.80%	55.65%	57.37%	58.98%
91.00%	39.87%	42.76%	45.43%	47.90%	50.18%	52.28%	54.24%	56.06%	57.75%	59.33%
93.00%	40.53%	43.38%	46.01%	48.44%	50.68%	52.76%	54.68%	56.47%	58.13%	59.69%
95.00%	41.18%	44.00%	46.59%	48.98%	51.19%	53.23%	55.12%	56.88%	58.52%	60.05%
97.00%	41.84%	44.61%	47.17%	49.52%	51.69%	53.70%	55.57%	57.30%	58.91%	60.41%
99.00%	42.49%	45.23%	47.74%	50.06%	52.20%	54.18%	56.01%	57.71%	59.30%	60.78%
101.00%	43.13%	45.84%	48.32%	50.60%	52.70%	54.65%	56.45%	58.13%	59.69%	61.14%

TABLE 10.2 Real Options Value—3-Year Maturity

Maturity	3	Year(s)	Risk-Free Rate	5%						
Profitability Ratio (% in-the-money)										
Volatility	−99%	−90.00%	−80.00%	−70.00%	−60.00%	−50.00%	−40.00%	−30.00%	−20.00%	−10.00%	0.00%
1.00%	0.00%	0.00%	0.00%	0.00%	0.00%	0.00%	0.00%	0.00%	0.00%	4.37%	13.93%
3.00%	0.00%	0.00%	0.00%	0.00%	0.00%	0.00%	0.00%	0.00%	0.19%	4.92%	13.93%
5.00%	0.00%	0.00%	0.00%	0.00%	0.00%	0.00%	0.00%	0.03%	1.00%	6.00%	14.06%
7.00%	0.00%	0.00%	0.00%	0.00%	0.00%	0.00%	0.01%	0.24%	2.11%	7.23%	14.51%
9.00%	0.00%	0.00%	0.00%	0.00%	0.00%	0.00%	0.07%	0.74%	3.35%	8.51%	15.22%
11.00%	0.00%	0.00%	0.00%	0.00%	0.00%	0.02%	0.26%	1.49%	4.65%	9.81%	16.10%
13.00%	0.00%	0.00%	0.00%	0.00%	0.00%	0.08%	0.62%	2.42%	5.99%	11.12%	17.08%
15.00%	0.00%	0.00%	0.00%	0.00%	0.02%	0.22%	1.16%	3.47%	7.35%	12.44%	18.13%
17.00%	0.00%	0.00%	0.00%	0.00%	0.06%	0.49%	1.86%	4.62%	8.72%	13.76%	19.22%
19.00%	0.00%	0.00%	0.00%	0.01%	0.16%	0.88%	2.70%	5.84%	10.10%	15.08%	20.35%
21.00%	0.00%	0.00%	0.00%	0.03%	0.33%	1.40%	3.65%	7.10%	11.48%	16.40%	21.50%
23.00%	0.00%	0.00%	0.00%	0.08%	0.60%	2.05%	4.68%	8.40%	12.86%	17.72%	22.67%
25.00%	0.00%	0.00%	0.01%	0.18%	0.96%	2.80%	5.80%	9.72%	14.25%	19.04%	23.84%
27.00%	0.00%	0.00%	0.02%	0.32%	1.43%	3.66%	6.97%	11.07%	15.63%	20.35%	25.02%
29.00%	0.00%	0.00%	0.05%	0.54%	1.99%	4.60%	8.18%	12.43%	17.00%	21.65%	26.21%
31.00%	0.00%	0.00%	0.11%	0.83%	2.65%	5.61%	9.44%	13.79%	18.37%	22.96%	27.40%
33.00%	0.00%	0.00%	0.19%	1.20%	3.40%	6.69%	10.73%	15.17%	19.74%	24.25%	28.59%
35.00%	0.00%	0.01%	0.32%	1.65%	4.23%	7.82%	12.04%	16.55%	21.10%	25.54%	29.78%
37.00%	0.00%	0.02%	0.50%	2.18%	5.14%	9.01%	13.38%	17.93%	22.46%	26.83%	30.96%
39.00%	0.00%	0.04%	0.73%	2.80%	6.11%	10.23%	14.73%	19.31%	23.81%	28.10%	32.15%
41.00%	0.00%	0.07%	1.03%	3.49%	7.15%	11.48%	16.09%	20.69%	25.15%	29.37%	33.33%
43.00%	0.00%	0.12%	1.38%	4.26%	8.24%	12.77%	17.46%	22.07%	26.49%	30.64%	34.50%
45.00%	0.00%	0.19%	1.81%	5.10%	9.38%	14.08%	18.83%	23.44%	27.81%	31.89%	35.67%
47.00%	0.00%	0.28%	2.30%	6.00%	10.56%	15.40%	20.21%	24.81%	29.13%	33.14%	36.83%
49.00%	0.00%	0.41%	2.87%	6.96%	11.77%	16.75%	21.59%	26.18%	30.44%	34.38%	37.99%
51.00%	0.00%	0.58%	3.50%	7.97%	13.02%	18.10%	22.98%	27.53%	31.74%	35.61%	39.14%
53.00%	0.00%	0.79%	4.20%	9.04%	14.29%	19.47%	24.36%	28.88%	33.03%	36.82%	40.28%
55.00%	0.00%	1.05%	4.96%	10.15%	15.59%	20.84%	25.73%	30.22%	34.31%	38.03%	41.42%
57.00%	0.00%	1.36%	5.78%	11.31%	16.91%	22.22%	27.11%	31.55%	35.58%	39.24%	42.55%
59.00%	0.00%	1.72%	6.66%	12.49%	18.25%	23.60%	28.47%	32.88%	36.84%	40.43%	43.66%
61.00%	0.00%	2.13%	7.59%	13.72%	19.60%	24.98%	29.84%	34.19%	38.09%	41.61%	44.77%
63.00%	0.00%	2.60%	8.58%	14.97%	20.96%	26.36%	31.19%	35.49%	39.33%	42.77%	45.87%
65.00%	0.01%	3.13%	9.61%	16.25%	22.33%	27.74%	32.54%	36.78%	40.56%	43.93%	46.96%
67.00%	0.01%	3.72%	10.69%	17.55%	23.70%	29.12%	33.87%	38.06%	41.77%	45.08%	48.04%
69.00%	0.02%	4.36%	11.81%	18.87%	25.08%	30.49%	35.20%	39.33%	42.98%	46.21%	49.11%
71.00%	0.03%	5.05%	12.96%	20.20%	26.46%	31.85%	36.52%	40.59%	44.17%	47.34%	50.17%
73.00%	0.05%	5.81%	14.15%	21.55%	27.84%	33.21%	37.83%	41.83%	45.35%	48.45%	51.22%
75.00%	0.08%	6.61%	15.37%	22.91%	29.23%	34.56%	39.12%	43.06%	46.51%	49.55%	52.25%
77.00%	0.11%	7.47%	16.62%	24.28%	30.60%	35.90%	40.40%	44.28%	47.66%	50.64%	53.28%
79.00%	0.16%	8.38%	17.90%	25.65%	31.98%	37.23%	41.68%	45.49%	48.80%	51.71%	54.29%
81.00%	0.21%	9.33%	19.19%	27.03%	33.35%	38.55%	42.93%	46.68%	49.93%	52.78%	55.30%
83.00%	0.29%	10.33%	20.50%	28.41%	34.71%	39.86%	44.18%	47.86%	51.04%	53.83%	56.29%
85.00%	0.38%	11.37%	21.83%	29.79%	36.06%	41.16%	45.41%	49.02%	52.14%	54.86%	57.27%
87.00%	0.49%	12.45%	23.18%	31.17%	37.41%	42.45%	46.63%	50.17%	53.22%	55.89%	58.23%
89.00%	0.62%	13.57%	24.53%	32.55%	38.74%	43.72%	47.83%	51.31%	54.30%	56.90%	59.19%
91.00%	0.78%	14.72%	25.90%	33.93%	40.07%	44.98%	49.02%	52.43%	55.35%	57.89%	60.13%
93.00%	0.97%	15.91%	27.27%	35.30%	41.38%	46.22%	50.20%	53.54%	56.40%	58.88%	61.06%
95.00%	1.19%	17.12%	28.65%	36.66%	42.69%	47.46%	51.36%	54.63%	57.42%	59.85%	61.97%
97.00%	1.44%	18.37%	30.03%	38.01%	43.98%	48.67%	52.50%	55.70%	58.44%	60.80%	62.88%
99.00%	1.72%	19.63%	31.41%	39.36%	45.25%	49.87%	53.63%	56.77%	59.44%	61.75%	63.77%
101.00%	2.04%	20.92%	32.79%	40.70%	46.52%	51.06%	54.74%	57.81%	60.42%	62.67%	64.65%

Note: Risk-free rate is 5 percent.

TABLE 10.2   Continued

Volatility	10.00%	20.00%	30.00%	40.00%	50.00%	60.00%	70.00%	80.00%	90.00%	100.00%
1.00%	21.75%	28.27%	33.79%	38.52%	42.62%	46.21%	49.37%	52.18%	54.70%	56.96%
3.00%	21.75%	28.27%	33.79%	38.52%	42.62%	46.21%	49.37%	52.18%	54.70%	56.96%
5.00%	21.76%	28.27%	33.79%	38.52%	42.62%	46.21%	49.37%	52.18%	54.70%	56.96%
7.00%	21.84%	28.28%	33.79%	38.52%	42.62%	46.21%	49.37%	52.18%	54.70%	56.96%
9.00%	22.09%	28.35%	33.81%	38.52%	42.62%	46.21%	49.37%	52.18%	54.70%	56.96%
11.00%	22.54%	28.54%	33.88%	38.55%	42.63%	46.21%	49.37%	52.18%	54.70%	56.96%
13.00%	23.14%	28.86%	34.03%	38.62%	42.66%	46.22%	49.38%	52.19%	54.70%	56.96%
15.00%	23.87%	29.32%	34.29%	38.76%	42.73%	46.26%	49.40%	52.19%	54.71%	56.97%
17.00%	24.69%	29.88%	34.66%	38.99%	42.87%	46.34%	49.44%	52.22%	54.72%	56.98%
19.00%	25.57%	30.53%	35.13%	39.31%	43.08%	46.48%	49.53%	52.28%	54.76%	57.00%
21.00%	26.51%	31.26%	35.67%	39.71%	43.37%	46.68%	49.67%	52.38%	54.83%	57.05%
23.00%	27.48%	32.05%	36.28%	40.18%	43.72%	46.95%	49.87%	52.52%	54.93%	57.12%
25.00%	28.49%	32.88%	36.96%	40.71%	44.14%	47.27%	50.12%	52.72%	55.08%	57.24%
27.00%	29.52%	33.75%	37.68%	41.30%	44.62%	47.66%	50.43%	52.96%	55.27%	57.39%
29.00%	30.56%	34.65%	38.44%	41.94%	45.15%	48.09%	50.78%	53.25%	55.51%	57.58%
31.00%	31.62%	35.57%	39.23%	42.61%	45.72%	48.57%	51.19%	53.59%	55.79%	57.82%
33.00%	32.68%	36.51%	40.05%	43.32%	46.33%	49.09%	51.63%	53.97%	56.11%	58.09%
35.00%	33.76%	37.46%	40.89%	44.06%	46.97%	49.65%	52.12%	54.38%	56.48%	58.41%
37.00%	34.84%	38.43%	41.75%	44.82%	47.64%	50.24%	52.63%	54.84%	56.87%	58.75%
39.00%	35.92%	39.41%	42.63%	45.60%	48.34%	50.85%	53.18%	55.32%	57.30%	59.13%
41.00%	37.00%	40.39%	43.52%	46.40%	49.05%	51.49%	53.75%	55.83%	57.75%	59.54%
43.00%	38.08%	41.38%	44.41%	47.21%	49.78%	52.15%	54.34%	56.36%	58.24%	59.97%
45.00%	39.16%	42.37%	45.32%	48.03%	50.53%	52.83%	54.96%	56.92%	58.74%	60.43%
47.00%	40.23%	43.36%	46.22%	48.86%	51.29%	53.52%	55.59%	57.50%	59.26%	60.90%
49.00%	41.31%	44.35%	47.14%	49.70%	52.05%	54.23%	56.23%	58.09%	59.81%	61.40%
51.00%	42.38%	45.34%	48.05%	50.54%	52.83%	54.94%	56.89%	58.69%	60.36%	61.92%
53.00%	43.44%	46.33%	48.97%	51.39%	53.61%	55.66%	57.56%	59.31%	60.93%	62.44%
55.00%	44.50%	47.31%	49.88%	52.24%	54.40%	56.39%	58.23%	59.94%	61.52%	62.99%
57.00%	45.55%	48.29%	50.79%	53.08%	55.19%	57.13%	58.92%	60.57%	62.11%	63.54%
59.00%	46.60%	49.27%	51.70%	53.93%	55.98%	57.87%	59.61%	61.22%	62.71%	64.10%
61.00%	47.64%	50.24%	52.61%	54.78%	56.77%	58.61%	60.30%	61.86%	63.32%	64.67%
63.00%	48.67%	51.21%	53.52%	55.63%	57.57%	59.35%	60.99%	62.52%	63.93%	65.25%
65.00%	49.69%	52.17%	54.42%	56.47%	58.36%	60.09%	61.69%	63.17%	64.55%	65.83%
67.00%	50.71%	53.12%	55.31%	57.31%	59.15%	60.84%	62.39%	63.83%	65.17%	66.41%
69.00%	51.71%	54.06%	56.20%	58.15%	59.94%	61.58%	63.09%	64.49%	65.79%	67.00%
71.00%	52.71%	55.00%	57.08%	58.98%	60.72%	62.32%	63.79%	65.15%	66.42%	67.60%
73.00%	53.70%	55.93%	57.96%	59.81%	61.50%	63.06%	64.49%	65.82%	67.05%	68.19%
75.00%	54.67%	56.85%	58.83%	60.63%	62.28%	63.79%	65.18%	66.47%	67.67%	68.79%
77.00%	55.64%	57.77%	59.69%	61.45%	63.05%	64.52%	65.88%	67.13%	68.30%	69.38%
79.00%	56.60%	58.67%	60.55%	62.25%	63.81%	65.25%	66.57%	67.79%	68.92%	69.97%
81.00%	57.54%	59.57%	61.39%	63.06%	64.57%	65.97%	67.25%	68.44%	69.54%	70.57%
83.00%	58.48%	60.45%	62.23%	63.85%	65.33%	66.68%	67.93%	69.09%	70.16%	71.16%
85.00%	59.41%	61.33%	63.06%	64.64%	66.07%	67.39%	68.61%	69.73%	70.78%	71.75%
87.00%	60.32%	62.19%	63.88%	65.41%	66.81%	68.10%	69.28%	70.37%	71.39%	72.33%
89.00%	61.22%	63.05%	64.69%	66.18%	67.55%	68.80%	69.95%	71.01%	72.00%	72.91%
91.00%	62.11%	63.89%	65.49%	66.95%	68.27%	69.49%	70.61%	71.64%	72.60%	73.49%
93.00%	62.99%	64.72%	66.28%	67.70%	68.99%	70.17%	71.26%	72.27%	73.20%	74.06%
95.00%	63.86%	65.55%	67.07%	68.44%	69.70%	70.85%	71.91%	72.88%	73.79%	74.63%
97.00%	64.72%	66.36%	67.84%	69.18%	70.40%	71.52%	72.55%	73.50%	74.38%	75.20%
99.00%	65.56%	67.16%	68.60%	69.90%	71.09%	72.18%	73.18%	74.10%	74.96%	75.76%
101.00%	66.39%	67.95%	69.35%	70.62%	71.77%	72.83%	73.81%	74.70%	75.54%	76.31%

TABLE 10.3 Real Options Value—5-Year Maturity

Maturity	5	Year(s)	Risk-Free Rate 5%							
Profitability Ratio (% in-the-money)										
Volatility	**-99%**	**-90.00%**	**-80.00%**	**-70.00%**	**-60.00%**	**-50.00%**	**-40.00%**	**-30.00%**	**-20.00%**	**-10.00%**	**0.00%**
1.00%	0.00%	0.00%	0.00%	0.00%	0.00%	0.00%	0.00%	0.00%	2.77%	13.47%	22.12%
3.00%	0.00%	0.00%	0.00%	0.00%	0.00%	0.00%	0.00%	0.17%	4.17%	13.50%	22.12%
5.00%	0.00%	0.00%	0.00%	0.00%	0.00%	0.00%	0.04%	1.07%	5.85%	13.95%	22.16%
7.00%	0.00%	0.00%	0.00%	0.00%	0.00%	0.01%	0.35%	2.43%	7.57%	14.86%	22.44%
9.00%	0.00%	0.00%	0.00%	0.00%	0.00%	0.12%	1.05%	3.99%	9.30%	16.05%	23.03%
11.00%	0.00%	0.00%	0.00%	0.00%	0.04%	0.43%	2.07%	5.66%	11.04%	17.39%	23.86%
13.00%	0.00%	0.00%	0.00%	0.01%	0.15%	1.00%	3.32%	7.38%	12.78%	18.81%	24.87%
15.00%	0.00%	0.00%	0.00%	0.03%	0.41%	1.80%	4.74%	9.14%	14.51%	20.28%	26.00%
17.00%	0.00%	0.00%	0.00%	0.12%	0.84%	2.82%	6.27%	10.91%	16.24%	21.78%	27.21%
19.00%	0.00%	0.00%	0.02%	0.29%	1.46%	4.01%	7.88%	12.69%	17.96%	23.31%	28.49%
21.00%	0.00%	0.00%	0.05%	0.58%	2.26%	5.34%	9.56%	14.47%	19.67%	24.84%	29.80%
23.00%	0.00%	0.00%	0.13%	1.00%	3.22%	6.78%	11.27%	16.26%	21.38%	26.39%	31.14%
25.00%	0.00%	0.00%	0.26%	1.57%	4.33%	8.30%	13.01%	18.04%	23.07%	27.93%	32.50%
27.00%	0.00%	0.01%	0.48%	2.29%	5.57%	9.90%	14.77%	19.81%	24.76%	29.47%	33.88%
29.00%	0.00%	0.04%	0.80%	3.15%	6.92%	11.55%	16.55%	21.58%	26.43%	31.01%	35.26%
31.00%	0.00%	0.08%	1.23%	4.14%	8.35%	13.24%	18.33%	23.33%	28.10%	32.54%	36.65%
33.00%	0.00%	0.16%	1.77%	5.24%	9.87%	14.96%	20.11%	25.08%	29.75%	34.07%	38.04%
35.00%	0.00%	0.28%	2.43%	6.46%	11.44%	16.71%	21.90%	26.81%	31.38%	35.59%	39.43%
37.00%	0.00%	0.46%	3.21%	7.77%	13.07%	18.48%	23.67%	28.53%	33.00%	37.09%	40.81%
39.00%	0.00%	0.70%	4.11%	9.17%	14.74%	20.25%	25.45%	30.24%	34.61%	38.59%	42.19%
41.00%	0.00%	1.03%	5.11%	10.64%	16.45%	22.03%	27.21%	31.93%	36.20%	40.07%	43.56%
43.00%	0.00%	1.44%	6.22%	12.18%	18.18%	23.82%	28.96%	33.60%	37.78%	41.54%	44.92%
45.00%	0.00%	1.94%	7.42%	13.77%	19.94%	25.60%	30.70%	35.26%	39.34%	42.99%	46.27%
47.00%	0.00%	2.53%	8.71%	15.41%	21.71%	27.38%	32.42%	36.90%	40.88%	44.43%	47.61%
49.00%	0.01%	3.23%	10.07%	17.09%	23.48%	29.15%	34.13%	38.52%	42.40%	45.86%	48.94%
51.00%	0.01%	4.02%	11.51%	18.79%	25.27%	30.91%	35.82%	40.12%	43.91%	47.26%	50.25%
53.00%	0.03%	4.90%	13.01%	20.53%	27.05%	32.66%	37.50%	41.71%	45.40%	48.65%	51.55%
55.00%	0.05%	5.88%	14.57%	22.28%	28.83%	34.39%	39.15%	43.27%	46.86%	50.03%	52.84%
57.00%	0.08%	6.95%	16.17%	24.05%	30.61%	36.11%	40.79%	44.81%	48.31%	51.38%	54.10%
59.00%	0.12%	8.10%	17.82%	25.83%	32.38%	37.81%	42.40%	46.33%	49.74%	52.72%	55.36%
61.00%	0.19%	9.33%	19.50%	27.61%	34.13%	39.50%	43.99%	47.83%	51.14%	54.04%	56.59%
63.00%	0.28%	10.64%	21.21%	29.39%	35.88%	41.16%	45.56%	49.30%	52.52%	55.33%	57.81%
65.00%	0.39%	12.02%	22.95%	31.17%	37.61%	42.80%	47.11%	50.76%	53.89%	56.61%	59.01%
67.00%	0.55%	13.46%	24.70%	32.95%	39.32%	44.42%	48.64%	52.19%	55.23%	57.87%	60.19%
69.00%	0.74%	14.96%	26.47%	34.72%	41.01%	46.02%	50.14%	53.59%	56.55%	59.11%	61.36%
71.00%	0.99%	16.51%	28.25%	36.48%	42.69%	47.60%	51.61%	54.97%	57.84%	60.32%	62.50%
73.00%	1.28%	18.11%	30.03%	38.22%	44.34%	49.15%	53.06%	56.33%	59.11%	61.52%	63.63%
75.00%	1.63%	19.75%	31.81%	39.95%	45.97%	50.67%	54.49%	57.67%	60.36%	62.69%	64.73%
77.00%	2.04%	21.42%	33.60%	41.66%	47.58%	52.17%	55.89%	58.97%	61.59%	63.85%	65.82%
79.00%	2.52%	23.12%	35.37%	43.35%	49.16%	53.65%	57.26%	60.26%	62.79%	64.98%	66.88%
81.00%	3.06%	24.85%	37.14%	45.03%	50.71%	55.10%	58.61%	61.52%	63.97%	66.09%	67.93%
83.00%	3.68%	26.60%	38.90%	46.67%	52.25%	56.52%	59.93%	62.75%	65.13%	67.17%	68.95%
85.00%	4.37%	28.36%	40.64%	48.30%	53.75%	57.91%	61.23%	63.96%	66.26%	68.24%	69.96%
87.00%	5.13%	30.13%	42.37%	49.90%	55.23%	59.27%	62.50%	65.14%	67.37%	69.28%	70.94%
89.00%	5.97%	31.92%	44.08%	51.48%	56.68%	60.61%	63.74%	66.30%	68.46%	70.30%	71.90%
91.00%	6.88%	33.70%	45.77%	53.02%	58.10%	61.92%	64.95%	67.44%	69.52%	71.30%	72.84%
93.00%	7.87%	35.48%	47.43%	54.55%	59.49%	63.20%	66.14%	68.54%	70.55%	72.27%	73.76%
95.00%	8.93%	37.26%	49.08%	56.04%	60.85%	64.46%	67.30%	69.62%	71.57%	73.23%	74.66%
97.00%	10.06%	39.03%	50.70%	57.50%	62.18%	65.68%	68.44%	70.68%	72.56%	74.16%	75.54%
99.00%	11.26%	40.79%	52.29%	58.94%	63.49%	66.88%	69.54%	71.71%	73.52%	75.07%	76.40%
101.00%	12.52%	42.54%	53.86%	60.34%	64.76%	68.05%	70.62%	72.72%	74.47%	75.95%	77.24%

Note: Risk-free rate is 5 percent.

TABLE 10.3 Continued

Volatility	10.00%	20.00%	30.00%	40.00%	50.00%	60.00%	70.00%	80.00%	90.00%	100.00%
1.00%	29.20%	35.10%	40.09%	44.37%	48.08%	51.32%	54.19%	56.73%	59.01%	61.06%
3.00%	29.20%	35.10%	40.09%	44.37%	48.08%	51.32%	54.19%	56.73%	59.01%	61.06%
5.00%	29.20%	35.10%	40.09%	44.37%	48.08%	51.32%	54.19%	56.73%	59.01%	61.06%
7.00%	29.26%	35.11%	40.09%	44.37%	48.08%	51.32%	54.19%	56.73%	59.01%	61.06%
9.00%	29.50%	35.19%	40.12%	44.38%	48.08%	51.33%	54.19%	56.73%	59.01%	61.06%
11.00%	29.95%	35.41%	40.22%	44.42%	48.10%	51.33%	54.19%	56.73%	59.01%	61.06%
13.00%	30.60%	35.80%	40.44%	44.55%	48.17%	51.37%	54.21%	56.74%	59.02%	61.06%
15.00%	31.40%	36.35%	40.80%	44.77%	48.31%	51.46%	54.26%	56.78%	59.04%	61.08%
17.00%	32.33%	37.03%	41.29%	45.11%	48.55%	51.62%	54.37%	56.85%	59.09%	61.11%
19.00%	33.35%	37.82%	41.89%	45.57%	48.88%	51.86%	54.56%	56.98%	59.18%	61.18%
21.00%	34.43%	38.70%	42.59%	46.11%	49.31%	52.20%	54.81%	57.18%	59.34%	61.30%
23.00%	35.57%	39.64%	43.36%	46.75%	49.82%	52.61%	55.14%	57.45%	59.55%	61.47%
25.00%	36.75%	40.64%	44.21%	47.45%	50.41%	53.10%	55.55%	57.78%	59.83%	61.70%
27.00%	37.95%	41.69%	45.10%	48.22%	51.06%	53.65%	56.02%	58.18%	60.16%	61.99%
29.00%	39.18%	42.77%	46.05%	49.04%	51.77%	54.26%	56.55%	58.64%	60.56%	62.33%
31.00%	40.42%	43.87%	47.02%	49.89%	52.52%	54.92%	57.13%	59.15%	61.01%	62.72%
33.00%	41.68%	44.99%	48.02%	50.79%	53.31%	55.63%	57.75%	59.70%	61.50%	63.16%
35.00%	42.94%	46.13%	49.05%	51.71%	54.14%	56.37%	58.41%	60.30%	62.03%	63.64%
37.00%	44.20%	47.28%	50.09%	52.65%	54.99%	57.14%	59.11%	60.93%	62.60%	64.15%
39.00%	45.46%	48.43%	51.14%	53.60%	55.86%	57.93%	59.83%	61.58%	63.20%	64.70%
41.00%	46.72%	49.59%	52.20%	54.58%	56.75%	58.75%	60.58%	62.27%	63.83%	65.28%
43.00%	47.98%	50.75%	53.26%	55.56%	57.65%	59.58%	61.34%	62.98%	64.48%	65.88%
45.00%	49.23%	51.90%	54.33%	56.54%	58.57%	60.42%	62.13%	63.70%	65.15%	66.50%
47.00%	50.47%	53.06%	55.40%	57.53%	59.48%	61.27%	62.92%	64.44%	65.84%	67.14%
49.00%	51.71%	54.20%	56.47%	58.53%	60.41%	62.13%	63.72%	65.19%	66.54%	67.80%
51.00%	52.93%	55.34%	57.53%	59.52%	61.33%	63.00%	64.53%	65.94%	67.25%	68.47%
53.00%	54.14%	56.48%	58.59%	60.51%	62.26%	63.87%	65.34%	66.71%	67.97%	69.14%
55.00%	55.34%	57.60%	59.64%	61.49%	63.18%	64.73%	66.16%	67.48%	68.70%	69.83%
57.00%	56.53%	58.71%	60.68%	62.47%	64.11%	65.60%	66.98%	68.25%	69.42%	70.52%
59.00%	57.71%	59.82%	61.72%	63.45%	65.02%	66.47%	67.79%	69.02%	70.15%	71.21%
61.00%	58.87%	60.90%	62.74%	64.41%	65.93%	67.33%	68.61%	69.79%	70.89%	71.90%
63.00%	60.01%	61.98%	63.76%	65.37%	66.84%	68.18%	69.42%	70.56%	71.62%	72.60%
65.00%	61.14%	63.04%	64.76%	66.32%	67.73%	69.03%	70.22%	71.32%	72.34%	73.29%
67.00%	62.25%	64.09%	65.75%	67.25%	68.62%	69.87%	71.02%	72.09%	73.07%	73.98%
69.00%	63.35%	65.13%	66.73%	68.18%	69.50%	70.71%	71.82%	72.84%	73.79%	74.67%
71.00%	64.43%	66.15%	67.69%	69.09%	70.37%	71.53%	72.60%	73.59%	74.50%	75.35%
73.00%	65.49%	67.15%	68.64%	69.99%	71.22%	72.35%	73.38%	74.33%	75.21%	76.03%
75.00%	66.53%	68.13%	69.58%	70.88%	72.07%	73.15%	74.15%	75.06%	75.91%	76.70%
77.00%	67.56%	69.10%	70.50%	71.75%	72.90%	73.94%	74.90%	75.79%	76.61%	77.37%
79.00%	68.56%	70.06%	71.40%	72.61%	73.72%	74.72%	75.65%	76.50%	77.29%	78.03%
81.00%	69.55%	70.99%	72.29%	73.46%	74.52%	75.49%	76.39%	77.21%	77.97%	78.68%
83.00%	70.52%	71.91%	73.16%	74.29%	75.31%	76.25%	77.11%	77.90%	78.64%	79.32%
85.00%	71.47%	72.81%	74.02%	75.10%	76.09%	76.99%	77.82%	78.59%	79.29%	79.95%
87.00%	72.40%	73.69%	74.86%	75.90%	76.86%	77.73%	78.52%	79.26%	79.94%	80.57%
89.00%	73.31%	74.56%	75.68%	76.69%	77.61%	78.44%	79.21%	79.92%	80.57%	81.18%
91.00%	74.20%	75.41%	76.48%	77.46%	78.34%	79.15%	79.89%	80.57%	81.20%	81.78%
93.00%	75.07%	76.23%	77.27%	78.21%	79.06%	79.84%	80.55%	81.20%	81.81%	82.37%
95.00%	75.93%	77.04%	78.05%	78.95%	79.77%	80.51%	81.20%	81.83%	82.41%	82.95%
97.00%	76.76%	77.84%	78.80%	79.67%	80.46%	81.17%	81.83%	82.44%	83.00%	83.52%
99.00%	77.57%	78.61%	79.54%	80.37%	81.13%	81.82%	82.45%	83.04%	83.58%	84.08%
101.00%	78.37%	79.36%	80.26%	81.06%	81.79%	82.45%	83.06%	83.62%	84.14%	84.62%

TABLE 10.4 Real Options Value—7-Year Maturity

Maturity	7	Year(s)	Risk-Free Rate	5%							

Volatility	−99%	−90.00%	−80.00%	−70.00%	−60.00%	−50.00%	−40.00%	−30.00%	−20.00%	−10.00%	0.00%
1.00%	0.00%	0.00%	0.00%	0.00%	0.00%	0.00%	0.00%	0.76%	11.91%	21.70%	29.53%
3.00%	0.00%	0.00%	0.00%	0.00%	0.00%	0.00%	0.07%	2.85%	12.09%	21.70%	29.53%
5.00%	0.00%	0.00%	0.00%	0.00%	0.00%	0.02%	0.78%	4.96%	13.03%	21.85%	29.55%
7.00%	0.00%	0.00%	0.00%	0.00%	0.01%	0.27%	2.13%	7.07%	14.46%	22.41%	29.71%
9.00%	0.00%	0.00%	0.00%	0.00%	0.09%	0.94%	3.83%	9.18%	16.10%	23.36%	30.16%
11.00%	0.00%	0.00%	0.00%	0.02%	0.38%	2.01%	5.71%	11.28%	17.85%	24.56%	30.88%
13.00%	0.00%	0.00%	0.00%	0.11%	0.94%	3.39%	7.70%	13.37%	19.65%	25.93%	31.84%
15.00%	0.00%	0.00%	0.01%	0.34%	1.79%	4.99%	9.74%	15.45%	21.49%	27.41%	32.95%
17.00%	0.00%	0.00%	0.06%	0.75%	2.91%	6.75%	11.82%	17.52%	23.34%	28.95%	34.18%
19.00%	0.00%	0.00%	0.18%	1.38%	4.25%	8.63%	13.92%	19.58%	25.20%	30.54%	35.49%
21.00%	0.00%	0.01%	0.41%	2.23%	5.78%	10.59%	16.03%	21.62%	27.06%	32.16%	36.87%
23.00%	0.00%	0.03%	0.77%	3.29%	7.45%	12.61%	18.14%	23.65%	28.91%	33.80%	38.28%
25.00%	0.00%	0.08%	1.30%	4.53%	9.24%	14.66%	20.25%	25.67%	30.76%	35.45%	39.73%
27.00%	0.00%	0.17%	2.00%	5.94%	11.12%	16.75%	22.35%	27.66%	32.59%	37.10%	41.20%
29.00%	0.00%	0.33%	2.87%	7.49%	13.07%	18.85%	24.43%	29.64%	34.42%	38.75%	42.68%
31.00%	0.00%	0.59%	3.91%	9.17%	15.08%	20.96%	26.50%	31.60%	36.22%	40.40%	44.16%
33.00%	0.00%	0.94%	5.11%	10.95%	17.13%	23.07%	28.56%	33.54%	38.02%	42.04%	45.65%
35.00%	0.00%	1.43%	6.45%	12.81%	19.20%	25.18%	30.59%	35.45%	39.79%	43.67%	47.14%
37.00%	0.00%	2.04%	7.93%	14.74%	21.30%	27.27%	32.61%	37.34%	41.54%	45.28%	48.61%
39.00%	0.00%	2.79%	9.52%	16.73%	23.41%	29.36%	34.60%	39.21%	43.27%	46.88%	50.08%
41.00%	0.01%	3.68%	11.22%	18.76%	25.52%	31.42%	36.56%	41.05%	44.98%	48.46%	51.54%
43.00%	0.02%	4.70%	13.00%	20.82%	27.63%	33.47%	38.50%	42.86%	46.67%	50.02%	52.99%
45.00%	0.04%	5.86%	14.87%	22.91%	29.73%	35.50%	40.42%	44.65%	48.33%	51.56%	54.42%
47.00%	0.07%	7.14%	16.79%	25.01%	31.82%	37.50%	42.30%	46.41%	49.97%	53.08%	55.83%
49.00%	0.12%	8.55%	18.77%	27.12%	33.89%	39.47%	44.16%	48.14%	51.58%	54.58%	57.22%
51.00%	0.20%	10.06%	20.80%	29.23%	35.95%	41.42%	45.98%	49.84%	53.17%	56.06%	58.60%
53.00%	0.32%	11.68%	22.85%	31.34%	37.98%	43.34%	47.77%	51.52%	54.72%	57.51%	59.95%
55.00%	0.48%	13.38%	24.94%	33.43%	39.98%	45.22%	49.53%	53.16%	56.25%	58.94%	61.29%
57.00%	0.70%	15.17%	27.03%	35.52%	41.96%	47.08%	51.26%	54.77%	57.75%	60.34%	62.60%
59.00%	0.99%	17.03%	29.14%	37.58%	43.91%	48.90%	52.96%	56.34%	59.22%	61.71%	63.88%
61.00%	1.34%	18.95%	31.25%	39.62%	45.83%	50.69%	54.62%	57.89%	60.67%	63.06%	65.14%
63.00%	1.78%	20.92%	33.36%	41.64%	47.72%	52.44%	56.25%	59.40%	62.08%	64.38%	66.38%
65.00%	2.31%	22.93%	35.46%	43.63%	49.57%	54.15%	57.84%	60.88%	63.46%	65.67%	67.59%
67.00%	2.93%	24.98%	37.55%	45.59%	51.38%	55.83%	59.39%	62.33%	64.81%	66.93%	68.78%
69.00%	3.65%	27.06%	39.62%	47.52%	53.16%	57.47%	60.91%	63.74%	66.13%	68.17%	69.94%
71.00%	4.47%	29.15%	41.66%	49.42%	54.91%	59.08%	62.40%	65.12%	67.41%	69.37%	71.07%
73.00%	5.40%	31.25%	43.69%	51.28%	56.61%	60.65%	63.85%	66.47%	68.67%	70.55%	72.18%
75.00%	6.44%	33.36%	45.68%	53.10%	58.27%	62.17%	65.26%	67.78%	69.89%	71.70%	73.26%
77.00%	7.58%	35.47%	47.65%	54.88%	59.90%	63.66%	66.63%	69.06%	71.09%	72.82%	74.31%
79.00%	8.82%	37.58%	49.58%	56.62%	61.48%	65.12%	67.97%	70.30%	72.25%	73.91%	75.34%
81.00%	10.16%	39.67%	51.47%	58.33%	63.03%	66.53%	69.28%	71.51%	73.38%	74.97%	76.34%
83.00%	11.60%	41.74%	53.33%	59.99%	64.53%	67.90%	70.54%	72.69%	74.48%	76.00%	77.31%
85.00%	13.13%	43.80%	55.15%	61.61%	65.99%	69.24%	71.77%	73.83%	75.54%	77.00%	78.25%
87.00%	14.74%	45.83%	56.93%	63.19%	67.42%	70.54%	72.97%	74.94%	76.58%	77.97%	79.17%
89.00%	16.43%	47.83%	58.67%	64.73%	68.80%	71.79%	74.13%	76.01%	77.58%	78.91%	80.06%
91.00%	18.20%	49.80%	60.37%	66.22%	70.14%	73.02%	75.25%	77.06%	78.56%	79.83%	80.92%
93.00%	20.03%	51.74%	62.02%	67.67%	71.44%	74.20%	76.34%	78.07%	79.50%	80.71%	81.76%
95.00%	21.93%	53.64%	63.63%	69.08%	72.70%	75.34%	77.39%	79.05%	80.41%	81.57%	82.57%
97.00%	23.87%	55.50%	65.19%	70.44%	73.92%	76.45%	78.41%	79.99%	81.30%	82.40%	83.35%
99.00%	25.86%	57.32%	66.71%	71.77%	75.10%	77.52%	79.40%	80.90%	82.15%	83.20%	84.11%
101.00%	27.88%	59.10%	68.19%	73.05%	76.24%	78.56%	80.35%	81.79%	82.98%	83.98%	84.84%

Note: Risk-free rate is 5 percent.

TABLE 10.4 Continued

Volatility	10.00%	20.00%	30.00%	40.00%	50.00%	60.00%	70.00%	80.00%	90.00%	100.00%
1.00%	35.94%	41.28%	45.79%	49.67%	53.02%	55.96%	58.55%	60.85%	62.91%	64.77%
3.00%	35.94%	41.28%	45.79%	49.67%	53.02%	55.96%	58.55%	60.85%	62.91%	64.77%
5.00%	35.94%	41.28%	45.79%	49.67%	53.02%	55.96%	58.55%	60.85%	62.91%	64.77%
7.00%	35.98%	41.28%	45.79%	49.67%	53.02%	55.96%	58.55%	60.85%	62.91%	64.77%
9.00%	36.16%	41.36%	45.82%	49.67%	53.02%	55.96%	58.55%	60.85%	62.91%	64.77%
11.00%	36.57%	41.57%	45.93%	49.73%	53.05%	55.97%	58.55%	60.85%	62.91%	64.77%
13.00%	37.19%	41.96%	46.17%	49.87%	53.14%	56.02%	58.58%	60.87%	62.92%	64.77%
15.00%	38.00%	42.53%	46.56%	50.14%	53.31%	56.14%	58.66%	60.92%	62.96%	64.80%
17.00%	38.95%	43.24%	47.09%	50.53%	53.60%	56.35%	58.82%	61.04%	63.04%	64.86%
19.00%	40.01%	44.08%	47.75%	51.04%	54.00%	56.66%	59.06%	61.22%	63.18%	64.97%
21.00%	41.15%	45.02%	48.52%	51.67%	54.51%	57.07%	59.38%	61.49%	63.40%	65.14%
23.00%	42.36%	46.04%	49.37%	52.38%	55.10%	57.56%	59.80%	61.83%	63.69%	65.38%
25.00%	43.61%	47.13%	50.30%	53.18%	55.78%	58.14%	60.29%	62.25%	64.05%	65.69%
27.00%	44.90%	48.26%	51.29%	54.03%	56.53%	58.79%	60.86%	62.75%	64.48%	66.06%
29.00%	46.22%	49.42%	52.32%	54.94%	57.33%	59.50%	61.48%	63.30%	64.96%	66.50%
31.00%	47.55%	50.62%	53.38%	55.90%	58.18%	60.26%	62.16%	63.91%	65.51%	66.99%
33.00%	48.90%	51.83%	54.48%	56.88%	59.07%	61.06%	62.88%	64.56%	66.10%	67.52%
35.00%	50.25%	53.06%	55.59%	57.89%	59.98%	61.90%	63.65%	65.25%	66.73%	68.10%
37.00%	51.60%	54.29%	56.72%	58.92%	60.93%	62.76%	64.44%	65.98%	67.40%	68.71%
39.00%	52.95%	55.53%	57.86%	59.97%	61.89%	63.64%	65.25%	66.73%	68.10%	69.36%
41.00%	54.30%	56.77%	59.00%	61.02%	62.86%	64.55%	66.09%	67.51%	68.82%	70.03%
43.00%	55.63%	58.01%	60.15%	62.08%	63.85%	65.46%	66.94%	68.30%	69.56%	70.72%
45.00%	56.96%	59.24%	61.29%	63.15%	64.84%	66.38%	67.80%	69.11%	70.31%	71.43%
47.00%	58.27%	60.46%	62.43%	64.21%	65.83%	67.31%	68.67%	69.92%	71.08%	72.15%
49.00%	59.57%	61.67%	63.56%	65.27%	66.82%	68.24%	69.54%	70.74%	71.85%	72.88%
51.00%	60.85%	62.87%	64.68%	66.32%	67.81%	69.17%	70.42%	71.57%	72.63%	73.62%
53.00%	62.12%	64.05%	65.79%	67.36%	68.79%	70.09%	71.29%	72.39%	73.41%	74.36%
55.00%	63.37%	65.22%	66.89%	68.39%	69.76%	71.01%	72.16%	73.22%	74.20%	75.10%
57.00%	64.59%	66.37%	67.97%	69.42%	70.73%	71.93%	73.03%	74.04%	74.98%	75.85%
59.00%	65.80%	67.51%	69.04%	70.43%	71.68%	72.83%	73.89%	74.86%	75.75%	76.59%
61.00%	66.99%	68.62%	70.09%	71.42%	72.63%	73.73%	74.74%	75.67%	76.53%	77.32%
63.00%	68.15%	69.72%	71.13%	72.40%	73.56%	74.61%	75.58%	76.47%	77.29%	78.05%
65.00%	69.29%	70.80%	72.15%	73.37%	74.47%	75.48%	76.41%	77.26%	78.05%	78.78%
67.00%	70.41%	71.85%	73.15%	74.31%	75.37%	76.34%	77.22%	78.04%	78.80%	79.50%
69.00%	71.50%	72.88%	74.12%	75.24%	76.26%	77.18%	78.03%	78.81%	79.53%	80.20%
71.00%	72.57%	73.90%	75.08%	76.15%	77.12%	78.01%	78.82%	79.57%	80.26%	80.90%
73.00%	73.61%	74.88%	76.02%	77.04%	77.97%	78.82%	79.60%	80.31%	80.97%	81.58%
75.00%	74.63%	75.85%	76.94%	77.92%	78.80%	79.61%	80.36%	81.04%	81.67%	82.26%
77.00%	75.63%	76.79%	77.83%	78.77%	79.62%	80.39%	81.10%	81.75%	82.36%	82.92%
79.00%	76.60%	77.71%	78.71%	79.60%	80.41%	81.15%	81.83%	82.45%	83.03%	83.57%
81.00%	77.54%	78.61%	79.56%	80.41%	81.19%	81.89%	82.54%	83.14%	83.69%	84.20%
83.00%	78.46%	79.48%	80.39%	81.20%	81.94%	82.62%	83.24%	83.81%	84.33%	84.82%
85.00%	79.35%	80.33%	81.19%	81.97%	82.68%	83.32%	83.91%	84.46%	84.96%	85.42%
87.00%	80.22%	81.15%	81.98%	82.72%	83.40%	84.01%	84.58%	85.09%	85.57%	86.01%
89.00%	81.06%	81.95%	82.74%	83.45%	84.09%	84.68%	85.22%	85.71%	86.17%	86.59%
91.00%	81.88%	82.73%	83.48%	84.16%	84.77%	85.33%	85.84%	86.31%	86.75%	87.15%
93.00%	82.67%	83.48%	84.20%	84.84%	85.43%	85.96%	86.45%	86.90%	87.31%	87.70%
95.00%	83.44%	84.21%	84.89%	85.51%	86.07%	86.57%	87.04%	87.47%	87.86%	88.23%
97.00%	84.18%	84.92%	85.57%	86.15%	86.69%	87.17%	87.61%	88.02%	88.39%	88.74%
99.00%	84.90%	85.60%	86.22%	86.78%	87.28%	87.74%	88.16%	88.55%	88.91%	89.24%
101.00%	85.60%	86.26%	86.85%	87.38%	87.86%	88.30%	88.70%	89.07%	89.41%	89.72%

TABLE 10.5 Real Options Value—10-Year Maturity

Maturity	10	Year(s)		Risk-Free Rate	5%					
Profitability Ratio (% in-the-money)										
Volatility	−99%	−90.00%	−80.00%	−70.00%	−60.00%	−50.00%	−40.00%	−30.00%	−20.00%	−10.00%	0.00%
1.00%	0.00%	0.00%	0.00%	0.00%	0.00%	0.00%	0.80%	13.35%	24.18%	32.61%	39.35%
3.00%	0.00%	0.00%	0.00%	0.00%	0.00%	0.08%	3.28%	13.61%	24.19%	32.61%	39.35%
5.00%	0.00%	0.00%	0.00%	0.00%	0.03%	0.93%	5.81%	14.81%	24.41%	32.63%	39.35%
7.00%	0.00%	0.00%	0.00%	0.01%	0.32%	2.56%	8.33%	16.56%	25.15%	32.88%	39.42%
9.00%	0.00%	0.00%	0.00%	0.09%	1.11%	4.62%	10.84%	18.54%	26.34%	33.48%	39.70%
11.00%	0.00%	0.00%	0.01%	0.39%	2.39%	6.89%	13.35%	20.63%	27.82%	34.42%	40.25%
13.00%	0.00%	0.00%	0.07%	1.02%	4.06%	9.29%	15.84%	22.77%	29.47%	35.60%	41.06%
15.00%	0.00%	0.00%	0.26%	2.01%	6.01%	11.75%	18.31%	24.95%	31.23%	36.96%	42.07%
17.00%	0.00%	0.01%	0.65%	3.33%	8.15%	14.25%	20.77%	27.13%	33.06%	38.44%	43.24%
19.00%	0.00%	0.05%	1.28%	4.93%	10.43%	16.77%	23.20%	29.32%	34.94%	40.00%	44.52%
21.00%	0.00%	0.16%	2.18%	6.76%	12.81%	19.29%	25.61%	31.50%	36.83%	41.62%	45.89%
23.00%	0.00%	0.36%	3.34%	8.78%	15.25%	21.81%	28.00%	33.66%	38.74%	43.28%	47.31%
25.00%	0.00%	0.71%	4.74%	10.95%	17.74%	24.31%	30.36%	35.81%	40.66%	44.96%	48.78%
27.00%	0.00%	1.23%	6.37%	13.24%	20.25%	26.80%	32.69%	37.93%	42.56%	46.66%	50.28%
29.00%	0.00%	1.94%	8.18%	15.61%	22.77%	29.26%	34.99%	40.03%	44.46%	48.36%	51.80%
31.00%	0.00%	2.85%	10.16%	18.04%	25.30%	31.69%	37.26%	42.11%	46.34%	50.06%	53.33%
33.00%	0.01%	3.97%	12.28%	20.52%	27.81%	34.09%	39.49%	44.15%	48.20%	51.74%	54.86%
35.00%	0.02%	5.29%	14.51%	23.03%	30.30%	36.46%	41.69%	46.17%	50.04%	53.42%	56.39%
37.00%	0.04%	6.79%	16.84%	25.54%	32.77%	38.79%	43.84%	48.15%	51.86%	55.08%	57.90%
39.00%	0.09%	8.48%	19.23%	28.07%	35.21%	41.08%	45.96%	50.10%	53.64%	56.72%	59.41%
41.00%	0.18%	10.32%	21.68%	30.58%	37.62%	43.32%	48.04%	52.01%	55.40%	58.33%	60.90%
43.00%	0.31%	12.30%	24.16%	33.08%	40.00%	45.53%	50.07%	53.88%	57.12%	59.92%	62.37%
45.00%	0.51%	14.41%	26.67%	35.56%	42.33%	47.69%	52.07%	55.71%	58.81%	61.48%	63.81%
47.00%	0.79%	16.62%	29.20%	38.01%	44.62%	49.81%	54.01%	57.51%	60.47%	63.02%	65.23%
49.00%	1.17%	18.92%	31.72%	40.43%	46.86%	51.87%	55.91%	59.26%	62.09%	64.52%	66.63%
51.00%	1.67%	21.30%	34.23%	42.80%	49.06%	53.89%	57.77%	60.97%	63.67%	65.99%	68.00%
53.00%	2.29%	23.73%	36.73%	45.14%	51.20%	55.86%	59.58%	62.64%	65.22%	67.42%	69.33%
55.00%	3.05%	26.20%	39.20%	47.43%	53.30%	57.78%	61.34%	64.27%	66.72%	68.82%	70.64%
57.00%	3.95%	28.70%	41.64%	49.67%	55.34%	59.64%	63.06%	65.85%	68.19%	70.19%	71.92%
59.00%	5.01%	31.22%	44.04%	51.85%	57.33%	61.46%	64.72%	67.39%	69.62%	71.52%	73.16%
61.00%	6.21%	33.74%	46.40%	53.99%	59.26%	63.22%	66.34%	68.88%	71.00%	72.81%	74.37%
63.00%	7.57%	36.26%	48.72%	56.07%	61.14%	64.93%	67.91%	70.33%	72.35%	74.06%	75.55%
65.00%	9.07%	38.76%	50.98%	58.09%	62.96%	66.59%	69.43%	71.73%	73.65%	75.28%	76.69%
67.00%	10.72%	41.24%	53.19%	60.06%	64.73%	68.19%	70.90%	73.09%	74.91%	76.46%	77.80%
69.00%	12.50%	43.70%	55.35%	61.97%	66.44%	69.75%	72.32%	74.41%	76.14%	77.61%	78.87%
71.00%	14.41%	46.11%	57.45%	63.82%	68.10%	71.25%	73.70%	75.68%	77.32%	78.71%	79.91%
73.00%	16.43%	48.49%	59.49%	65.60%	69.69%	72.70%	75.02%	76.90%	78.46%	79.78%	80.91%
75.00%	18.56%	50.82%	61.47%	67.33%	71.24%	74.09%	76.30%	78.09%	79.56%	80.81%	81.88%
77.00%	20.78%	53.10%	63.39%	69.00%	72.72%	75.44%	77.54%	79.22%	80.62%	81.80%	82.81%
79.00%	23.08%	55.32%	65.25%	70.61%	74.16%	76.73%	78.72%	80.32%	81.64%	82.76%	83.71%
81.00%	25.44%	57.49%	67.04%	72.16%	75.53%	77.98%	79.86%	81.37%	82.62%	83.68%	84.58%
83.00%	27.86%	59.59%	68.77%	73.66%	76.86%	79.17%	80.96%	82.39%	83.56%	84.56%	85.41%
85.00%	30.33%	61.64%	70.44%	75.09%	78.13%	80.32%	82.01%	83.36%	84.47%	85.41%	86.21%
87.00%	32.82%	63.61%	72.04%	76.47%	79.35%	81.42%	83.01%	84.29%	85.34%	86.22%	86.98%
89.00%	35.34%	65.53%	73.58%	77.79%	80.51%	82.47%	83.98%	85.18%	86.17%	87.00%	87.71%
91.00%	37.86%	67.38%	75.06%	79.05%	81.63%	83.48%	84.90%	86.03%	86.96%	87.74%	88.42%
93.00%	40.38%	69.16%	76.48%	80.26%	82.70%	84.44%	85.78%	86.84%	87.72%	88.46%	89.09%
95.00%	42.89%	70.87%	77.84%	81.42%	83.72%	85.36%	86.62%	87.62%	88.45%	89.14%	89.73%
97.00%	45.38%	72.52%	79.14%	82.52%	84.69%	86.24%	87.42%	88.36%	89.14%	89.79%	90.34%
99.00%	47.84%	74.10%	80.38%	83.57%	85.62%	87.07%	88.19%	89.07%	89.80%	90.40%	90.93%
101.00%	50.26%	75.61%	81.56%	84.58%	86.50%	87.87%	88.91%	89.74%	90.42%	90.99%	91.48%

Note: Risk-free rate is 5 percent.

TABLE 10.5   Continued

Volatility	10.00%	20.00%	30.00%	40.00%	50.00%	60.00%	70.00%	80.00%	90.00%	100.00%
1.00%	44.86%	49.46%	53.34%	56.68%	59.56%	62.09%	64.32%	66.30%	68.08%	69.67%
3.00%	44.86%	49.46%	53.34%	56.68%	59.56%	62.09%	64.32%	66.30%	68.08%	69.67%
5.00%	44.86%	49.46%	53.34%	56.68%	59.56%	62.09%	64.32%	66.30%	68.08%	69.67%
7.00%	44.88%	49.46%	53.34%	56.68%	59.56%	62.09%	64.32%	66.30%	68.08%	69.67%
9.00%	45.00%	49.51%	53.37%	56.69%	59.57%	62.09%	64.32%	66.30%	68.08%	69.67%
11.00%	45.32%	49.69%	53.46%	56.74%	59.60%	62.11%	64.33%	66.31%	68.08%	69.67%
13.00%	45.85%	50.04%	53.69%	56.88%	59.69%	62.17%	64.37%	66.33%	68.10%	69.69%
15.00%	46.59%	50.57%	54.07%	57.15%	59.88%	62.31%	64.47%	66.40%	68.15%	69.72%
17.00%	47.50%	51.27%	54.60%	57.56%	60.20%	62.55%	64.65%	66.55%	68.26%	69.81%
19.00%	48.54%	52.11%	55.28%	58.11%	60.63%	62.90%	64.93%	66.77%	68.44%	69.96%
21.00%	49.68%	53.06%	56.07%	58.76%	61.18%	63.35%	65.31%	67.09%	68.71%	70.18%
23.00%	50.90%	54.10%	56.96%	59.52%	61.83%	63.90%	65.79%	67.50%	69.05%	70.48%
25.00%	52.18%	55.22%	57.93%	60.36%	62.56%	64.54%	66.34%	67.98%	69.48%	70.85%
27.00%	53.51%	56.38%	58.96%	61.27%	63.36%	65.25%	66.97%	68.54%	69.98%	71.30%
29.00%	54.86%	57.59%	60.04%	62.24%	64.22%	66.03%	67.67%	69.17%	70.54%	71.81%
31.00%	56.24%	58.83%	61.15%	63.24%	65.13%	66.85%	68.41%	69.85%	71.16%	72.37%
33.00%	57.62%	60.09%	62.29%	64.28%	66.08%	67.71%	69.20%	70.57%	71.82%	72.98%
35.00%	59.01%	61.35%	63.45%	65.34%	67.05%	68.61%	70.03%	71.33%	72.52%	73.63%
37.00%	60.40%	62.63%	64.62%	66.42%	68.04%	69.52%	70.88%	72.12%	73.26%	74.31%
39.00%	61.79%	63.90%	65.80%	67.51%	69.05%	70.46%	71.75%	72.93%	74.02%	75.02%
41.00%	63.16%	65.17%	66.98%	68.60%	70.07%	71.41%	72.63%	73.76%	74.79%	75.75%
43.00%	64.52%	66.43%	68.15%	69.69%	71.09%	72.36%	73.53%	74.60%	75.58%	76.49%
45.00%	65.86%	67.68%	69.31%	70.78%	72.11%	73.32%	74.43%	75.44%	76.38%	77.25%
47.00%	67.18%	68.92%	70.46%	71.86%	73.12%	74.27%	75.33%	76.29%	77.18%	78.01%
49.00%	68.48%	70.13%	71.60%	72.93%	74.13%	75.22%	76.22%	77.14%	77.99%	78.77%
51.00%	69.76%	71.33%	72.73%	73.99%	75.13%	76.16%	77.11%	77.99%	78.79%	79.54%
53.00%	71.01%	72.50%	73.83%	75.03%	76.11%	77.10%	78.00%	78.83%	79.59%	80.30%
55.00%	72.24%	73.65%	74.91%	76.05%	77.08%	78.01%	78.87%	79.66%	80.38%	81.06%
57.00%	73.43%	74.78%	75.97%	77.05%	78.03%	78.92%	79.73%	80.48%	81.17%	81.80%
59.00%	74.60%	75.88%	77.01%	78.04%	78.96%	79.80%	80.57%	81.28%	81.94%	82.54%
61.00%	75.74%	76.95%	78.03%	79.00%	79.87%	80.67%	81.40%	82.08%	82.70%	83.27%
63.00%	76.84%	77.99%	79.01%	79.93%	80.77%	81.52%	82.22%	82.85%	83.44%	83.98%
65.00%	77.92%	79.01%	79.98%	80.85%	81.64%	82.35%	83.01%	83.61%	84.17%	84.68%
67.00%	78.96%	79.99%	80.91%	81.74%	82.48%	83.16%	83.78%	84.35%	84.88%	85.37%
69.00%	79.98%	80.95%	81.82%	82.60%	83.31%	83.95%	84.54%	85.08%	85.57%	86.04%
71.00%	80.95%	81.88%	82.70%	83.44%	84.11%	84.71%	85.27%	85.78%	86.25%	86.69%
73.00%	81.90%	82.77%	83.55%	84.25%	84.88%	85.46%	85.98%	86.46%	86.91%	87.32%
75.00%	82.82%	83.64%	84.38%	85.04%	85.63%	86.18%	86.67%	87.13%	87.55%	87.94%
77.00%	83.70%	84.48%	85.17%	85.80%	86.36%	86.87%	87.34%	87.77%	88.17%	88.53%
79.00%	84.55%	85.29%	85.94%	86.53%	87.06%	87.54%	87.98%	88.39%	88.76%	89.11%
81.00%	85.37%	86.06%	86.68%	87.24%	87.74%	88.19%	88.61%	88.99%	89.34%	89.67%
83.00%	86.16%	86.81%	87.39%	87.92%	88.39%	88.82%	89.21%	89.57%	89.90%	90.21%
85.00%	86.91%	87.53%	88.08%	88.57%	89.01%	89.42%	89.79%	90.13%	90.44%	90.73%
87.00%	87.64%	88.22%	88.74%	89.20%	89.62%	90.00%	90.34%	90.66%	90.96%	91.23%
89.00%	88.33%	88.88%	89.37%	89.80%	90.19%	90.55%	90.88%	91.18%	91.45%	91.71%
91.00%	89.00%	89.51%	89.97%	90.38%	90.75%	91.08%	91.39%	91.67%	91.93%	92.17%
93.00%	89.64%	90.12%	90.55%	90.93%	91.28%	91.59%	91.88%	92.15%	92.39%	92.62%
95.00%	90.25%	90.70%	91.10%	91.46%	91.79%	92.08%	92.35%	92.60%	92.83%	93.04%
97.00%	90.83%	91.25%	91.63%	91.97%	92.27%	92.55%	92.80%	93.03%	93.25%	93.45%
99.00%	91.38%	91.78%	92.13%	92.45%	92.73%	92.99%	93.23%	93.45%	93.65%	93.84%
101.00%	91.91%	92.28%	92.61%	92.91%	93.18%	93.42%	93.64%	93.85%	94.03%	94.21%

TABLE 10.6 Real Options Value—15-Year Maturity

Maturity	15	Year(s)		Risk-Free Rate	5%					
Profitability Ratio (% in-the-money)										
Volatility	**–99%**	**–90.00%**	**–80.00%**	**–70.00%**	**–60.00%**	**–50.00%**	**–40.00%**	**–30.00%**	**–20.00%**	**–10.00%**	**0.00%**
1.00%	0.00%	0.00%	0.00%	0.00%	0.00%	5.65%	21.27%	32.52%	40.95%	47.51%	52.76%
3.00%	0.00%	0.00%	0.00%	0.00%	0.43%	7.80%	21.35%	32.52%	40.95%	47.51%	52.76%
5.00%	0.00%	0.00%	0.00%	0.08%	2.27%	10.58%	22.17%	32.64%	40.97%	47.52%	52.76%
7.00%	0.00%	0.00%	0.01%	0.66%	4.84%	13.48%	23.75%	33.24%	41.16%	47.57%	52.78%
9.00%	0.00%	0.00%	0.12%	1.96%	7.70%	16.39%	25.76%	34.36%	41.71%	47.83%	52.90%
11.00%	0.00%	0.00%	0.52%	3.87%	10.71%	19.31%	27.98%	35.84%	42.63%	48.38%	53.22%
13.00%	0.00%	0.03%	1.36%	6.20%	13.77%	22.21%	30.31%	37.56%	43.84%	49.21%	53.78%
15.00%	0.00%	0.14%	2.66%	8.83%	16.86%	25.09%	32.71%	39.44%	45.27%	50.27%	54.56%
17.00%	0.00%	0.42%	4.39%	11.66%	19.95%	27.94%	35.13%	41.42%	46.84%	51.51%	55.53%
19.00%	0.00%	0.95%	6.47%	14.61%	23.02%	30.76%	37.57%	43.45%	48.52%	52.88%	56.65%
21.00%	0.00%	1.79%	8.85%	17.63%	26.06%	33.54%	39.99%	45.52%	50.27%	54.35%	57.89%
23.00%	0.00%	2.96%	11.46%	20.71%	29.07%	36.27%	42.40%	47.61%	52.06%	55.89%	59.20%
25.00%	0.00%	4.45%	14.24%	23.79%	32.04%	38.96%	44.78%	49.69%	53.87%	57.47%	60.58%
27.00%	0.02%	6.25%	17.14%	26.88%	34.95%	41.61%	47.13%	51.76%	55.70%	59.07%	61.99%
29.00%	0.05%	8.33%	20.14%	29.95%	37.82%	44.19%	49.44%	53.81%	57.52%	60.69%	63.44%
31.00%	0.13%	10.65%	23.19%	32.98%	40.63%	46.73%	51.70%	55.84%	59.33%	62.31%	64.89%
33.00%	0.27%	13.18%	26.27%	35.97%	43.37%	49.21%	53.93%	57.83%	61.12%	63.93%	66.35%
35.00%	0.50%	15.88%	29.36%	38.91%	46.06%	51.62%	56.10%	59.79%	62.88%	65.52%	67.81%
37.00%	0.87%	18.71%	32.44%	41.80%	48.67%	53.97%	58.22%	61.70%	64.62%	67.10%	69.25%
39.00%	1.39%	21.64%	35.49%	44.62%	51.22%	56.26%	60.28%	63.57%	66.31%	68.65%	70.67%
41.00%	2.11%	24.65%	38.51%	47.37%	53.69%	58.49%	62.29%	65.39%	67.97%	70.17%	72.07%
43.00%	3.03%	27.71%	41.47%	50.05%	56.09%	60.64%	64.24%	67.16%	69.59%	71.66%	73.44%
45.00%	4.17%	30.80%	44.38%	52.65%	58.41%	62.73%	66.12%	68.88%	71.17%	73.11%	74.78%
47.00%	5.54%	33.89%	47.22%	55.18%	60.66%	64.75%	67.95%	70.54%	72.70%	74.52%	76.09%
49.00%	7.15%	36.96%	49.99%	57.62%	62.83%	66.70%	69.72%	72.15%	74.18%	75.89%	77.36%
51.00%	8.98%	40.01%	52.69%	59.98%	64.93%	68.58%	71.42%	73.71%	75.61%	77.21%	78.59%
53.00%	11.03%	43.01%	55.30%	62.26%	66.94%	70.39%	73.06%	75.21%	76.99%	78.50%	79.79%
55.00%	13.28%	45.96%	57.82%	64.45%	68.88%	72.12%	74.64%	76.65%	78.32%	79.73%	80.94%
57.00%	15.70%	48.85%	60.26%	66.56%	70.74%	73.79%	76.15%	78.04%	79.60%	80.92%	82.05%
59.00%	18.30%	51.67%	62.61%	68.58%	72.52%	75.39%	77.60%	79.37%	80.83%	82.06%	83.12%
61.00%	21.03%	54.40%	64.87%	70.52%	74.23%	76.92%	78.99%	80.65%	82.01%	83.16%	84.15%
63.00%	23.87%	57.05%	67.04%	72.37%	75.86%	78.38%	80.32%	81.86%	83.14%	84.21%	85.13%
65.00%	26.81%	59.61%	69.11%	74.14%	77.41%	79.77%	81.58%	83.03%	84.22%	85.22%	86.07%
67.00%	29.82%	62.08%	71.09%	75.82%	78.89%	81.10%	82.79%	84.14%	85.24%	86.17%	86.97%
69.00%	32.88%	64.45%	72.99%	77.43%	80.30%	82.36%	83.94%	85.19%	86.22%	87.09%	87.83%
71.00%	35.96%	66.73%	74.79%	78.95%	81.64%	83.56%	85.03%	86.19%	87.15%	87.95%	88.64%
73.00%	39.05%	68.90%	76.50%	80.40%	82.91%	84.70%	86.06%	87.14%	88.03%	88.78%	89.42%
75.00%	42.12%	70.98%	78.13%	81.77%	84.11%	85.77%	87.04%	88.04%	88.87%	89.56%	90.15%
77.00%	45.17%	72.96%	79.67%	83.07%	85.24%	86.79%	87.96%	88.90%	89.66%	90.30%	90.85%
79.00%	48.18%	74.84%	81.13%	84.30%	86.31%	87.75%	88.84%	89.70%	90.41%	91.00%	91.51%
81.00%	51.13%	76.62%	82.50%	85.45%	87.32%	88.65%	89.66%	90.46%	91.11%	91.66%	92.13%
83.00%	54.01%	78.31%	83.80%	86.54%	88.28%	89.50%	90.44%	91.17%	91.78%	92.28%	92.71%
85.00%	56.81%	79.91%	85.02%	87.56%	89.17%	90.30%	91.16%	91.85%	92.40%	92.87%	93.26%
87.00%	59.53%	81.42%	86.17%	88.52%	90.01%	91.06%	91.85%	92.48%	92.99%	93.42%	93.78%
89.00%	62.15%	82.83%	87.25%	89.42%	90.79%	91.76%	92.49%	93.07%	93.54%	93.93%	94.27%
91.00%	64.67%	84.16%	88.26%	90.27%	91.53%	92.42%	93.09%	93.62%	94.05%	94.41%	94.72%
93.00%	67.09%	85.41%	89.20%	91.05%	92.21%	93.03%	93.65%	94.13%	94.53%	94.86%	95.15%
95.00%	69.41%	86.58%	90.08%	91.79%	92.85%	93.60%	94.17%	94.62%	94.98%	95.28%	95.54%
97.00%	71.61%	87.68%	90.90%	92.47%	93.45%	94.14%	94.66%	95.06%	95.40%	95.68%	95.91%
99.00%	73.70%	88.70%	91.67%	93.11%	94.00%	94.63%	95.11%	95.48%	95.79%	96.04%	96.26%
101.00%	75.69%	89.65%	92.38%	93.70%	94.52%	95.09%	95.53%	95.87%	96.15%	96.38%	96.58%

Note: Risk-free rate is 5 percent.

TABLE 10.6 Continued

Volatility	10.00%	20.00%	30.00%	40.00%	50.00%	60.00%	70.00%	80.00%	90.00%	100.00%
1.00%	57.06%	60.64%	63.66%	66.26%	68.51%	70.48%	72.21%	73.76%	75.14%	76.38%
3.00%	57.06%	60.64%	63.66%	66.26%	68.51%	70.48%	72.21%	73.76%	75.14%	76.38%
5.00%	57.06%	60.64%	63.66%	66.26%	68.51%	70.48%	72.21%	73.76%	75.14%	76.38%
7.00%	57.06%	60.64%	63.66%	66.26%	68.51%	70.48%	72.21%	73.76%	75.14%	76.38%
9.00%	57.11%	60.66%	63.68%	66.26%	68.51%	70.48%	72.21%	73.76%	75.14%	76.38%
11.00%	57.30%	60.77%	63.74%	66.30%	68.53%	70.49%	72.22%	73.76%	75.14%	76.38%
13.00%	57.68%	61.02%	63.91%	66.42%	68.61%	70.54%	72.26%	73.79%	75.16%	76.40%
15.00%	58.26%	61.45%	64.22%	66.65%	68.78%	70.67%	72.36%	73.86%	75.22%	76.44%
17.00%	59.02%	62.04%	64.69%	67.02%	69.08%	70.91%	72.54%	74.01%	75.33%	76.53%
19.00%	59.93%	62.79%	65.30%	67.52%	69.49%	71.25%	72.82%	74.25%	75.53%	76.70%
21.00%	60.96%	63.66%	66.03%	68.14%	70.02%	71.70%	73.21%	74.58%	75.82%	76.95%
23.00%	62.09%	64.63%	66.87%	68.87%	70.65%	72.25%	73.69%	75.00%	76.19%	77.27%
25.00%	63.29%	65.68%	67.80%	69.68%	71.37%	72.88%	74.26%	75.50%	76.64%	77.68%
27.00%	64.55%	66.79%	68.79%	70.56%	72.16%	73.59%	74.89%	76.08%	77.16%	78.15%
29.00%	65.84%	67.95%	69.83%	71.50%	73.00%	74.36%	75.59%	76.72%	77.74%	78.68%
31.00%	67.15%	69.14%	70.90%	72.48%	73.90%	75.18%	76.34%	77.40%	78.38%	79.27%
33.00%	68.47%	70.34%	72.00%	73.49%	74.82%	76.03%	77.13%	78.13%	79.05%	79.90%
35.00%	69.80%	71.56%	73.12%	74.52%	75.77%	76.91%	77.95%	78.89%	79.76%	80.56%
37.00%	71.12%	72.77%	74.24%	75.55%	76.74%	77.81%	78.79%	79.68%	80.50%	81.25%
39.00%	72.43%	73.98%	75.36%	76.60%	77.71%	78.72%	79.64%	80.48%	81.25%	81.96%
41.00%	73.72%	75.18%	76.48%	77.64%	78.68%	79.63%	80.49%	81.28%	82.01%	82.68%
43.00%	74.99%	76.36%	77.58%	78.67%	79.65%	80.54%	81.35%	82.09%	82.78%	83.41%
45.00%	76.24%	77.52%	78.66%	79.69%	80.61%	81.44%	82.21%	82.90%	83.55%	84.14%
47.00%	77.46%	78.66%	79.73%	80.69%	81.55%	82.34%	83.05%	83.71%	84.31%	84.87%
49.00%	78.64%	79.77%	80.77%	81.67%	82.48%	83.22%	83.89%	84.50%	85.06%	85.59%
51.00%	79.79%	80.85%	81.79%	82.63%	83.39%	84.08%	84.70%	85.28%	85.81%	86.30%
53.00%	80.91%	81.90%	82.78%	83.56%	84.27%	84.92%	85.51%	86.04%	86.54%	87.00%
55.00%	81.99%	82.92%	83.74%	84.47%	85.14%	85.74%	86.29%	86.79%	87.25%	87.68%
57.00%	83.03%	83.90%	84.66%	85.35%	85.97%	86.53%	87.05%	87.52%	87.95%	88.35%
59.00%	84.04%	84.84%	85.56%	86.20%	86.78%	87.31%	87.78%	88.22%	88.63%	89.00%
61.00%	85.00%	85.75%	86.42%	87.02%	87.56%	88.05%	88.50%	88.91%	89.28%	89.63%
63.00%	85.93%	86.63%	87.25%	87.81%	88.31%	88.77%	89.18%	89.57%	89.92%	90.24%
65.00%	86.81%	87.47%	88.05%	88.57%	89.03%	89.46%	89.85%	90.20%	90.53%	90.83%
67.00%	87.66%	88.27%	88.81%	89.29%	89.73%	90.12%	90.48%	90.81%	91.11%	91.40%
69.00%	88.47%	89.03%	89.53%	89.98%	90.39%	90.75%	91.09%	91.39%	91.68%	91.94%
71.00%	89.24%	89.76%	90.23%	90.64%	91.02%	91.36%	91.67%	91.95%	92.22%	92.46%
73.00%	89.97%	90.46%	90.89%	91.27%	91.62%	91.94%	92.22%	92.49%	92.73%	92.96%
75.00%	90.67%	91.12%	91.51%	91.87%	92.19%	92.49%	92.75%	93.00%	93.22%	93.43%
77.00%	91.32%	91.74%	92.11%	92.44%	92.74%	93.01%	93.25%	93.48%	93.69%	93.88%
79.00%	91.95%	92.33%	92.67%	92.98%	93.25%	93.50%	93.73%	93.94%	94.13%	94.31%
81.00%	92.53%	92.89%	93.20%	93.49%	93.74%	93.97%	94.18%	94.37%	94.55%	94.71%
83.00%	93.09%	93.42%	93.71%	93.97%	94.20%	94.41%	94.61%	94.78%	94.95%	95.10%
85.00%	93.61%	93.91%	94.18%	94.42%	94.63%	94.83%	95.01%	95.17%	95.32%	95.46%
87.00%	94.10%	94.38%	94.62%	94.84%	95.04%	95.22%	95.39%	95.54%	95.67%	95.80%
89.00%	94.56%	94.81%	95.04%	95.24%	95.42%	95.59%	95.74%	95.88%	96.01%	96.12%
91.00%	94.99%	95.22%	95.43%	95.62%	95.78%	95.94%	96.07%	96.20%	96.32%	96.43%
93.00%	95.39%	95.61%	95.80%	95.97%	96.12%	96.26%	96.39%	96.50%	96.61%	96.71%
95.00%	95.77%	95.97%	96.14%	96.30%	96.44%	96.56%	96.68%	96.79%	96.88%	96.97%
97.00%	96.12%	96.30%	96.46%	96.60%	96.73%	96.85%	96.95%	97.05%	97.14%	97.22%
99.00%	96.45%	96.61%	96.76%	96.89%	97.00%	97.11%	97.21%	97.29%	97.38%	97.45%
101.00%	96.75%	96.90%	97.03%	97.15%	97.26%	97.35%	97.44%	97.52%	97.60%	97.67%

TABLE 10.7 Real Options Value—30-Year Maturity

Maturity	30	Year(s)		Risk-Free Rate 5%							
Profitability Ratio (% in-the-money)											
Volatility	–99%	–90.00%	–80.00%	–70.00%	–60.00%	–50.00%	–40.00%	–30.00%	–20.00%	–10.00%	0.00%
1.00%	0.00%	0.00%	0.05%	25.62%	44.22%	55.37%	62.81%	68.12%	72.11%	75.21%	77.69%
3.00%	0.00%	0.00%	2.62%	25.82%	44.22%	55.37%	62.81%	68.12%	72.11%	75.21%	77.69%
5.00%	0.00%	0.02%	6.64%	27.30%	44.34%	55.38%	62.81%	68.12%	72.11%	75.21%	77.69%
7.00%	0.00%	0.37%	10.94%	29.75%	45.00%	55.54%	62.85%	68.13%	72.11%	75.21%	77.69%
9.00%	0.00%	1.57%	15.31%	32.67%	46.31%	56.06%	63.06%	68.22%	72.15%	75.22%	77.69%
11.00%	0.00%	3.71%	19.66%	35.80%	48.08%	57.01%	63.56%	68.49%	72.30%	75.31%	77.74%
13.00%	0.00%	6.63%	23.98%	39.03%	50.16%	58.30%	64.37%	69.00%	72.63%	75.53%	77.89%
15.00%	0.01%	10.13%	28.22%	42.28%	52.43%	59.86%	65.45%	69.76%	73.16%	75.91%	78.17%
17.00%	0.04%	14.03%	32.38%	45.51%	54.80%	61.59%	66.72%	70.71%	73.89%	76.47%	78.61%
19.00%	0.18%	18.17%	36.44%	48.70%	57.23%	63.44%	68.15%	71.83%	74.77%	77.18%	79.18%
21.00%	0.50%	22.46%	40.40%	51.83%	59.66%	65.36%	69.67%	73.06%	75.78%	78.01%	79.88%
23.00%	1.13%	26.82%	44.23%	54.88%	62.08%	67.30%	71.26%	74.37%	76.87%	78.94%	80.67%
25.00%	2.15%	31.19%	47.94%	57.84%	64.47%	69.25%	72.88%	75.73%	78.03%	79.94%	81.53%
27.00%	3.64%	35.51%	51.51%	60.70%	66.79%	71.18%	74.50%	77.11%	79.23%	80.98%	82.45%
29.00%	5.62%	39.75%	54.94%	63.46%	69.06%	73.07%	76.11%	78.51%	80.45%	82.05%	83.41%
31.00%	8.09%	43.88%	58.22%	66.10%	71.24%	74.92%	77.70%	79.89%	81.66%	83.13%	84.38%
33.00%	11.01%	47.89%	61.36%	68.63%	73.35%	76.71%	79.25%	81.25%	82.87%	84.21%	85.35%
35.00%	14.34%	51.74%	64.35%	71.04%	75.36%	78.43%	80.75%	82.57%	84.05%	85.28%	86.32%
37.00%	18.02%	55.44%	67.18%	73.34%	77.28%	80.08%	82.19%	83.85%	85.20%	86.32%	87.27%
39.00%	21.96%	58.96%	69.87%	75.51%	79.11%	81.66%	83.58%	85.09%	86.31%	87.33%	88.19%
41.00%	26.11%	62.31%	72.40%	77.56%	80.84%	83.15%	84.90%	86.27%	87.38%	88.31%	89.09%
43.00%	30.39%	65.48%	74.78%	79.49%	82.47%	84.57%	86.15%	87.39%	88.40%	89.24%	89.95%
45.00%	34.74%	68.47%	77.01%	81.30%	84.00%	85.90%	87.34%	88.46%	89.37%	90.13%	90.77%
47.00%	39.11%	71.28%	79.09%	82.99%	85.44%	87.16%	88.45%	89.47%	90.29%	90.98%	91.56%
49.00%	43.44%	73.90%	81.04%	84.57%	86.78%	88.33%	89.50%	90.41%	91.16%	91.77%	92.30%
51.00%	47.69%	76.35%	82.84%	86.04%	88.03%	89.43%	90.48%	91.30%	91.97%	92.52%	92.99%
53.00%	51.82%	78.63%	84.52%	87.40%	89.19%	90.44%	91.39%	92.12%	92.72%	93.22%	93.64%
55.00%	55.80%	80.74%	86.06%	88.65%	90.26%	91.39%	92.23%	92.89%	93.43%	93.87%	94.25%
57.00%	59.62%	82.68%	87.49%	89.81%	91.25%	92.26%	93.01%	93.60%	94.08%	94.48%	94.82%
59.00%	63.24%	84.47%	88.79%	90.87%	92.16%	93.06%	93.73%	94.26%	94.68%	95.04%	95.34%
61.00%	66.67%	86.12%	89.99%	91.85%	92.99%	93.79%	94.39%	94.86%	95.24%	95.55%	95.82%
63.00%	69.88%	87.62%	91.08%	92.73%	93.75%	94.46%	95.00%	95.41%	95.75%	96.03%	96.27%
65.00%	72.88%	88.99%	92.07%	93.54%	94.45%	95.08%	95.55%	95.91%	96.21%	96.46%	96.67%
67.00%	75.67%	90.23%	92.98%	94.28%	95.08%	95.63%	96.05%	96.37%	96.64%	96.86%	97.04%
69.00%	78.25%	91.36%	93.79%	94.94%	95.65%	96.14%	96.50%	96.79%	97.02%	97.21%	97.38%
71.00%	80.61%	92.38%	94.53%	95.54%	96.16%	96.59%	96.91%	97.16%	97.37%	97.54%	97.68%
73.00%	82.78%	93.29%	95.19%	96.08%	96.62%	97.00%	97.28%	97.50%	97.68%	97.83%	97.96%
75.00%	84.76%	94.11%	95.78%	96.56%	97.04%	97.37%	97.61%	97.81%	97.96%	98.09%	98.20%
77.00%	86.55%	94.85%	96.31%	96.99%	97.41%	97.70%	97.91%	98.08%	98.22%	98.33%	98.43%
79.00%	88.17%	95.50%	96.78%	97.37%	97.74%	97.99%	98.18%	98.32%	98.44%	98.54%	98.62%
81.00%	89.63%	96.09%	97.20%	97.72%	98.03%	98.25%	98.41%	98.54%	98.64%	98.73%	98.80%
83.00%	90.93%	96.60%	97.57%	98.02%	98.29%	98.48%	98.62%	98.73%	98.82%	98.90%	98.96%
85.00%	92.10%	97.06%	97.90%	98.28%	98.52%	98.68%	98.81%	98.90%	98.98%	99.04%	99.10%
87.00%	93.14%	97.46%	98.18%	98.52%	98.72%	98.86%	98.97%	99.05%	99.12%	99.17%	99.22%
89.00%	94.06%	97.81%	98.44%	98.73%	98.90%	99.02%	99.11%	99.18%	99.24%	99.29%	99.33%
91.00%	94.87%	98.12%	98.66%	98.91%	99.06%	99.16%	99.24%	99.30%	99.35%	99.39%	99.42%
93.00%	95.58%	98.39%	98.85%	99.06%	99.19%	99.28%	99.35%	99.40%	99.44%	99.48%	99.50%
95.00%	96.21%	98.63%	99.02%	99.20%	99.31%	99.39%	99.44%	99.49%	99.52%	99.55%	99.58%
97.00%	96.76%	98.83%	99.17%	99.32%	99.41%	99.48%	99.53%	99.56%	99.59%	99.62%	99.64%
99.00%	97.23%	99.01%	99.29%	99.42%	99.50%	99.56%	99.60%	99.63%	99.65%	99.68%	99.69%
101.00%	97.65%	99.16%	99.40%	99.51%	99.58%	99.62%	99.66%	99.69%	99.71%	99.72%	99.74%

Note: Risk-free rate is 5 percent.

TABLE 10.7 Continued

Volatility	10.00%	20.00%	30.00%	40.00%	50.00%	60.00%	70.00%	80.00%	90.00%	100.00%
1.00%	79.72%	81.41%	82.84%	84.06%	85.12%	86.05%	86.87%	87.60%	88.26%	88.84%
3.00%	79.72%	81.41%	82.84%	84.06%	85.12%	86.05%	86.87%	87.60%	88.26%	88.84%
5.00%	79.72%	81.41%	82.84%	84.06%	85.12%	86.05%	86.87%	87.60%	88.26%	88.84%
7.00%	79.72%	81.41%	82.84%	84.06%	85.12%	86.05%	86.87%	87.60%	88.26%	88.84%
9.00%	79.72%	81.41%	82.84%	84.06%	85.12%	86.05%	86.87%	87.60%	88.26%	88.84%
11.00%	79.75%	81.43%	82.85%	84.07%	85.13%	86.06%	86.88%	87.61%	88.26%	88.84%
13.00%	79.85%	81.49%	82.90%	84.10%	85.15%	86.08%	86.89%	87.62%	88.26%	88.85%
15.00%	80.06%	81.65%	83.02%	84.20%	85.23%	86.13%	86.94%	87.65%	88.29%	88.87%
17.00%	80.40%	81.92%	83.24%	84.37%	85.37%	86.25%	87.03%	87.73%	88.36%	88.93%
19.00%	80.87%	82.31%	83.56%	84.65%	85.60%	86.45%	87.20%	87.88%	88.49%	89.04%
21.00%	81.46%	82.81%	83.99%	85.01%	85.92%	86.73%	87.45%	88.09%	88.68%	89.21%
23.00%	82.14%	83.40%	84.50%	85.47%	86.32%	87.08%	87.77%	88.38%	88.94%	89.44%
25.00%	82.90%	84.07%	85.10%	86.00%	86.80%	87.51%	88.15%	88.73%	89.26%	89.74%
27.00%	83.71%	84.80%	85.75%	86.59%	87.33%	88.00%	88.60%	89.14%	89.63%	90.08%
29.00%	84.57%	85.57%	86.45%	87.22%	87.91%	88.53%	89.09%	89.59%	90.05%	90.47%
31.00%	85.44%	86.36%	87.17%	87.89%	88.53%	89.10%	89.61%	90.08%	90.51%	90.90%
33.00%	86.33%	87.17%	87.92%	88.57%	89.16%	89.69%	90.16%	90.60%	90.99%	91.35%
35.00%	87.21%	87.99%	88.67%	89.27%	89.81%	90.29%	90.73%	91.13%	91.49%	91.83%
37.00%	88.08%	88.79%	89.41%	89.96%	90.46%	90.90%	91.30%	91.67%	92.00%	92.31%
39.00%	88.94%	89.58%	90.15%	90.65%	91.10%	91.51%	91.87%	92.21%	92.52%	92.80%
41.00%	89.76%	90.35%	90.87%	91.33%	91.74%	92.11%	92.44%	92.75%	93.02%	93.28%
43.00%	90.56%	91.10%	91.56%	91.98%	92.35%	92.69%	92.99%	93.27%	93.53%	93.76%
45.00%	91.33%	91.81%	92.23%	92.61%	92.95%	93.25%	93.53%	93.78%	94.01%	94.23%
47.00%	92.06%	92.49%	92.88%	93.22%	93.52%	93.80%	94.05%	94.28%	94.49%	94.68%
49.00%	92.75%	93.14%	93.48%	93.79%	94.07%	94.32%	94.54%	94.75%	94.94%	95.11%
51.00%	93.40%	93.75%	94.06%	94.34%	94.59%	94.81%	95.01%	95.20%	95.37%	95.53%
53.00%	94.01%	94.32%	94.60%	94.85%	95.08%	95.28%	95.46%	95.63%	95.78%	95.92%
55.00%	94.58%	94.86%	95.11%	95.33%	95.53%	95.71%	95.88%	96.03%	96.17%	96.29%
57.00%	95.11%	95.36%	95.59%	95.78%	95.96%	96.12%	96.27%	96.40%	96.53%	96.64%
59.00%	95.60%	95.83%	96.02%	96.20%	96.36%	96.51%	96.64%	96.76%	96.87%	96.97%
61.00%	96.05%	96.25%	96.43%	96.59%	96.73%	96.86%	96.98%	97.08%	97.18%	97.27%
63.00%	96.47%	96.65%	96.81%	96.95%	97.07%	97.19%	97.29%	97.38%	97.47%	97.55%
65.00%	96.85%	97.01%	97.15%	97.27%	97.38%	97.49%	97.58%	97.66%	97.74%	97.81%
67.00%	97.20%	97.34%	97.46%	97.57%	97.67%	97.76%	97.84%	97.91%	97.98%	98.05%
69.00%	97.52%	97.64%	97.75%	97.85%	97.93%	98.01%	98.08%	98.15%	98.21%	98.26%
71.00%	97.81%	97.91%	98.01%	98.09%	98.17%	98.24%	98.30%	98.36%	98.41%	98.46%
73.00%	98.07%	98.16%	98.24%	98.32%	98.38%	98.44%	98.50%	98.55%	98.60%	98.64%
75.00%	98.30%	98.38%	98.45%	98.52%	98.58%	98.63%	98.68%	98.72%	98.76%	98.80%
77.00%	98.51%	98.58%	98.64%	98.70%	98.75%	98.80%	98.84%	98.88%	98.91%	98.95%
79.00%	98.70%	98.76%	98.81%	98.86%	98.91%	98.95%	98.98%	99.02%	99.05%	99.08%
81.00%	98.86%	98.92%	98.97%	99.01%	99.05%	99.08%	99.11%	99.14%	99.17%	99.19%
83.00%	99.01%	99.06%	99.10%	99.14%	99.17%	99.20%	99.23%	99.25%	99.28%	99.30%
85.00%	99.14%	99.18%	99.22%	99.25%	99.28%	99.31%	99.33%	99.35%	99.37%	99.39%
87.00%	99.26%	99.29%	99.33%	99.35%	99.38%	99.40%	99.42%	99.44%	99.46%	99.47%
89.00%	99.36%	99.39%	99.42%	99.44%	99.46%	99.48%	99.50%	99.52%	99.53%	99.54%
91.00%	99.45%	99.48%	99.50%	99.52%	99.54%	99.55%	99.57%	99.58%	99.60%	99.61%
93.00%	99.53%	99.55%	99.57%	99.59%	99.60%	99.62%	99.63%	99.64%	99.65%	99.66%
95.00%	99.60%	99.62%	99.63%	99.65%	99.66%	99.67%	99.68%	99.69%	99.70%	99.71%
97.00%	99.66%	99.67%	99.69%	99.70%	99.71%	99.72%	99.73%	99.74%	99.75%	99.75%
99.00%	99.71%	99.72%	99.73%	99.74%	99.75%	99.76%	99.77%	99.78%	99.78%	99.79%
101.00%	99.75%	99.76%	99.77%	99.78%	99.79%	99.80%	99.81%	99.81%	99.82%	99.82%

IMPLIED VOLATILITY TABLES

Tables 10.8 and 10.9 show the implied volatility of a project based on management's estimated minimum or maximum values of an asset at the end of the maturity term. The columns list the maximum step-size ratio and minimum step-size ratio. The rows list the maturity of the option. The risk-free rate or implementation costs are irrelevant in this analysis. Notice that the higher (lower) the step-size ratio on the maximum (minimum) value, the higher (lower) the volatility. In addition, the longer the maturity, with the same step-size ratio, the lower the implied volatility.

Example

Suppose management agrees that the maximum possible asset value of a particular project with a strategic option with 5-year expiration is $300 million at the end of this 5-year horizon. Further, suppose the net present value of the project is currently valued at $100 million. Find the implied volatility of this project.

Using the implied volatility table for maximum values, the maximum step size is $300 million divided by $100 million or 3.0, with a 5-year maturity. The resulting implied volatility of the project is found to be 21.97 percent. Another way to look at it is to build a simple five-step lattice (Figure 10.1), with a starting asset value of $100 million, a volatility of 21.97 percent, with a 5-year maturity.

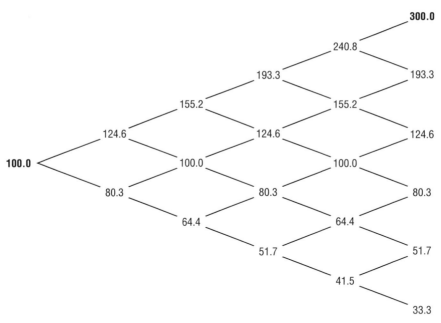

FIGURE 10.1 Simple five-step lattice.

TABLE 10.8 Implied Volatility—Maximum Terminal Values

Maturity	Maximum Step Size Ratio (Max/Now)									
	1.50	2.00	2.50	3.00	3.50	4.00	4.50	5.00	5.50	6.00
0.25	162.19%	277.26%	366.52%	439.44%	501.11%	554.52%	601.63%	643.78%	681.90%	716.70%
0.50	81.09%	138.63%	183.26%	219.72%	250.55%	277.26%	300.82%	321.89%	340.95%	358.35%
0.75	54.06%	92.42%	122.17%	146.48%	167.04%	184.84%	200.54%	214.59%	227.30%	238.90%
1.00	40.55%	69.31%	91.63%	109.86%	125.28%	138.63%	150.41%	160.94%	170.47%	179.18%
1.25	32.44%	55.45%	73.30%	87.89%	100.22%	110.90%	120.33%	128.76%	136.38%	143.34%
1.50	27.03%	46.21%	61.09%	73.24%	83.52%	92.42%	100.27%	107.30%	113.65%	119.45%
1.75	23.17%	39.61%	52.36%	62.78%	71.59%	79.22%	85.95%	91.97%	97.41%	102.39%
2.00	20.27%	34.66%	45.81%	54.93%	62.64%	69.31%	75.20%	80.47%	85.24%	89.59%
2.25	18.02%	30.81%	40.72%	48.83%	55.68%	61.61%	66.85%	71.53%	75.77%	79.63%
2.50	16.22%	27.73%	36.65%	43.94%	50.11%	55.45%	60.16%	64.38%	68.19%	71.67%
2.75	14.74%	25.21%	33.32%	39.95%	45.56%	50.41%	54.69%	58.53%	61.99%	65.15%
3.00	13.52%	23.10%	30.54%	36.62%	41.76%	46.21%	50.14%	53.65%	56.82%	59.73%
3.25	12.48%	21.33%	28.19%	33.80%	38.55%	42.66%	46.28%	49.52%	52.45%	55.13%
3.50	11.58%	19.80%	26.18%	31.39%	35.79%	39.61%	42.97%	45.98%	48.71%	51.19%
3.75	10.81%	18.48%	24.43%	29.30%	33.41%	36.97%	40.11%	42.92%	45.46%	47.78%
4.00	10.14%	17.33%	22.91%	27.47%	31.32%	34.66%	37.60%	40.24%	42.62%	44.79%
4.25	9.54%	16.31%	21.56%	25.85%	29.48%	32.62%	35.39%	37.87%	40.11%	42.16%
4.50	9.01%	15.40%	20.36%	24.41%	27.84%	30.81%	33.42%	35.77%	37.88%	39.82%
4.75	8.54%	14.59%	19.29%	23.13%	26.37%	29.19%	31.66%	33.88%	35.89%	37.72%
5.00	8.11%	13.86%	18.33%	21.97%	25.06%	27.73%	30.08%	32.19%	34.09%	35.84%
5.25	7.72%	13.20%	17.45%	20.93%	23.86%	26.41%	28.65%	30.66%	32.47%	34.13%
5.50	7.37%	12.60%	16.66%	19.97%	22.78%	25.21%	27.35%	29.26%	31.00%	32.58%
5.75	7.05%	12.05%	15.94%	19.11%	21.79%	24.11%	26.16%	27.99%	29.65%	31.16%
6.00	6.76%	11.55%	15.27%	18.31%	20.88%	23.10%	25.07%	26.82%	28.41%	29.86%
6.25	6.49%	11.09%	14.66%	17.58%	20.04%	22.18%	24.07%	25.75%	27.28%	28.67%
6.50	6.24%	10.66%	14.10%	16.90%	19.27%	21.33%	23.14%	24.76%	26.23%	27.57%
6.75	6.01%	10.27%	13.57%	16.28%	18.56%	20.54%	22.28%	23.84%	25.26%	26.54%
7.00	5.79%	9.90%	13.09%	15.69%	17.90%	19.80%	21.49%	22.99%	24.35%	25.60%
7.25	5.59%	9.56%	12.64%	15.15%	17.28%	19.12%	20.75%	22.20%	23.51%	24.71%
7.50	5.41%	9.24%	12.22%	14.65%	16.70%	18.48%	20.05%	21.46%	22.73%	23.89%
7.75	5.23%	8.94%	11.82%	14.18%	16.16%	17.89%	19.41%	20.77%	22.00%	23.12%
8.00	5.07%	8.66%	11.45%	13.73%	15.66%	17.33%	18.80%	20.12%	21.31%	22.40%
8.25	4.91%	8.40%	11.11%	13.32%	15.19%	16.80%	18.23%	19.51%	20.66%	21.72%
8.50	4.77%	8.15%	10.78%	12.92%	14.74%	16.31%	17.70%	18.93%	20.06%	21.08%
8.75	4.63%	7.92%	10.47%	12.56%	14.32%	15.84%	17.19%	18.39%	19.48%	20.48%
9.00	4.51%	7.70%	10.18%	12.21%	13.92%	15.40%	16.71%	17.88%	18.94%	19.91%
9.25	4.38%	7.49%	9.91%	11.88%	13.54%	14.99%	16.26%	17.40%	18.43%	19.37%
9.50	4.27%	7.30%	9.65%	11.56%	13.19%	14.59%	15.83%	16.94%	17.94%	18.86%
9.75	4.16%	7.11%	9.40%	11.27%	12.85%	14.22%	15.43%	16.51%	17.48%	18.38%
10.00	4.05%	6.93%	9.16%	10.99%	12.53%	13.86%	15.04%	16.09%	17.05%	17.92%
10.25	3.96%	6.76%	8.94%	10.72%	12.22%	13.52%	14.67%	15.70%	16.63%	17.48%
10.50	3.86%	6.60%	8.73%	10.46%	11.93%	13.20%	14.32%	15.33%	16.24%	17.06%
10.75	3.77%	6.45%	8.52%	10.22%	11.65%	12.90%	13.99%	14.97%	15.86%	16.67%
11.00	3.69%	6.30%	8.33%	9.99%	11.39%	12.60%	13.67%	14.63%	15.50%	16.29%
11.25	3.60%	6.16%	8.14%	9.77%	11.14%	12.32%	13.37%	14.31%	15.15%	15.93%
11.50	3.53%	6.03%	7.97%	9.55%	10.89%	12.05%	13.08%	14.00%	14.82%	15.58%
11.75	3.45%	5.90%	7.80%	9.35%	10.66%	11.80%	12.80%	13.70%	14.51%	15.25%
12.00	3.38%	5.78%	7.64%	9.16%	10.44%	11.55%	12.53%	13.41%	14.21%	14.93%

TABLE 10.8 Continued

Maturity	6.50	7.00	7.50	8.00	8.50	9.00	9.50	10.00	10.50	11.00
0.25	748.72%	778.36%	805.96%	831.78%	856.03%	878.89%	900.52%	921.03%	940.55%	959.16%
0.50	374.36%	389.18%	402.98%	415.89%	428.01%	439.44%	450.26%	460.52%	470.28%	479.58%
0.75	249.57%	259.45%	268.65%	277.26%	285.34%	292.96%	300.17%	307.01%	313.52%	319.72%
1.00	187.18%	194.59%	201.49%	207.94%	214.01%	219.72%	225.13%	230.26%	235.14%	239.79%
1.25	149.74%	155.67%	161.19%	166.36%	171.21%	175.78%	180.10%	184.21%	188.11%	191.83%
1.50	124.79%	129.73%	134.33%	138.63%	142.67%	146.48%	150.09%	153.51%	156.76%	159.86%
1.75	106.96%	111.19%	115.14%	118.83%	122.29%	125.56%	128.65%	131.58%	134.36%	137.02%
2.00	93.59%	97.30%	100.75%	103.97%	107.00%	109.86%	112.56%	115.13%	117.57%	119.89%
2.25	83.19%	86.48%	89.55%	92.42%	95.11%	97.65%	100.06%	102.34%	104.51%	106.57%
2.50	74.87%	77.84%	80.60%	83.18%	85.60%	87.89%	90.05%	92.10%	94.06%	95.92%
2.75	68.07%	70.76%	73.27%	75.62%	77.82%	79.90%	81.87%	83.73%	85.50%	87.20%
3.00	62.39%	64.86%	67.16%	69.31%	71.34%	73.24%	75.04%	76.75%	78.38%	79.93%
3.25	57.59%	59.87%	62.00%	63.98%	65.85%	67.61%	69.27%	70.85%	72.35%	73.78%
3.50	53.48%	55.60%	57.57%	59.41%	61.14%	62.78%	64.32%	65.79%	67.18%	68.51%
3.75	49.91%	51.89%	53.73%	55.45%	57.07%	58.59%	60.03%	61.40%	62.70%	63.94%
4.00	46.80%	48.65%	50.37%	51.99%	53.50%	54.93%	56.28%	57.56%	58.78%	59.95%
4.25	44.04%	45.79%	47.41%	48.93%	50.35%	51.70%	52.97%	54.18%	55.33%	56.42%
4.50	41.60%	43.24%	44.78%	46.21%	47.56%	48.83%	50.03%	51.17%	52.25%	53.29%
4.75	39.41%	40.97%	42.42%	43.78%	45.05%	46.26%	47.40%	48.48%	49.50%	50.48%
5.00	37.44%	38.92%	40.30%	41.59%	42.80%	43.94%	45.03%	46.05%	47.03%	47.96%
5.25	35.65%	37.06%	38.38%	39.61%	40.76%	41.85%	42.88%	43.86%	44.79%	45.67%
5.50	34.03%	35.38%	36.63%	37.81%	38.91%	39.95%	40.93%	41.87%	42.75%	43.60%
5.75	32.55%	33.84%	35.04%	36.16%	37.22%	38.21%	39.15%	40.04%	40.89%	41.70%
6.00	31.20%	32.43%	33.58%	34.66%	35.67%	36.62%	37.52%	38.38%	39.19%	39.96%
6.25	29.95%	31.13%	32.24%	33.27%	34.24%	35.16%	36.02%	36.84%	37.62%	38.37%
6.50	28.80%	29.94%	31.00%	31.99%	32.92%	33.80%	34.64%	35.42%	36.18%	36.89%
6.75	27.73%	28.83%	29.85%	30.81%	31.70%	32.55%	33.35%	34.11%	34.84%	35.52%
7.00	26.74%	27.80%	28.78%	29.71%	30.57%	31.39%	32.16%	32.89%	33.59%	34.26%
7.25	25.82%	26.84%	27.79%	28.68%	29.52%	30.31%	31.05%	31.76%	32.43%	33.07%
7.50	24.96%	25.95%	26.87%	27.73%	28.53%	29.30%	30.02%	30.70%	31.35%	31.97%
7.75	24.15%	25.11%	26.00%	26.83%	27.61%	28.35%	29.05%	29.71%	30.34%	30.94%
8.00	23.40%	24.32%	25.19%	25.99%	26.75%	27.47%	28.14%	28.78%	29.39%	29.97%
8.25	22.69%	23.59%	24.42%	25.21%	25.94%	26.63%	27.29%	27.91%	28.50%	29.07%
8.50	22.02%	22.89%	23.70%	24.46%	25.18%	25.85%	26.49%	27.09%	27.66%	28.21%
8.75	21.39%	22.24%	23.03%	23.77%	24.46%	25.11%	25.73%	26.32%	26.87%	27.40%
9.00	20.80%	21.62%	22.39%	23.10%	23.78%	24.41%	25.01%	25.58%	26.13%	26.64%
9.25	20.24%	21.04%	21.78%	22.48%	23.14%	23.75%	24.34%	24.89%	25.42%	25.92%
9.50	19.70%	20.48%	21.21%	21.89%	22.53%	23.13%	23.70%	24.24%	24.75%	25.24%
9.75	19.20%	19.96%	20.67%	21.33%	21.95%	22.54%	23.09%	23.62%	24.12%	24.59%
10.00	18.72%	19.46%	20.15%	20.79%	21.40%	21.97%	22.51%	23.03%	23.51%	23.98%
10.25	18.26%	18.98%	19.66%	20.29%	20.88%	21.44%	21.96%	22.46%	22.94%	23.39%
10.50	17.83%	18.53%	19.19%	19.80%	20.38%	20.93%	21.44%	21.93%	22.39%	22.84%
10.75	17.41%	18.10%	18.74%	19.34%	19.91%	20.44%	20.94%	21.42%	21.87%	22.31%
11.00	17.02%	17.69%	18.32%	18.90%	19.46%	19.97%	20.47%	20.93%	21.38%	21.80%
11.25	16.64%	17.30%	17.91%	18.48%	19.02%	19.53%	20.01%	20.47%	20.90%	21.31%
11.50	16.28%	16.92%	17.52%	18.08%	18.61%	19.11%	19.58%	20.02%	20.45%	20.85%
11.75	15.93%	16.56%	17.15%	17.70%	18.21%	18.70%	19.16%	19.60%	20.01%	20.41%
12.00	15.60%	16.22%	16.79%	17.33%	17.83%	18.31%	18.76%	19.19%	19.59%	19.98%

TABLE 10.9   Implied Volatility—Minimum Terminal Values

Maturity	Minimum Step Size Ratio (Min/Now)									
	0.05	0.10	0.15	0.20	0.25	0.30	0.35	0.40	0.45	0.50
0.25	1198.29%	921.03%	758.85%	643.78%	554.52%	481.59%	419.93%	366.52%	319.40%	277.26%
0.50	599.15%	460.52%	379.42%	321.89%	277.26%	240.79%	209.96%	183.26%	159.70%	138.63%
0.75	399.43%	307.01%	252.95%	214.59%	184.84%	160.53%	139.98%	122.17%	106.47%	92.42%
1.00	299.57%	230.26%	189.71%	160.94%	138.63%	120.40%	104.98%	91.63%	79.85%	69.31%
1.25	239.66%	184.21%	151.77%	128.76%	110.90%	96.32%	83.99%	73.30%	63.88%	55.45%
1.50	199.72%	153.51%	126.47%	107.30%	92.42%	80.26%	69.99%	61.09%	53.23%	46.21%
1.75	171.18%	131.58%	108.41%	91.97%	79.22%	68.80%	59.99%	52.36%	45.63%	39.61%
2.00	149.79%	115.13%	94.86%	80.47%	69.31%	60.20%	52.49%	45.81%	39.93%	34.66%
2.25	133.14%	102.34%	84.32%	71.53%	61.61%	53.51%	46.66%	40.72%	35.49%	30.81%
2.50	119.83%	92.10%	75.88%	64.38%	55.45%	48.16%	41.99%	36.65%	31.94%	27.73%
2.75	108.94%	83.73%	68.99%	58.53%	50.41%	43.78%	38.18%	33.32%	29.04%	25.21%
3.00	99.86%	76.75%	63.24%	53.65%	46.21%	40.13%	34.99%	30.54%	26.62%	23.10%
3.25	92.18%	70.85%	58.37%	49.52%	42.66%	37.05%	32.30%	28.19%	24.57%	21.33%
3.50	85.59%	65.79%	54.20%	45.98%	39.61%	34.40%	29.99%	26.18%	22.81%	19.80%
3.75	79.89%	61.40%	50.59%	42.92%	36.97%	32.11%	28.00%	24.43%	21.29%	18.48%
4.00	74.89%	57.56%	47.43%	40.24%	34.66%	30.10%	26.25%	22.91%	19.96%	17.33%
4.25	70.49%	54.18%	44.64%	37.87%	32.62%	28.33%	24.70%	21.56%	18.79%	16.31%
4.50	66.57%	51.17%	42.16%	35.77%	30.81%	26.75%	23.33%	20.36%	17.74%	15.40%
4.75	63.07%	48.48%	39.94%	33.88%	29.19%	25.35%	22.10%	19.29%	16.81%	14.59%
5.00	59.91%	46.05%	37.94%	32.19%	27.73%	24.08%	21.00%	18.33%	15.97%	13.86%
5.25	57.06%	43.86%	36.14%	30.66%	26.41%	22.93%	20.00%	17.45%	15.21%	13.20%
5.50	54.47%	41.87%	34.49%	29.26%	25.21%	21.89%	19.09%	16.66%	14.52%	12.60%
5.75	52.10%	40.04%	32.99%	27.99%	24.11%	20.94%	18.26%	15.94%	13.89%	12.05%
6.00	49.93%	38.38%	31.62%	26.82%	23.10%	20.07%	17.50%	15.27%	13.31%	11.55%
6.25	47.93%	36.84%	30.35%	25.75%	22.18%	19.26%	16.80%	14.66%	12.78%	11.09%
6.50	46.09%	35.42%	29.19%	24.76%	21.33%	18.52%	16.15%	14.10%	12.28%	10.66%
6.75	44.38%	34.11%	28.11%	23.84%	20.54%	17.84%	15.55%	13.57%	11.83%	10.27%
7.00	42.80%	32.89%	27.10%	22.99%	19.80%	17.20%	15.00%	13.09%	11.41%	9.90%
7.25	41.32%	31.76%	26.17%	22.20%	19.12%	16.61%	14.48%	12.64%	11.01%	9.56%
7.50	39.94%	30.70%	25.29%	21.46%	18.48%	16.05%	14.00%	12.22%	10.65%	9.24%
7.75	38.65%	29.71%	24.48%	20.77%	17.89%	15.54%	13.55%	11.82%	10.30%	8.94%
8.00	37.45%	28.78%	23.71%	20.12%	17.33%	15.05%	13.12%	11.45%	9.98%	8.66%
8.25	36.31%	27.91%	23.00%	19.51%	16.80%	14.59%	12.73%	11.11%	9.68%	8.40%
8.50	35.24%	27.09%	22.32%	18.93%	16.31%	14.16%	12.35%	10.78%	9.39%	8.15%
8.75	34.24%	26.32%	21.68%	18.39%	15.84%	13.76%	12.00%	10.47%	9.13%	7.92%
9.00	33.29%	25.58%	21.08%	17.88%	15.40%	13.38%	11.66%	10.18%	8.87%	7.70%
9.25	32.39%	24.89%	20.51%	17.40%	14.99%	13.02%	11.35%	9.91%	8.63%	7.49%
9.50	31.53%	24.24%	19.97%	16.94%	14.59%	12.67%	11.05%	9.65%	8.41%	7.30%
9.75	30.73%	23.62%	19.46%	16.51%	14.22%	12.35%	10.77%	9.40%	8.19%	7.11%
10.00	29.96%	23.03%	18.97%	16.09%	13.86%	12.04%	10.50%	9.16%	7.99%	6.93%
10.25	29.23%	22.46%	18.51%	15.70%	13.52%	11.75%	10.24%	8.94%	7.79%	6.76%
10.50	28.53%	21.93%	18.07%	15.33%	13.20%	11.47%	10.00%	8.73%	7.60%	6.60%
10.75	27.87%	21.42%	17.65%	14.97%	12.90%	11.20%	9.77%	8.52%	7.43%	6.45%
11.00	27.23%	20.93%	17.25%	14.63%	12.60%	10.95%	9.54%	8.33%	7.26%	6.30%
11.25	26.63%	20.47%	16.86%	14.31%	12.32%	10.70%	9.33%	8.14%	7.10%	6.16%
11.50	26.05%	20.02%	16.50%	14.00%	12.05%	10.47%	9.13%	7.97%	6.94%	6.03%
11.75	25.50%	19.60%	16.15%	13.70%	11.80%	10.25%	8.93%	7.80%	6.80%	5.90%
12.00	24.96%	19.19%	15.81%	13.41%	11.55%	10.03%	8.75%	7.64%	6.65%	5.78%

TABLE 10.9 Continued

Maturity	0.55	0.60	0.65	0.70	0.75	0.80	0.85	0.90	0.95	0.99
0.25	239.13%	204.33%	172.31%	142.67%	115.07%	89.26%	65.01%	42.14%	20.52%	4.02%
0.50	119.57%	102.17%	86.16%	71.33%	57.54%	44.63%	32.50%	21.07%	10.26%	2.01%
0.75	79.71%	68.11%	57.44%	47.56%	38.36%	29.75%	21.67%	14.05%	6.84%	1.34%
1.00	59.78%	51.08%	43.08%	35.67%	28.77%	22.31%	16.25%	10.54%	5.13%	1.01%
1.25	47.83%	40.87%	34.46%	28.53%	23.01%	17.85%	13.00%	8.43%	4.10%	0.80%
1.50	39.86%	34.06%	28.72%	23.78%	19.18%	14.88%	10.83%	7.02%	3.42%	0.67%
1.75	34.16%	29.19%	24.62%	20.38%	16.44%	12.75%	9.29%	6.02%	2.93%	0.57%
2.00	29.89%	25.54%	21.54%	17.83%	14.38%	11.16%	8.13%	5.27%	2.56%	0.50%
2.25	26.57%	22.70%	19.15%	15.85%	12.79%	9.92%	7.22%	4.68%	2.28%	0.45%
2.50	23.91%	20.43%	17.23%	14.27%	11.51%	8.93%	6.50%	4.21%	2.05%	0.40%
2.75	21.74%	18.58%	15.66%	12.97%	10.46%	8.11%	5.91%	3.83%	1.87%	0.37%
3.00	19.93%	17.03%	14.36%	11.89%	9.59%	7.44%	5.42%	3.51%	1.71%	0.34%
3.25	18.39%	15.72%	13.25%	10.97%	8.85%	6.87%	5.00%	3.24%	1.58%	0.31%
3.50	17.08%	14.60%	12.31%	10.19%	8.22%	6.38%	4.64%	3.01%	1.47%	0.29%
3.75	15.94%	13.62%	11.49%	9.51%	7.67%	5.95%	4.33%	2.81%	1.37%	0.27%
4.00	14.95%	12.77%	10.77%	8.92%	7.19%	5.58%	4.06%	2.63%	1.28%	0.25%
4.25	14.07%	12.02%	10.14%	8.39%	6.77%	5.25%	3.82%	2.48%	1.21%	0.24%
4.50	13.29%	11.35%	9.57%	7.93%	6.39%	4.96%	3.61%	2.34%	1.14%	0.22%
4.75	12.59%	10.75%	9.07%	7.51%	6.06%	4.70%	3.42%	2.22%	1.08%	0.21%
5.00	11.96%	10.22%	8.62%	7.13%	5.75%	4.46%	3.25%	2.11%	1.03%	0.20%
5.25	11.39%	9.73%	8.21%	6.79%	5.48%	4.25%	3.10%	2.01%	0.98%	0.19%
5.50	10.87%	9.29%	7.83%	6.48%	5.23%	4.06%	2.95%	1.92%	0.93%	0.18%
5.75	10.40%	8.88%	7.49%	6.20%	5.00%	3.88%	2.83%	1.83%	0.89%	0.17%
6.00	9.96%	8.51%	7.18%	5.94%	4.79%	3.72%	2.71%	1.76%	0.85%	0.17%
6.25	9.57%	8.17%	6.89%	5.71%	4.60%	3.57%	2.60%	1.69%	0.82%	0.16%
6.50	9.20%	7.86%	6.63%	5.49%	4.43%	3.43%	2.50%	1.62%	0.79%	0.15%
6.75	8.86%	7.57%	6.38%	5.28%	4.26%	3.31%	2.41%	1.56%	0.76%	0.15%
7.00	8.54%	7.30%	6.15%	5.10%	4.11%	3.19%	2.32%	1.51%	0.73%	0.14%
7.25	8.25%	7.05%	5.94%	4.92%	3.97%	3.08%	2.24%	1.45%	0.71%	0.14%
7.50	7.97%	6.81%	5.74%	4.76%	3.84%	2.98%	2.17%	1.40%	0.68%	0.13%
7.75	7.71%	6.59%	5.56%	4.60%	3.71%	2.88%	2.10%	1.36%	0.66%	0.13%
8.00	7.47%	6.39%	5.38%	4.46%	3.60%	2.79%	2.03%	1.32%	0.64%	0.13%
8.25	7.25%	6.19%	5.22%	4.32%	3.49%	2.70%	1.97%	1.28%	0.62%	0.12%
8.50	7.03%	6.01%	5.07%	4.20%	3.38%	2.63%	1.91%	1.24%	0.60%	0.12%
8.75	6.83%	5.84%	4.92%	4.08%	3.29%	2.55%	1.86%	1.20%	0.59%	0.11%
9.00	6.64%	5.68%	4.79%	3.96%	3.20%	2.48%	1.81%	1.17%	0.57%	0.11%
9.25	6.46%	5.52%	4.66%	3.86%	3.11%	2.41%	1.76%	1.14%	0.55%	0.11%
9.50	6.29%	5.38%	4.53%	3.75%	3.03%	2.35%	1.71%	1.11%	0.54%	0.11%
9.75	6.13%	5.24%	4.42%	3.66%	2.95%	2.29%	1.67%	1.08%	0.53%	0.10%
10.00	5.98%	5.11%	4.31%	3.57%	2.88%	2.23%	1.63%	1.05%	0.51%	0.10%
10.25	5.83%	4.98%	4.20%	3.48%	2.81%	2.18%	1.59%	1.03%	0.50%	0.10%
10.50	5.69%	4.87%	4.10%	3.40%	2.74%	2.13%	1.55%	1.00%	0.49%	0.10%
10.75	5.56%	4.75%	4.01%	3.32%	2.68%	2.08%	1.51%	0.98%	0.48%	0.09%
11.00	5.43%	4.64%	3.92%	3.24%	2.62%	2.03%	1.48%	0.96%	0.47%	0.09%
11.25	5.31%	4.54%	3.83%	3.17%	2.56%	1.98%	1.44%	0.94%	0.46%	0.09%
11.50	5.20%	4.44%	3.75%	3.10%	2.50%	1.94%	1.41%	0.92%	0.45%	0.09%
11.75	5.09%	4.35%	3.67%	3.04%	2.45%	1.90%	1.38%	0.90%	0.44%	0.09%
12.00	4.98%	4.26%	3.59%	2.97%	2.40%	1.86%	1.35%	0.88%	0.43%	0.08%

DIVIDEND IMPACT TABLES

Tables 10.10 through 10.12 list the impact of a dividend on an American option. The columns list the volatility of the underlying asset, whereas the rows list the dividend payout as a percentage of asset value. The resulting values show the reduction in option value from a base case with no dividends. Notice that as volatility increases, the reduction in option value becomes less. In retrospect, when the dividend rate increases, the reduction in option value increases.

Example

Calculate the impact to an option's value if a 1.55 percent dividend exists on a 5-year real option with 10 percent volatility.

1. Assume both asset value and implementation costs are at $100 million.
2. What if both asset value and implementation costs are now $350 million?
3. Find the effect if asset value is $120 million but implementation cost is $100 million.

Answers

1. Based on the table for at-the-money options, the impact is −27.19 percent. This is simply the difference in option value, where the real option value on an American call is $23.42 for zero dividends and $17.05 for the 1.55 percent dividend. The change from $23.42 to $17.05 is simply −27.19 percent.
2. The same −27.19 percent applies as the option is still at-the-money.
3. Using the table for 20 percent in-the-money, the reduction is −20.48 percent.

TABLE 10.10 Dividend Impact—At-the-Money Options

Maturity	5 Years		Risk-Free Rate	5%						
Volatility (at-the-money)										
Dividend	5.00%	10.00%	15.00%	20.00%	25.00%	30.00%	35.00%	40.00%	45.00%	50.00%
0.05%	-1.11%	-0.95%	-0.79%	-0.67%	-0.59%	-0.53%	-0.48%	-0.45%	-0.42%	-0.39%
0.15%	-3.33%	-2.83%	-2.35%	-2.00%	-1.76%	-1.58%	-1.44%	-1.33%	-1.25%	-1.18%
0.25%	-5.53%	-4.70%	-3.89%	-3.32%	-2.92%	-2.62%	-2.39%	-2.21%	-2.07%	-1.96%
0.35%	-7.72%	-6.54%	-5.42%	-4.63%	-4.06%	-3.65%	-3.33%	-3.09%	-2.89%	-2.73%
0.45%	-9.89%	-8.37%	-6.93%	-5.92%	-5.20%	-4.67%	-4.27%	-3.96%	-3.70%	-3.49%
0.55%	-12.05%	-10.18%	-8.43%	-7.20%	-6.33%	-5.69%	-5.20%	-4.81%	-4.50%	-4.24%
0.65%	-14.19%	-11.96%	-9.92%	-8.48%	-7.45%	-6.70%	-6.12%	-5.67%	-5.30%	-4.99%
0.75%	-16.32%	-13.73%	-11.38%	-9.73%	-8.56%	-7.69%	-7.03%	-6.51%	-6.08%	-5.72%
0.85%	-18.43%	-15.48%	-12.84%	-10.98%	-9.66%	-8.68%	-7.94%	-7.34%	-6.86%	-6.44%
0.95%	-20.52%	-17.21%	-14.27%	-12.21%	-10.75%	-9.66%	-8.83%	-8.17%	-7.62%	-7.16%
1.05%	-22.60%	-18.93%	-15.70%	-13.44%	-11.83%	-10.64%	-9.72%	-8.98%	-8.37%	-7.85%
1.15%	-24.66%	-20.62%	-17.10%	-14.65%	-12.90%	-11.60%	-10.59%	-9.78%	-9.11%	-8.54%
1.25%	-26.70%	-22.29%	-18.50%	-15.84%	-13.95%	-12.55%	-11.46%	-10.58%	-9.84%	-9.21%
1.35%	-28.72%	-23.94%	-19.87%	-17.03%	-15.00%	-13.49%	-12.31%	-11.36%	-10.56%	-9.87%
1.45%	-30.72%	-25.58%	-21.23%	-18.20%	-16.04%	-14.42%	-13.15%	-12.12%	-11.26%	-10.52%
1.55%	-32.71%	-27.19%	-22.58%	-19.37%	-17.06%	-15.34%	-13.98%	-12.88%	-11.95%	-11.15%
1.65%	-34.67%	-28.78%	-23.91%	-20.51%	-18.08%	-16.24%	-14.80%	-13.62%	-12.63%	-11.77%
1.75%	-36.61%	-30.36%	-25.23%	-21.65%	-19.08%	-17.13%	-15.60%	-14.34%	-13.29%	-12.38%
1.85%	-38.53%	-31.91%	-26.53%	-22.77%	-20.07%	-18.01%	-16.39%	-15.06%	-13.94%	-12.98%
1.95%	-40.43%	-33.44%	-27.81%	-23.88%	-21.04%	-18.88%	-17.17%	-15.76%	-14.58%	-13.56%
2.05%	-42.31%	-34.95%	-29.08%	-24.98%	-22.00%	-19.73%	-17.93%	-16.45%	-15.20%	-14.13%
2.15%	-44.16%	-36.45%	-30.34%	-26.06%	-22.95%	-20.57%	-18.67%	-17.12%	-15.81%	-14.69%
2.25%	-45.99%	-37.92%	-31.57%	-27.13%	-23.88%	-21.39%	-19.41%	-17.78%	-16.41%	-15.24%
2.35%	-47.79%	-39.37%	-32.80%	-28.18%	-24.79%	-22.20%	-20.12%	-18.42%	-16.99%	-15.78%
2.45%	-49.57%	-40.80%	-34.00%	-29.21%	-25.69%	-22.99%	-20.83%	-19.05%	-17.57%	-16.30%
2.55%	-51.32%	-42.21%	-35.19%	-30.23%	-26.58%	-23.76%	-21.51%	-19.67%	-18.13%	-16.82%
2.65%	-53.04%	-43.60%	-36.36%	-31.23%	-27.44%	-24.52%	-22.19%	-20.27%	-18.68%	-17.33%
2.75%	-54.74%	-44.97%	-37.51%	-32.21%	-28.29%	-25.26%	-22.84%	-20.86%	-19.22%	-17.82%
2.85%	-56.41%	-46.31%	-38.64%	-33.18%	-29.12%	-25.99%	-23.49%	-21.44%	-19.74%	-18.31%
2.95%	-58.05%	-47.64%	-39.75%	-34.12%	-29.93%	-26.70%	-24.12%	-22.01%	-20.26%	-18.80%
3.05%	-59.66%	-48.94%	-40.84%	-35.04%	-30.73%	-27.39%	-24.73%	-22.57%	-20.77%	-19.27%
3.15%	-61.24%	-50.22%	-41.91%	-35.95%	-31.50%	-28.07%	-25.33%	-23.11%	-21.27%	-19.74%
3.25%	-62.79%	-51.47%	-42.96%	-36.83%	-32.26%	-28.72%	-25.92%	-23.64%	-21.77%	-20.20%
3.35%	-64.30%	-52.70%	-43.98%	-37.69%	-32.99%	-29.37%	-26.49%	-24.17%	-22.25%	-20.66%
3.45%	-65.79%	-53.90%	-44.97%	-38.52%	-33.71%	-30.00%	-27.06%	-24.68%	-22.73%	-21.11%
3.55%	-67.24%	-55.08%	-45.94%	-39.34%	-34.41%	-30.61%	-27.61%	-25.19%	-23.20%	-21.56%
3.65%	-68.65%	-56.23%	-46.89%	-40.13%	-35.08%	-31.21%	-28.15%	-25.68%	-23.67%	-22.00%
3.75%	-70.03%	-57.34%	-47.80%	-40.89%	-35.74%	-31.79%	-28.68%	-26.17%	-24.13%	-22.44%
3.85%	-71.38%	-58.42%	-48.69%	-41.64%	-36.39%	-32.36%	-29.20%	-26.66%	-24.59%	-22.88%
3.95%	-72.68%	-59.47%	-49.55%	-42.35%	-37.01%	-32.92%	-29.71%	-27.14%	-25.04%	-23.32%
4.05%	-73.95%	-60.48%	-50.37%	-43.05%	-37.62%	-33.47%	-30.22%	-27.61%	-25.50%	-23.75%
4.15%	-75.17%	-61.45%	-51.17%	-43.73%	-38.22%	-34.01%	-30.72%	-28.09%	-25.95%	-24.19%
4.25%	-76.35%	-62.38%	-51.93%	-44.38%	-38.80%	-34.54%	-31.21%	-28.55%	-26.40%	-24.63%
4.35%	-77.47%	-63.27%	-52.66%	-45.02%	-39.37%	-35.06%	-31.70%	-29.02%	-26.85%	-25.06%
4.45%	-78.54%	-64.11%	-53.37%	-45.63%	-39.92%	-35.58%	-32.19%	-29.49%	-27.30%	-25.50%
4.55%	-79.54%	-64.91%	-54.05%	-46.24%	-40.48%	-36.10%	-32.68%	-29.95%	-27.75%	-25.94%
4.65%	-80.47%	-65.66%	-54.70%	-46.83%	-41.02%	-36.61%	-33.16%	-30.42%	-28.20%	-26.38%
4.75%	-81.31%	-66.37%	-55.34%	-47.41%	-41.56%	-37.12%	-33.65%	-30.89%	-28.66%	-26.82%

Note: Maturity is 5 years and risk-free rate is 5 percent.

TABLE 10.10 Continued

Dividend	55.00%	60.00%	65.00%	70.00%	75.00%	80.00%	85.00%	90.00%	95.00%	99.00%
0.05%	-0.37%	-0.36%	-0.34%	-0.33%	-0.32%	-0.31%	-0.31%	-0.30%	-0.29%	-0.29%
0.15%	-1.12%	-1.07%	-1.03%	-0.99%	-0.96%	-0.93%	-0.90%	-0.88%	-0.85%	-0.83%
0.25%	-1.86%	-1.78%	-1.71%	-1.64%	-1.58%	-1.53%	-1.48%	-1.43%	-1.38%	-1.35%
0.35%	-2.59%	-2.47%	-2.37%	-2.28%	-2.19%	-2.11%	-2.03%	-1.96%	-1.89%	-1.84%
0.45%	-3.31%	-3.16%	-3.02%	-2.89%	-2.78%	-2.67%	-2.57%	-2.47%	-2.38%	-2.31%
0.55%	-4.02%	-3.83%	-3.66%	-3.50%	-3.35%	-3.22%	-3.09%	-2.97%	-2.86%	-2.77%
0.65%	-4.72%	-4.49%	-4.28%	-4.09%	-3.91%	-3.75%	-3.59%	-3.45%	-3.31%	-3.21%
0.75%	-5.41%	-5.14%	-4.89%	-4.66%	-4.45%	-4.26%	-4.08%	-3.91%	-3.76%	-3.64%
0.85%	-6.09%	-5.77%	-5.48%	-5.22%	-4.98%	-4.76%	-4.56%	-4.37%	-4.19%	-4.07%
0.95%	-6.75%	-6.39%	-6.07%	-5.77%	-5.50%	-5.25%	-5.02%	-4.81%	-4.62%	-4.48%
1.05%	-7.40%	-7.00%	-6.63%	-6.30%	-6.00%	-5.73%	-5.48%	-5.25%	-5.04%	-4.89%
1.15%	-8.04%	-7.59%	-7.19%	-6.83%	-6.50%	-6.19%	-5.92%	-5.67%	-5.45%	-5.29%
1.25%	-8.66%	-8.17%	-7.73%	-7.34%	-6.98%	-6.65%	-6.36%	-6.09%	-5.85%	-5.68%
1.35%	-9.27%	-8.74%	-8.26%	-7.84%	-7.45%	-7.10%	-6.78%	-6.50%	-6.25%	-6.07%
1.45%	-9.87%	-9.30%	-8.78%	-8.32%	-7.91%	-7.54%	-7.21%	-6.91%	-6.65%	-6.46%
1.55%	-10.46%	-9.84%	-9.29%	-8.80%	-8.36%	-7.97%	-7.62%	-7.31%	-7.04%	-6.84%
1.65%	-11.03%	-10.37%	-9.79%	-9.27%	-8.81%	-8.40%	-8.03%	-7.71%	-7.42%	-7.22%
1.75%	-11.59%	-10.90%	-10.28%	-9.73%	-9.25%	-8.82%	-8.44%	-8.10%	-7.80%	-7.59%
1.85%	-12.14%	-11.41%	-10.76%	-10.19%	-9.68%	-9.23%	-8.84%	-8.49%	-8.19%	-7.97%
1.95%	-12.68%	-11.91%	-11.23%	-10.63%	-10.11%	-9.64%	-9.23%	-8.88%	-8.56%	-8.34%
2.05%	-13.21%	-12.40%	-11.69%	-11.07%	-10.53%	-10.05%	-9.63%	-9.26%	-8.94%	-8.72%
2.15%	-13.72%	-12.88%	-12.15%	-11.50%	-10.94%	-10.45%	-10.02%	-9.64%	-9.32%	-9.09%
2.25%	-14.23%	-13.36%	-12.60%	-11.93%	-11.35%	-10.85%	-10.41%	-10.02%	-9.69%	-9.46%
2.35%	-14.73%	-13.82%	-13.04%	-12.36%	-11.76%	-11.24%	-10.79%	-10.40%	-10.06%	-9.83%
2.45%	-15.22%	-14.28%	-13.48%	-12.77%	-12.17%	-11.64%	-11.18%	-10.78%	-10.44%	-10.19%
2.55%	-15.70%	-14.74%	-13.91%	-13.19%	-12.57%	-12.03%	-11.56%	-11.16%	-10.81%	-10.56%
2.65%	-16.17%	-15.19%	-14.33%	-13.60%	-12.97%	-12.42%	-11.94%	-11.53%	-11.18%	-10.93%
2.75%	-16.64%	-15.63%	-14.76%	-14.01%	-13.36%	-12.80%	-12.32%	-11.91%	-11.55%	-11.30%
2.85%	-17.10%	-16.06%	-15.18%	-14.41%	-13.76%	-13.19%	-12.70%	-12.28%	-11.92%	-11.67%
2.95%	-17.55%	-16.50%	-15.59%	-14.82%	-14.15%	-13.58%	-13.08%	-12.66%	-12.29%	-12.03%
3.05%	-18.00%	-16.92%	-16.00%	-15.22%	-14.54%	-13.96%	-13.46%	-13.03%	-12.66%	-12.40%
3.15%	-18.45%	-17.35%	-16.41%	-15.62%	-14.93%	-14.35%	-13.84%	-13.41%	-13.03%	-12.77%
3.25%	-18.88%	-17.77%	-16.82%	-16.02%	-15.32%	-14.73%	-14.22%	-13.78%	-13.40%	-13.14%
3.35%	-19.32%	-18.19%	-17.23%	-16.41%	-15.71%	-15.12%	-14.60%	-14.16%	-13.78%	-13.51%
3.45%	-19.75%	-18.61%	-17.64%	-16.81%	-16.10%	-15.50%	-14.98%	-14.54%	-14.15%	-13.88%
3.55%	-20.18%	-19.02%	-18.04%	-17.21%	-16.50%	-15.89%	-15.36%	-14.91%	-14.52%	-14.25%
3.65%	-20.61%	-19.44%	-18.45%	-17.60%	-16.89%	-16.27%	-15.74%	-15.29%	-14.89%	-14.62%
3.75%	-21.03%	-19.85%	-18.85%	-18.00%	-17.28%	-16.66%	-16.13%	-15.67%	-15.27%	-14.99%
3.85%	-21.46%	-20.26%	-19.25%	-18.40%	-17.67%	-17.05%	-16.51%	-16.05%	-15.64%	-15.36%
3.95%	-21.88%	-20.68%	-19.66%	-18.80%	-18.06%	-17.43%	-16.89%	-16.42%	-16.02%	-15.73%
4.05%	-22.30%	-21.09%	-20.07%	-19.20%	-18.46%	-17.82%	-17.28%	-16.80%	-16.39%	-16.10%
4.15%	-22.73%	-21.50%	-20.47%	-19.60%	-18.85%	-18.21%	-17.66%	-17.19%	-16.77%	-16.47%
4.25%	-23.15%	-21.92%	-20.88%	-20.00%	-19.25%	-18.60%	-18.05%	-17.57%	-17.15%	-16.85%
4.35%	-23.58%	-22.34%	-21.29%	-20.40%	-19.65%	-19.00%	-18.44%	-17.95%	-17.53%	-17.22%
4.45%	-24.00%	-22.75%	-21.70%	-20.81%	-20.05%	-19.39%	-18.83%	-18.34%	-17.91%	-17.60%
4.55%	-24.43%	-23.18%	-22.11%	-21.22%	-20.45%	-19.79%	-19.22%	-18.72%	-18.29%	-17.97%
4.65%	-24.86%	-23.60%	-22.53%	-21.62%	-20.85%	-20.19%	-19.61%	-19.11%	-18.67%	-18.35%
4.75%	-25.30%	-24.02%	-22.95%	-22.04%	-21.26%	-20.58%	-20.00%	-19.50%	-19.05%	-18.73%

TABLE 10.11 Dividend Impact—20 Percent Out-of-the-Money Options

Maturity	5 Years		Risk-Free Rate	5%					
Volatility (20% out-of-the-money)									
Dividend	**5.00%**	**10.00%**	**15.00%**	**20.00%**	**25.00%**	**30.00%**	**35.00%**	**40.00%**	**45.00%**	**50.00%**
0.05%	-2.61%	-1.45%	-1.03%	-0.81%	-0.68%	-0.59%	-0.53%	-0.48%	-0.45%	-0.42%
0.15%	-7.71%	-4.30%	-3.06%	-2.42%	-2.03%	-1.77%	-1.58%	-1.44%	-1.33%	-1.24%
0.25%	-12.63%	-7.09%	-5.06%	-4.00%	-3.36%	-2.93%	-2.62%	-2.39%	-2.21%	-2.07%
0.35%	-17.38%	-9.83%	-7.03%	-5.57%	-4.68%	-4.08%	-3.65%	-3.33%	-3.08%	-2.88%
0.45%	-21.96%	-12.51%	-8.97%	-7.12%	-5.99%	-5.22%	-4.68%	-4.27%	-3.95%	-3.69%
0.55%	-26.37%	-15.14%	-10.88%	-8.65%	-7.28%	-6.35%	-5.69%	-5.19%	-4.80%	-4.49%
0.65%	-30.61%	-17.71%	-12.76%	-10.16%	-8.56%	-7.47%	-6.70%	-6.11%	-5.65%	-5.28%
0.75%	-34.68%	-20.23%	-14.62%	-11.65%	-9.82%	-8.58%	-7.69%	-7.02%	-6.49%	-6.06%
0.85%	-38.59%	-22.69%	-16.44%	-13.12%	-11.07%	-9.68%	-8.68%	-7.92%	-7.32%	-6.83%
0.95%	-42.33%	-25.09%	-18.24%	-14.58%	-12.31%	-10.77%	-9.66%	-8.81%	-8.14%	-7.59%
1.05%	-45.90%	-27.45%	-20.01%	-16.01%	-13.54%	-11.85%	-10.62%	-9.69%	-8.95%	-8.34%
1.15%	-49.32%	-29.75%	-21.75%	-17.43%	-14.75%	-12.91%	-11.58%	-10.56%	-9.75%	-9.07%
1.25%	-52.58%	-32.00%	-23.46%	-18.83%	-15.94%	-13.97%	-12.53%	-11.42%	-10.53%	-9.80%
1.35%	-55.69%	-34.19%	-25.14%	-20.21%	-17.13%	-15.01%	-13.46%	-12.27%	-11.31%	-10.51%
1.45%	-58.64%	-36.33%	-26.80%	-21.58%	-18.30%	-16.04%	-14.39%	-13.10%	-12.07%	-11.21%
1.55%	-61.45%	-38.43%	-28.43%	-22.92%	-19.45%	-17.06%	-15.30%	-13.93%	-12.82%	-11.90%
1.65%	-64.11%	-40.47%	-30.03%	-24.25%	-20.60%	-18.07%	-16.20%	-14.74%	-13.56%	-12.58%
1.75%	-66.63%	-42.46%	-31.61%	-25.56%	-21.73%	-19.06%	-17.08%	-15.54%	-14.29%	-13.24%
1.85%	-69.02%	-44.40%	-33.15%	-26.86%	-22.84%	-20.04%	-17.96%	-16.33%	-15.00%	-13.89%
1.95%	-71.27%	-46.29%	-34.68%	-28.13%	-23.94%	-21.01%	-18.82%	-17.10%	-15.70%	-14.53%
2.05%	-73.40%	-48.14%	-36.17%	-29.39%	-25.02%	-21.96%	-19.67%	-17.86%	-16.39%	-15.16%
2.15%	-75.40%	-49.94%	-37.64%	-30.63%	-26.09%	-22.90%	-20.50%	-18.61%	-17.07%	-15.78%
2.25%	-77.28%	-51.69%	-39.09%	-31.85%	-27.15%	-23.83%	-21.32%	-19.35%	-17.74%	-16.39%
2.35%	-79.05%	-53.39%	-40.51%	-33.05%	-28.19%	-24.74%	-22.13%	-20.07%	-18.39%	-16.98%
2.45%	-80.70%	-55.05%	-41.90%	-34.23%	-29.21%	-25.63%	-22.92%	-20.78%	-19.03%	-17.57%
2.55%	-82.25%	-56.66%	-43.27%	-35.40%	-30.22%	-26.51%	-23.70%	-21.47%	-19.66%	-18.14%
2.65%	-83.70%	-58.23%	-44.61%	-36.54%	-31.21%	-27.38%	-24.46%	-22.16%	-20.27%	-18.71%
2.75%	-85.06%	-59.75%	-45.92%	-37.67%	-32.18%	-28.22%	-25.21%	-22.83%	-20.88%	-19.26%
2.85%	-86.32%	-61.23%	-47.22%	-38.77%	-33.13%	-29.06%	-25.95%	-23.48%	-21.48%	-19.81%
2.95%	-87.49%	-62.67%	-48.48%	-39.86%	-34.07%	-29.87%	-26.67%	-24.13%	-22.06%	-20.35%
3.05%	-88.58%	-64.07%	-49.72%	-40.93%	-34.99%	-30.68%	-27.38%	-24.76%	-22.64%	-20.88%
3.15%	-89.58%	-65.43%	-50.93%	-41.97%	-35.89%	-31.46%	-28.07%	-25.38%	-23.20%	-21.40%
3.25%	-90.52%	-66.74%	-52.12%	-43.00%	-36.77%	-32.23%	-28.75%	-25.99%	-23.76%	-21.92%
3.35%	-91.38%	-68.02%	-53.28%	-44.00%	-37.64%	-32.98%	-29.42%	-26.59%	-24.31%	-22.42%
3.45%	-92.18%	-69.25%	-54.42%	-44.98%	-38.48%	-33.72%	-30.07%	-27.18%	-24.85%	-22.93%
3.55%	-92.91%	-70.45%	-55.53%	-45.94%	-39.31%	-34.44%	-30.71%	-27.76%	-25.38%	-23.43%
3.65%	-93.59%	-71.61%	-56.61%	-46.88%	-40.12%	-35.15%	-31.34%	-28.33%	-25.91%	-23.92%
3.75%	-94.20%	-72.73%	-57.66%	-47.79%	-40.91%	-35.84%	-31.96%	-28.89%	-26.43%	-24.41%
3.85%	-94.77%	-73.81%	-58.69%	-48.68%	-41.68%	-36.51%	-32.56%	-29.45%	-26.94%	-24.89%
3.95%	-95.29%	-74.86%	-59.69%	-49.55%	-42.43%	-37.18%	-33.16%	-29.99%	-27.45%	-25.37%
4.05%	-95.77%	-75.87%	-60.65%	-50.39%	-43.16%	-37.83%	-33.75%	-30.53%	-27.96%	-25.85%
4.15%	-96.20%	-76.84%	-61.59%	-51.22%	-43.88%	-38.47%	-34.32%	-31.07%	-28.46%	-26.33%
4.25%	-96.59%	-77.77%	-62.50%	-52.02%	-44.58%	-39.09%	-34.90%	-31.60%	-28.96%	-26.80%
4.35%	-96.95%	-78.67%	-63.38%	-52.79%	-45.27%	-39.71%	-35.46%	-32.12%	-29.45%	-27.28%
4.45%	-97.27%	-79.52%	-64.23%	-53.55%	-45.94%	-40.32%	-36.02%	-32.65%	-29.95%	-27.75%
4.55%	-97.57%	-80.34%	-65.05%	-54.29%	-46.60%	-40.92%	-36.57%	-33.17%	-30.44%	-28.23%
4.65%	-97.83%	-81.12%	-65.85%	-55.01%	-47.25%	-41.51%	-37.12%	-33.68%	-30.93%	-28.70%
4.75%	-98.07%	-81.87%	-66.61%	-55.71%	-47.89%	-42.09%	-37.67%	-34.20%	-31.43%	-29.18%

Note: Maturity is 5 years and risk-free rate is 5 percent.

TABLE 10.11 Continued

Dividend	55.00%	60.00%	65.00%	70.00%	75.00%	80.00%	85.00%	90.00%	95.00%	99.00%
0.05%	-0.39%	-0.37%	-0.36%	-0.34%	-0.33%	-0.32%	-0.31%	-0.30%	-0.30%	-0.29%
0.15%	-1.17%	-1.12%	-1.07%	-1.03%	-0.99%	-0.96%	-0.93%	-0.90%	-0.87%	-0.85%
0.25%	-1.95%	-1.85%	-1.77%	-1.70%	-1.63%	-1.57%	-1.52%	-1.47%	-1.42%	-1.38%
0.35%	-2.72%	-2.58%	-2.46%	-2.36%	-2.26%	-2.18%	-2.10%	-2.02%	-1.95%	-1.89%
0.45%	-3.48%	-3.30%	-3.14%	-3.00%	-2.88%	-2.76%	-2.66%	-2.55%	-2.46%	-2.39%
0.55%	-4.23%	-4.00%	-3.81%	-3.64%	-3.48%	-3.33%	-3.20%	-3.07%	-2.95%	-2.86%
0.65%	-4.97%	-4.70%	-4.47%	-4.26%	-4.07%	-3.89%	-3.73%	-3.57%	-3.43%	-3.33%
0.75%	-5.70%	-5.38%	-5.11%	-4.86%	-4.64%	-4.43%	-4.24%	-4.06%	-3.90%	-3.78%
0.85%	-6.41%	-6.06%	-5.74%	-5.46%	-5.20%	-4.96%	-4.74%	-4.54%	-4.36%	-4.22%
0.95%	-7.12%	-6.72%	-6.36%	-6.04%	-5.74%	-5.48%	-5.23%	-5.01%	-4.81%	-4.66%
1.05%	-7.82%	-7.36%	-6.96%	-6.60%	-6.28%	-5.98%	-5.71%	-5.47%	-5.25%	-5.08%
1.15%	-8.50%	-8.00%	-7.56%	-7.16%	-6.80%	-6.48%	-6.19%	-5.92%	-5.68%	-5.50%
1.25%	-9.17%	-8.62%	-8.14%	-7.71%	-7.32%	-6.97%	-6.65%	-6.36%	-6.10%	-5.91%
1.35%	-9.83%	-9.23%	-8.71%	-8.24%	-7.82%	-7.44%	-7.10%	-6.80%	-6.52%	-6.32%
1.45%	-10.47%	-9.83%	-9.27%	-8.76%	-8.31%	-7.91%	-7.55%	-7.23%	-6.94%	-6.73%
1.55%	-11.11%	-10.42%	-9.82%	-9.28%	-8.80%	-8.37%	-7.99%	-7.65%	-7.35%	-7.13%
1.65%	-11.73%	-11.00%	-10.36%	-9.78%	-9.28%	-8.83%	-8.42%	-8.07%	-7.75%	-7.53%
1.75%	-12.34%	-11.57%	-10.88%	-10.28%	-9.75%	-9.27%	-8.85%	-8.48%	-8.16%	-7.92%
1.85%	-12.94%	-12.12%	-11.40%	-10.77%	-10.21%	-9.72%	-9.28%	-8.89%	-8.56%	-8.31%
1.95%	-13.53%	-12.67%	-11.91%	-11.25%	-10.67%	-10.15%	-9.70%	-9.30%	-8.95%	-8.70%
2.05%	-14.11%	-13.21%	-12.42%	-11.72%	-11.12%	-10.58%	-10.12%	-9.71%	-9.35%	-9.09%
2.15%	-14.68%	-13.73%	-12.91%	-12.19%	-11.56%	-11.01%	-10.53%	-10.11%	-9.74%	-9.48%
2.25%	-15.24%	-14.25%	-13.40%	-12.65%	-12.00%	-11.44%	-10.94%	-10.51%	-10.13%	-9.87%
2.35%	-15.79%	-14.76%	-13.88%	-13.11%	-12.44%	-11.86%	-11.35%	-10.91%	-10.52%	-10.25%
2.45%	-16.33%	-15.27%	-14.35%	-13.56%	-12.87%	-12.27%	-11.76%	-11.30%	-10.91%	-10.64%
2.55%	-16.86%	-15.76%	-14.82%	-14.01%	-13.30%	-12.69%	-12.16%	-11.70%	-11.30%	-11.02%
2.65%	-17.38%	-16.25%	-15.28%	-14.45%	-13.73%	-13.10%	-12.56%	-12.09%	-11.69%	-11.40%
2.75%	-17.90%	-16.74%	-15.74%	-14.89%	-14.15%	-13.51%	-12.96%	-12.49%	-12.07%	-11.78%
2.85%	-18.41%	-17.21%	-16.20%	-15.32%	-14.57%	-13.92%	-13.36%	-12.88%	-12.46%	-12.17%
2.95%	-18.91%	-17.69%	-16.65%	-15.75%	-14.99%	-14.33%	-13.76%	-13.27%	-12.85%	-12.55%
3.05%	-19.40%	-18.15%	-17.09%	-16.18%	-15.41%	-14.74%	-14.16%	-13.66%	-13.23%	-12.93%
3.15%	-19.89%	-18.62%	-17.54%	-16.61%	-15.82%	-15.14%	-14.56%	-14.05%	-13.62%	-13.31%
3.25%	-20.38%	-19.08%	-17.98%	-17.04%	-16.24%	-15.55%	-14.96%	-14.45%	-14.01%	-13.69%
3.35%	-20.85%	-19.53%	-18.41%	-17.46%	-16.65%	-15.95%	-15.35%	-14.84%	-14.39%	-14.08%
3.45%	-21.33%	-19.99%	-18.85%	-17.89%	-17.06%	-16.36%	-15.75%	-15.23%	-14.78%	-14.46%
3.55%	-21.80%	-20.44%	-19.28%	-18.31%	-17.47%	-16.76%	-16.15%	-15.62%	-15.16%	-14.84%
3.65%	-22.27%	-20.88%	-19.72%	-18.73%	-17.89%	-17.17%	-16.55%	-16.01%	-15.55%	-15.23%
3.75%	-22.73%	-21.33%	-20.15%	-19.15%	-18.30%	-17.57%	-16.94%	-16.41%	-15.94%	-15.61%
3.85%	-23.19%	-21.78%	-20.58%	-19.57%	-18.71%	-17.97%	-17.34%	-16.80%	-16.33%	-15.99%
3.95%	-23.65%	-22.22%	-21.01%	-19.99%	-19.12%	-18.38%	-17.74%	-17.19%	-16.72%	-16.38%
4.05%	-24.11%	-22.66%	-21.44%	-20.41%	-19.54%	-18.79%	-18.14%	-17.59%	-17.10%	-16.76%
4.15%	-24.57%	-23.11%	-21.88%	-20.83%	-19.95%	-19.19%	-18.54%	-17.98%	-17.49%	-17.15%
4.25%	-25.03%	-23.55%	-22.31%	-21.26%	-20.36%	-19.60%	-18.95%	-18.38%	-17.89%	-17.53%
4.35%	-25.49%	-23.99%	-22.74%	-21.68%	-20.78%	-20.01%	-19.35%	-18.78%	-18.28%	-17.92%
4.45%	-25.94%	-24.44%	-23.17%	-22.11%	-21.20%	-20.42%	-19.75%	-19.17%	-18.67%	-18.31%
4.55%	-26.40%	-24.88%	-23.61%	-22.53%	-21.62%	-20.83%	-20.16%	-19.57%	-19.06%	-18.70%
4.65%	-26.86%	-25.33%	-24.04%	-22.96%	-22.04%	-21.24%	-20.56%	-19.97%	-19.45%	-19.09%
4.75%	-27.32%	-25.78%	-24.48%	-23.39%	-22.46%	-21.66%	-20.97%	-20.37%	-19.85%	-19.48%

TABLE 10.12 Dividend Impact—20 Percent In-the-Money Options

Maturity	5 Years		Risk-Free Rate		5%				
Volatility (20% in-the-money)									
Dividend	**5.00%**	**10.00%**	**15.00%**	**20.00%**	**25.00%**	**30.00%**	**35.00%**	**40.00%**	**45.00%**	**50.00%**
0.05%	-0.71%	-0.69%	-0.64%	-0.58%	-0.52%	-0.48%	-0.45%	-0.42%	-0.40%	-0.38%
0.15%	-2.13%	-2.07%	-1.90%	-1.72%	-1.57%	-1.44%	-1.34%	-1.25%	-1.19%	-1.13%
0.25%	-3.54%	-3.44%	-3.16%	-2.86%	-2.60%	-2.39%	-2.22%	-2.08%	-1.97%	-1.87%
0.35%	-4.94%	-4.81%	-4.41%	-3.99%	-3.63%	-3.34%	-3.10%	-2.91%	-2.75%	-2.61%
0.45%	-6.34%	-6.16%	-5.65%	-5.11%	-4.65%	-4.27%	-3.97%	-3.72%	-3.52%	-3.34%
0.55%	-7.73%	-7.51%	-6.88%	-6.22%	-5.66%	-5.21%	-4.84%	-4.53%	-4.28%	-4.06%
0.65%	-9.11%	-8.84%	-8.10%	-7.32%	-6.66%	-6.13%	-5.69%	-5.33%	-5.03%	-4.77%
0.75%	-10.48%	-10.17%	-9.31%	-8.42%	-7.66%	-7.05%	-6.54%	-6.13%	-5.77%	-5.46%
0.85%	-11.85%	-11.49%	-10.51%	-9.50%	-8.65%	-7.95%	-7.38%	-6.91%	-6.50%	-6.15%
0.95%	-13.21%	-12.80%	-11.70%	-10.58%	-9.63%	-8.85%	-8.22%	-7.68%	-7.22%	-6.82%
1.05%	-14.57%	-14.10%	-12.89%	-11.65%	-10.60%	-9.74%	-9.04%	-8.44%	-7.93%	-7.47%
1.15%	-15.92%	-15.40%	-14.06%	-12.71%	-11.56%	-10.63%	-9.85%	-9.19%	-8.62%	-8.12%
1.25%	-17.26%	-16.68%	-15.23%	-13.76%	-12.52%	-11.50%	-10.65%	-9.92%	-9.30%	-8.74%
1.35%	-18.59%	-17.96%	-16.38%	-14.80%	-13.46%	-12.36%	-11.43%	-10.65%	-9.96%	-9.36%
1.45%	-19.92%	-19.22%	-17.53%	-15.83%	-14.40%	-13.21%	-12.21%	-11.36%	-10.61%	-9.96%
1.55%	-21.24%	-20.48%	-18.67%	-16.85%	-15.32%	-14.04%	-12.97%	-12.05%	-11.25%	-10.55%
1.65%	-22.56%	-21.73%	-19.79%	-17.87%	-16.23%	-14.86%	-13.72%	-12.73%	-11.87%	-11.12%
1.75%	-23.86%	-22.97%	-20.91%	-18.87%	-17.13%	-15.67%	-14.45%	-13.40%	-12.48%	-11.68%
1.85%	-25.16%	-24.20%	-22.02%	-19.86%	-18.01%	-16.47%	-15.16%	-14.05%	-13.08%	-12.23%
1.95%	-26.46%	-25.42%	-23.11%	-20.83%	-18.88%	-17.25%	-15.87%	-14.68%	-13.66%	-12.76%
2.05%	-27.74%	-26.63%	-24.20%	-21.79%	-19.74%	-18.01%	-16.55%	-15.30%	-14.22%	-13.28%
2.15%	-29.03%	-27.83%	-25.27%	-22.74%	-20.58%	-18.76%	-17.22%	-15.91%	-14.78%	-13.79%
2.25%	-30.30%	-29.02%	-26.33%	-23.67%	-21.40%	-19.49%	-17.88%	-16.50%	-15.32%	-14.29%
2.35%	-31.57%	-30.20%	-27.37%	-24.59%	-22.21%	-20.21%	-18.52%	-17.08%	-15.85%	-14.78%
2.45%	-32.83%	-31.37%	-28.40%	-25.49%	-23.00%	-20.90%	-19.14%	-17.64%	-16.36%	-15.25%
2.55%	-34.08%	-32.53%	-29.41%	-26.37%	-23.77%	-21.58%	-19.75%	-18.19%	-16.86%	-15.72%
2.65%	-35.33%	-33.68%	-30.41%	-27.23%	-24.52%	-22.24%	-20.34%	-18.73%	-17.35%	-16.18%
2.75%	-36.57%	-34.81%	-31.39%	-28.07%	-25.25%	-22.89%	-20.91%	-19.25%	-17.84%	-16.63%
2.85%	-37.80%	-35.92%	-32.34%	-28.89%	-25.96%	-23.52%	-21.47%	-19.76%	-18.31%	-17.07%
2.95%	-39.03%	-37.02%	-33.28%	-29.69%	-26.65%	-24.12%	-22.02%	-20.26%	-18.77%	-17.51%
3.05%	-40.24%	-38.09%	-34.19%	-30.47%	-27.32%	-24.71%	-22.55%	-20.74%	-19.22%	-17.93%
3.15%	-41.45%	-39.15%	-35.07%	-31.22%	-27.97%	-25.29%	-23.07%	-21.22%	-19.67%	-18.36%
3.25%	-42.65%	-40.17%	-35.93%	-31.94%	-28.60%	-25.85%	-23.57%	-21.69%	-20.11%	-18.77%
3.35%	-43.83%	-41.17%	-36.75%	-32.64%	-29.21%	-26.39%	-24.07%	-22.14%	-20.54%	-19.19%
3.45%	-44.99%	-42.14%	-37.55%	-33.32%	-29.79%	-26.91%	-24.55%	-22.59%	-20.96%	-19.59%
3.55%	-46.12%	-43.07%	-38.32%	-33.97%	-30.36%	-27.42%	-25.02%	-23.03%	-21.38%	-20.00%
3.65%	-47.22%	-43.96%	-39.05%	-34.59%	-30.91%	-27.92%	-25.48%	-23.47%	-21.80%	-20.40%
3.75%	-48.27%	-44.81%	-39.74%	-35.19%	-31.44%	-28.41%	-25.93%	-23.90%	-22.21%	-20.81%
3.85%	-49.26%	-45.60%	-40.41%	-35.76%	-31.96%	-28.88%	-26.38%	-24.33%	-22.63%	-21.21%
3.95%	-50.18%	-46.35%	-41.03%	-36.31%	-32.45%	-29.34%	-26.82%	-24.75%	-23.03%	-21.61%
4.05%	-51.00%	-47.04%	-41.62%	-36.83%	-32.94%	-29.80%	-27.25%	-25.17%	-23.44%	-22.01%
4.15%	-51.70%	-47.66%	-42.17%	-37.34%	-33.41%	-30.25%	-27.68%	-25.58%	-23.85%	-22.41%
4.25%	-52.25%	-48.23%	-42.70%	-37.83%	-33.87%	-30.69%	-28.11%	-26.00%	-24.26%	-22.81%
4.35%	-52.63%	-48.73%	-43.19%	-38.30%	-34.33%	-31.13%	-28.54%	-26.42%	-24.67%	-23.21%
4.45%	-52.80%	-49.18%	-43.65%	-38.76%	-34.77%	-31.56%	-28.96%	-26.84%	-25.08%	-23.62%
4.55%	-52.75%	-49.57%	-44.10%	-39.21%	-35.22%	-32.00%	-29.39%	-27.26%	-25.50%	-24.03%
4.65%	-52.52%	-49.92%	-44.53%	-39.66%	-35.67%	-32.44%	-29.82%	-27.68%	-25.91%	-24.44%
4.75%	-52.52%	-50.25%	-44.96%	-40.11%	-36.11%	-32.88%	-30.26%	-28.11%	-26.34%	-24.86%

Note: Maturity is 5 years and risk-free rate is 5 percent.

TABLE 10.12 Continued

Dividend	55.00%	60.00%	65.00%	70.00%	75.00%	80.00%	85.00%	90.00%	95.00%	99.00%
0.05%	-0.36%	-0.35%	-0.34%	-0.33%	-0.32%	-0.31%	-0.30%	-0.29%	-0.29%	-0.28%
0.15%	-1.08%	-1.04%	-1.00%	-0.97%	-0.94%	-0.91%	-0.88%	-0.86%	-0.84%	-0.82%
0.25%	-1.79%	-1.72%	-1.65%	-1.60%	-1.54%	-1.49%	-1.44%	-1.40%	-1.35%	-1.32%
0.35%	-2.49%	-2.39%	-2.30%	-2.21%	-2.13%	-2.05%	-1.98%	-1.91%	-1.85%	-1.80%
0.45%	-3.18%	-3.05%	-2.92%	-2.81%	-2.70%	-2.60%	-2.50%	-2.41%	-2.32%	-2.25%
0.55%	-3.87%	-3.69%	-3.53%	-3.39%	-3.25%	-3.12%	-3.00%	-2.88%	-2.77%	-2.69%
0.65%	-4.53%	-4.32%	-4.13%	-3.95%	-3.78%	-3.63%	-3.48%	-3.34%	-3.21%	-3.12%
0.75%	-5.19%	-4.94%	-4.71%	-4.50%	-4.30%	-4.12%	-3.95%	-3.79%	-3.64%	-3.53%
0.85%	-5.83%	-5.54%	-5.28%	-5.03%	-4.81%	-4.60%	-4.40%	-4.22%	-4.06%	-3.94%
0.95%	-6.45%	-6.13%	-5.83%	-5.55%	-5.30%	-5.06%	-4.85%	-4.65%	-4.47%	-4.33%
1.05%	-7.07%	-6.70%	-6.36%	-6.06%	-5.77%	-5.52%	-5.28%	-5.06%	-4.87%	-4.72%
1.15%	-7.67%	-7.26%	-6.89%	-6.55%	-6.24%	-5.96%	-5.70%	-5.47%	-5.26%	-5.11%
1.25%	-8.25%	-7.80%	-7.40%	-7.03%	-6.69%	-6.39%	-6.12%	-5.87%	-5.65%	-5.49%
1.35%	-8.82%	-8.34%	-7.90%	-7.50%	-7.14%	-6.81%	-6.52%	-6.26%	-6.03%	-5.86%
1.45%	-9.38%	-8.85%	-8.38%	-7.96%	-7.57%	-7.23%	-6.92%	-6.65%	-6.40%	-6.23%
1.55%	-9.92%	-9.36%	-8.86%	-8.41%	-8.00%	-7.64%	-7.32%	-7.03%	-6.78%	-6.60%
1.65%	-10.45%	-9.86%	-9.32%	-8.85%	-8.42%	-8.04%	-7.71%	-7.41%	-7.15%	-6.96%
1.75%	-10.97%	-10.34%	-9.78%	-9.28%	-8.83%	-8.44%	-8.09%	-7.78%	-7.52%	-7.32%
1.85%	-11.48%	-10.81%	-10.22%	-9.70%	-9.24%	-8.83%	-8.47%	-8.16%	-7.88%	-7.69%
1.95%	-11.97%	-11.28%	-10.66%	-10.12%	-9.64%	-9.22%	-8.85%	-8.53%	-8.24%	-8.05%
2.05%	-12.46%	-11.73%	-11.09%	-10.53%	-10.04%	-9.60%	-9.22%	-8.89%	-8.61%	-8.40%
2.15%	-12.93%	-12.18%	-11.51%	-10.93%	-10.43%	-9.98%	-9.60%	-9.26%	-8.97%	-8.76%
2.25%	-13.40%	-12.61%	-11.93%	-11.33%	-10.81%	-10.36%	-9.97%	-9.62%	-9.33%	-9.12%
2.35%	-13.85%	-13.04%	-12.34%	-11.73%	-11.20%	-10.74%	-10.33%	-9.99%	-9.69%	-9.47%
2.45%	-14.30%	-13.47%	-12.75%	-12.12%	-11.58%	-11.11%	-10.70%	-10.35%	-10.04%	-9.83%
2.55%	-14.74%	-13.89%	-13.15%	-12.51%	-11.96%	-11.48%	-11.07%	-10.71%	-10.40%	-10.19%
2.65%	-15.17%	-14.30%	-13.54%	-12.90%	-12.33%	-11.85%	-11.43%	-11.07%	-10.76%	-10.54%
2.75%	-15.59%	-14.70%	-13.94%	-13.28%	-12.71%	-12.22%	-11.80%	-11.43%	-11.12%	-10.90%
2.85%	-16.01%	-15.11%	-14.33%	-13.66%	-13.08%	-12.59%	-12.16%	-11.79%	-11.47%	-11.25%
2.95%	-16.43%	-15.51%	-14.72%	-14.04%	-13.46%	-12.95%	-12.52%	-12.15%	-11.83%	-11.61%
3.05%	-16.84%	-15.90%	-15.10%	-14.42%	-13.83%	-13.32%	-12.89%	-12.51%	-12.19%	-11.96%
3.15%	-17.24%	-16.29%	-15.48%	-14.79%	-14.20%	-13.69%	-13.25%	-12.88%	-12.55%	-12.32%
3.25%	-17.64%	-16.68%	-15.87%	-15.17%	-14.57%	-14.06%	-13.62%	-13.24%	-12.91%	-12.68%
3.35%	-18.04%	-17.07%	-16.25%	-15.54%	-14.94%	-14.43%	-13.98%	-13.60%	-13.27%	-13.03%
3.45%	-18.44%	-17.46%	-16.63%	-15.92%	-15.31%	-14.79%	-14.35%	-13.96%	-13.63%	-13.39%
3.55%	-18.83%	-17.85%	-17.01%	-16.30%	-15.69%	-15.16%	-14.71%	-14.33%	-13.99%	-13.75%
3.65%	-19.23%	-18.23%	-17.39%	-16.67%	-16.06%	-15.53%	-15.08%	-14.69%	-14.35%	-14.11%
3.75%	-19.62%	-18.62%	-17.77%	-17.05%	-16.43%	-15.90%	-15.45%	-15.06%	-14.71%	-14.47%
3.85%	-20.01%	-19.01%	-18.15%	-17.43%	-16.81%	-16.28%	-15.82%	-15.42%	-15.08%	-14.83%
3.95%	-20.41%	-19.40%	-18.54%	-17.81%	-17.18%	-16.65%	-16.19%	-15.79%	-15.44%	-15.19%
4.05%	-20.80%	-19.78%	-18.92%	-18.19%	-17.56%	-17.02%	-16.56%	-16.16%	-15.80%	-15.55%
4.15%	-21.20%	-20.17%	-19.31%	-18.57%	-17.94%	-17.40%	-16.93%	-16.53%	-16.17%	-15.92%
4.25%	-21.59%	-20.57%	-19.70%	-18.96%	-18.32%	-17.78%	-17.31%	-16.90%	-16.54%	-16.28%
4.35%	-21.99%	-20.96%	-20.09%	-19.34%	-18.71%	-18.16%	-17.68%	-17.27%	-16.90%	-16.64%
4.45%	-22.39%	-21.36%	-20.48%	-19.73%	-19.09%	-18.54%	-18.06%	-17.64%	-17.27%	-17.01%
4.55%	-22.80%	-21.76%	-20.88%	-20.12%	-19.48%	-18.92%	-18.44%	-18.02%	-17.64%	-17.37%
4.65%	-23.20%	-22.16%	-21.27%	-20.52%	-19.87%	-19.31%	-18.82%	-18.39%	-18.01%	-17.74%
4.75%	-23.61%	-22.57%	-21.67%	-20.91%	-20.26%	-19.69%	-19.20%	-18.77%	-18.38%	-18.11%

Case Studies

MORE, FASTER, CHEAPER—THE SIREN
CALL OF UPSTREAM R&D

The following is contributed by Jaswant Singh Sihra, Senior Strategic Planning Advisor, Halliburton Company, Houston, Texas. Founded in 1919, Halliburton is a public company traded on the New York Stock Exchange, and is one of the world's largest providers of products and services to the petroleum and energy industries. The company serves its customers with a broad range of products and services through its Energy Services Group, and Engineering and Construction Group business segments. Halliburton has operations in 120 countries, has 82,000 employees worldwide, and recorded 2001 sales of US$13 billion.

There has arguably never been a time when the energy industry has faced a future of such tremendous potential coupled with such significant uncertainty as it does today. Value chain shifts have blurred the lines of demarcation between what has traditionally been known as the "upstream" side and the "downstream" side. The increasingly interconnected, global nature of the business; deregulation; the opening and growth of fledgling and established economies, respectively; shifting geopolitical landscapes; and climatic changes are just a few of the many events that have combined to create a long-term environment of growing energy demand coupled with great uncertainty. To fuel this insatiable appetite for energy, the industry has focused its attention on the two cheapest sources of energy: oil and gas.

Proven worldwide crude oil reserves are currently estimated at approximately 1 trillion barrels.[1] However, worldwide consumption is currently 75 million barrels per day and is expected to surpass 110 million barrels per day by 2020.[2] This uptrend in consumption is occurring while reserve replacement is following a downward trend from an average of 70 billion barrels of oil reserves added per year in the 1960s to today's average of approximately

20 billion barrels.[3] Additionally, the size of newly discovered reserves de-
creased from 200 million barrels to 50 million barrels during this 30-year
time interval.[4]

   This dichotomy has led to the siren call of the upstream energy business:
more, faster, and cheaper. Never has there been a more pressing need for a
greater abundance of oil and gas reserves that can be found and developed
more cheaply and delivered to an ever-hungry market faster. Unlike the
opening scene depicted in a once popular American television show, gone
are the days where one could seemingly fire a rifle into the ground, pierce a
large shallow lake of crude oil, and then enjoy prolific production for many
years. Most of the new discoveries outside of the Middle East are found in
increasingly remote locations where complex geology is the norm. With this
fact in mind, as the global demand curve continues to head north while the
global supply curve goes south, how will the industry (exclusive of the acts
of OPEC) manage to keep the market's equilibrium price for oil and gas at
a level where global economic growth is sustainable? The answer quite
clearly is through the application of advanced technology.

   It is widely accepted that most of the large-scale gains that the energy
industry has enjoyed in recent years are attributable to the leaps made in
technology development. Examples include the use of three- and four-
dimensional (time-lapse) seismic technology, so-called intelligent well com-
pletions, and directional drilling. These and many other advances have
greatly accelerated reservoir drainage, increased the probability of drilling
and completing a successful well, and facilitated the redevelopment of
mature fields allowing the drainage of previously bypassed reserves or reserves that simply could not be produced due to technology limitations at
the time the wells were completed. However, this advancement has indeed
been a double-edged sword because the greatly increased depletion rates resulting from better technology has resulted in a treadmill effect where many
energy companies are completing more wells just to keep up production at
current or slightly above current levels. This condition is especially true in
mature provinces such as the lower 48 states and the Gulf of Mexico continental shelf areas of the United States and the U.K. sector of the North Sea.

   To further complicate matters, the industry is answering the relentless
call of the "Capital Gods" of the world's financial markets. In the age of the
flashy dot-coms and biotechs, the energy industry has found its paltry
historical returns of single to low double-digits insufficient to attract the capital necessary for large-scale growth.[5] To this end, industry participants—
namely, the integrated energy companies and the service companies that
support their operations—are retrenching and attempting to refocus on
areas of core competencies. Mergers have become *the* way as economy of
scale is the name of the game. For energy companies it has simply become
more efficient to buy reserves than to find them. Likewise for service com-

panies it has become more economical to buy technical capabilities than to develop them. Additionally, efforts are ongoing with both players trying to wring out any potential inefficiencies that remain from operations.

Nowhere has this capital utilization rationalization process been more apparent and far-reaching than in the area of technology development. The resulting actions have created a shift in technology development that is every bit as dramatic as the great continental rift that broke apart Pangea. Upstream R&D investment over the past decade has been following a downward trend. Furthermore, the R&D load borne by service companies has been increasing annually for the past 30 years. In 1970 service companies accounted for approximately 20 percent of the industry's R&D spending with the integrated energy companies accounting for the bulk of the remaining 80 percent.[6] This work was primarily pure and so-called blue sky in nature. Today, greater than 40 percent of the industry's R&D spend belongs to the service companies and is application-driven. Currently, there are no indications that this trend will be arrested. Additionally, an increasing portion of the remaining 60 percent is being spread over jointly funded projects that involve service companies, universities, and the integrated energy companies.[7] In short, energy companies have elected to focus their efforts on managing their resources so that they may extract the most value from their assets—namely, reserves. They intend to do this by leveraging what is arguably the most valuable asset of the service companies—namely, technology.

Faced with the same capital constraints, service companies must adapt to this rapidly changing and evolving role. Further, this metamorphosis must be managed strategically within the context of an industry that continues to see a significant compression in the periods between business cycles and an increasing amplitude during the cycles. This circumstance means there is an increasing need for developing more expensive technology with greater associated risks and shorter expected product life cycles. This new role and the associated macrofactors previously stated have created problems in risk management, portfolio management, and technology valuation that simply cannot be addressed effectively using traditional methods and techniques. For example, how does one value a new downhole robotic sensor being developed by two ex-service-company engineers in their garage that has the potential to totally change the way a North Sea reservoir is produced? Should a large, integrated service company license the rights to the promising technology, buy the technology, develop its own or leap-frog it with the pet project being touted by "Jim's skunk works group down the hall"? If purchasing is the preferred option, how much is the technology worth today given the fact that its targeted market does not exist today? If everyone in the technology department feels the technology is strategic, yet no matter how much the numbers are massaged the project's NPV is extremely negative, how can management be convinced to proceed with the project? These are difficult questions that must be answered amid Wall Street screams for increased capital efficiency.

Real options analysis is quickly becoming a tool through which these types of questions are framed and subsequently answered. It allows one to focus on the strategic pathways inherent in any technology development project instead of the straight-line journey previously used to arrive at a project's NPV, payback, and IRR. Rather than replacing these metrics, real options analysis coupled with stochastic processes simply adds an increased level of sophistication and robustness into the decision-making process.

As technology development projects get increasingly more difficult, capital gets more scarce, and industry fundamentals become more dynamic, successful integrated service companies must adopt more sophisticated, disciplined, and quantitative processes for their R&D efforts. These systems must be robust, provide great flexibility and bring together all stakeholders—marketing, engineering, and strategic planning. Real options analysis is a very powerful tool that goes a long way toward satisfying these objectives.

Notes

1. BP Amoco data taken from "Exploration Frontiers for New Century Determined by Technology, Politics," *OGJ*, December 1999.
2. *International Energy Outlook 2000*, U.S. Energy Information Administration (EIA), 1999.
3. See note 1.
4. Ibid.
5. Dow Jones Industrial Group Averages, *Wall Street Journal*, February 2000.
6. "Research & Development—New Technology Solves Problems," *Hart's E&P*, October 2002.
7. Ibid.

REAL OPTIONS ANALYSIS APPLIED TO VALUING START-UP ENTITIES: THE DIGITAL NEWS, INC.

Indran Purushothaman (indran_purushothaman@yahoo.com), the author of this contribution, is a New York–based corporate finance adviser, specializing in undertaking financial analysis and valuation assignments across a range of investments, including start-ups.

The Valuation Challenge

Venture capitalists (VCs) face an unprecedented challenge in evaluating start-up entities in the current market environment. The existing financial analytical tools and frameworks available to analysts, unfortunately, have not kept up with the breakneck pace of economic change and the high level of uncertainty. The two key techniques, discounted cash flows (DCF) analysis and relative measures, do not adequately address the complexities arising from an uncertain business environment, turbulent financial markets, globalization, and emergence of new growth technologies. Nonetheless, financial analysis remains a critical component of the investment cycle, as both the VCs and start-up management team of target entities need to agree both on a value to determine how much capital should be raised and on the equity ownership structure.

In the post Internet-bubble era, as the markets became more nervous about investing into tech-based entities and the competition for funds intensified, VCs began to impose more restrictive terms on the management team and demanded a greater slice of the equity to compensate for their risk capital. This case study discusses the application of the real options analysis approach to value an Internet start-up that successfully raised $3 million in late 2002 in the midst of one of our toughest capital-raising markets.[1]

Real Options Analysis

Real options are an extension of financial options theory, but applied to situations involving real assets like mining projects, real estates, patents, R&D projects, and investment projects. A company that has a real option has essentially acquired the right but not an obligation to make a value-accretive decision. This right comes at a cost and typically the management team would have a limited window of opportunity within which to exercise the right. Underpinning the real options approach is a learning model assumption, where the option holder (management team) will make better and more informed strategic decisions, as some of the levels of uncertainty are resolved with the passage of time. For example, a VC may create for itself strategic value through setting up contractual agreements with a barrier option, where, for the promise of an initial funding, it has the right of first refusal, but not the obligation, to invest in a later round of funding should the investee company meet management-set milestones.

Deficiencies in Existing Methodologies

In many instances the value of a start-up entity is a function of the amount that VCs wish to invest and the level of ownership they desire. For example, if the VC is willing to invest $1.2 million and requires 30 percent ownership of the entity, then the value of the entity is essentially $4 million. The other key driver is related to liquidity and demand, where prices simply skyrocket in competitive bidding during times when VCs are fighting off each other to fund ideas. However, regardless of how much the entity was finally valued, there is always some financial analysis undertaken.

One common approach to valuing a target adopted by VCs is to use an earnings multiplier. The earnings of the exit year are projected and that amount is then multiplied with an earnings multiplier to arrive at an exit price. The problem with this methodology, and with relative valuations, is that it assumes that the comparables selected reflect the cash flows and risks of the entity valued, which is often difficult to determine for start-up entities with no historical track record. The other major assumption is that the market on which the comparable multiplier is based accurately reflects the underlying value of its stocks. Clearly, using a comparable derived from the prices of Internet stocks at the height of the tech boom in early 2000 would result in a very high and overvalued investment. In comparison, a DCF approach adds several layers of depth to the analysis as it involves forecasting cash flows and through the use of a discount rate, brings into the analysis the concept of risk. However, DCF analysis assumes a static investment decision, and assumes that decisions are made upfront with no recourse for management to alter the path and underlying cash flows mid-stream. Also building on the risk/reward principle, DCF analysis handles highly volatile cash flows by discounting them more severely than less volatile steams. Collectively, these flaws result in the understating of the fair value of a project, potentially resulting in a good project being rejected.

Real options analysis recognizes that there exist several paths that a management team may take to execute its strategy, which in itself may have to be modified mid-stream, to achieve its desired goals. Indeed, an innovative business plan should identify key decision points and options available to management, revealing the extent that management has sought to build strategic flexibility into its operations. Real options analysis seeks out and values these strategic flexibility options. Real options analysis builds on the strengths of DCF, as it is based on future cash flows and growth rates, and focuses on risk, but it enhances the analysis by providing a framework that conceptualizes and values managerial flexibility. Unlike DCF techniques where the expected cash flows are fixed, real options analysis adopts the notion of an active net present value (NPV), whose expected value trajectory is controllable by management. Real options analysis looks at active NPV as a sum of the passive NPV and the value of the embedded options. A key assumption of this methodology is that management is competent and capable of executing its options, should they be in-the-money (otherwise these options would be worthless).

The Digital News, Inc.

The presentation now turns to how real options analysis is applied as a framework to understand the sources of value and assess the fair value of the New York–based Internet start-up, The Digital News, Inc. (TDN). The timing of this analysis is about one year after commencement of operations and just prior to the first round of VC funding.

TDN syndicates broadcast quality video footage of corporate and public news releases to the media. TDN provides TV journalists and other program makers with a central destination to search, preview, acquire, or trade broadcast-quality video from a wide variety of sources. Content providers (mainly Fortune 1000 and global institutions) benefit from using TDN's proprietary platform as an efficient and convenient means to disseminate video news globally. The idea for creating this platform came from the journalism and advertising backgrounds of the two founding partners. As a team they ran a multinational public relations enterprise for 12 years. A key component of the earlier business was to create video news releases for major corporations and distribute them to TV stations. They found the distribution element of the chain to be the most challenging area of their business. The rapid rise of the Internet and ensuing high-speed broadband technologies presented an ideal means for distributing broadcast-quality video online.

After having been in operation for a year, TDN has made inroads in terms of building a functional prototype and found itself with a small but growing client base. However, to expand its client base, broaden its service offering, build a technologically robust platform, and establish relationships with the TV media rooms, it required more funds. Hence it was seeking its first round of VC funding. Following the first round of financing, TDN's management envisioned that it will require further funding, provided that certain targets are met, though the timing and magnitude of these additional funds are unknown. Those funds would be utilized to fuel expansion through acquisitions and enhance its technical capabilities. Clearly, if there is no market or if the technical platform fails to meet expectations, investors will not be compelled to make any further investment. The exit plan is scheduled for sometime in year five where it is expected that the investor's interest will be liquidated most likely via a trade sale rather than an initial public offering (IPO).

Framing The Digital News's Real Options

The real options process adopted here is essentially in accordance with the steps outlined by Mun in *Real Options Analysis* (Wiley, 2002), except that I have framed the real options first before presenting the financial analysis. A closer review of TDN's business model reveals that the management team has the ability, at various milestones, to abandon the project, delay initiatives, or expand services. The model essentially reflects a series of options on options, known as a *sequential compound option*, where the latter options depend on the successful execution of the earlier ones. Given that VCs will have board representation and will play a hands-on role on key decisions, one could suggest that the VCs essentially have the same real options as the management team. Indeed, by staging their investment and having written into their contractual agreement a first right of refusal to further funding, the VCs have acquired the flexibility to continue funding TDN.

Unfortunately, computing a sequential compound option is a rather complex task as it involves identifying the various embedded options and deciphering their relationship to each other. This task is made more difficult when either the time horizon for the execution of the second option or the amount required for the second investment is unclear. Indeed in this case TDN may turn out to be self-funding and not require additional funds. Rather than attempting the impossible task of valuing every conceivable option embedded in TDN, I have taken a macroview and framed the following American Expansion Option: By promising to provide the first round of funding and writing into the financing agreements a first right of refusal, the VCs have purchased the right, but not the obligation, to provide additional funds should TDN need more capital. However, should they feel that the outlook for TDN is not promising, they are not obliged to provide any further funds. Either way, by having the first right of refusal and making that initial investment they have acquired the right to benefit from the cash flows generated by TDN. This is an American option as TDN could seek additional funds at anytime within the assumed time frame of five years.

Financial Analysis and Modeling

The first step is to undertake a DCF analysis to arrive at the enterprise value. The key elements of the DCF analysis were to (a) forecast the free cash flow for an explicit forecast period (eight years); (b) determine the continuing value; (c) determine the discount rate; and (d) discount the cash flows and aggregate the discounted cash flows less the capital injection by investors to arrive at the NPV. The static valuation of TDN's future profitability using a DCF model is found to be $38 million.[2] The real options analysis undertaken here used the Real Option Analysis Toolkit software created by Johnathan Mun and Decisioneering. The appropriate option model to use in this case is a closed-form approximation of an American call option because the management team could decide to expand the operations anytime and accordingly seek to raise funds as and when it requires. The core inputs of this analysis are:

- Expansion factor—TDN will double its net cash flow
- Time to expiry—anytime over the next five years
- Volatility—implied volatility of 45 percent
- Risk-free rate—5 percent assumed
- Implementation cost (exercise price)—the amount of additional funds required—assumed to be $20 million to fund acquisition

Based on the preceding assumptions and using the backward induction technique, the lattice is calculated back to obtain a value of $63 million for the firm inclusive of the expansion option. As the underlying static value of TDN was $38 million, the cost for the VC of acquiring another investment with similar cash flows and risk is $(2 \times \$38) - \$20 = \$56$ million; that is, the value of twice its current operations less the acquisition costs. The $56 million is the static NPV without flexibility of the expanded operation. The additional $7 million is the real option value. In other words, the growth option embedded in TDN contributed an additional 12.5 percent to a static valuation analysis.

Conclusion

The analysis did show that by using the traditional valuation methods, the VC would have undervalued TDN and potentially might have missed investing in a lucrative venture. However, I believe the main benefit of undertaking a real options analysis for the VCs is that it forces them to think and identify what options exist in the investee entity or how they may create options within their investment. Seek to invest in entities that provide the greatest investment opportunity. The key benefit for the management teams of start-ups seeking to raise funds by undertaking such analysis is that it provides them with a powerful negotiating tool to highlight to potential investors the array of options embedded in their business. It also helps them extract better terms from VCs in terms of equity ownership ratio.

Notes

1. I used the real options approach to analyze the business and to help the management team articulate its business case to VCs during the capital-raising phase. However, in this case study, the analysis has been flipped around and is done from the perspective of a venture capitalist wanting to value the business.
2. To maintain confidentiality, the underlying numbers used to produce the results quoted in this case study are not the actual numbers; however, I am willing to share the thought process and technique used to obtain the results.

About the CD-ROM

INTRODUCTION

The enclosed CD-ROM contains the Real Options Analysis Toolkit trial software (limited version), a trial version of Crystal Ball 2000 Monte Carlo simulation software, sample Excel worksheets on real options, and sample problems in the book.

CD-ROM TABLE OF CONTENTS

Directory Name	File Name	Description
Real Options Analysis Toolkit	setup.exe	Installs the Real Options Analysis Toolkit
Crystal Ball Simulation Software	setup.exe	Installs the Crystal Ball Simulation software
Workbook Exercises	*.xls	Sample Excel Real Options exercise spreadsheets
Answers	*.xls	Sample Excel Real Options answer spreadsheets

MINIMUM SYSTEM REQUIREMENTS

- IBM PC or compatible computer with Pentium II or higher processor
- 64 MB RAM (128 MB RAM recommended)
- 75 MB hard-disk space
- CD-ROM drive
- SVGA monitor with 256 Color
- Excel 2000, XP, or later
- Windows 2000, XP, or later

TECHNICAL NOTES

- Make sure you have logged in with Administrative rights on the computer before installing the Real Options Analysis Toolkit. Most home computers have these rights automatically set. For other computers, check with your company's IT professional.
- Certain computer settings may require rebooting your computer between setups or reinserting the CD-ROM after the reboot.
- Certain foreign Regional Settings on your computer may deactivate the Custom Lattice in the Real Options Analysis Toolkit software. To reactivate, make sure the Regional Settings are set to English (USA).
- Contact www.crystalball.com to obtain a free registration code to extend your trial period of the software.
- Make sure your Excel Macro security settings are set to medium or low to allow the software's macros to run.

HOW TO INSTALL THE SOFTWARE
ONTO YOUR COMPUTER

There are two separate setup programs available in the CD-ROM. They are the Real Options Analysis Toolkit software and the Crystal Ball 2000 simulation software. You will need to run both setup programs separately. To run the setup programs, follow these instructions. Refer to Chapter 1 in the book for detailed step-by-step installation instructions.

1. Insert the enclosed Real Options CD-ROM into the CD-ROM drive of your computer.
2. Open Windows Explorer and locate the folders on the CD-ROM drive.
3. Open the *Crystal Ball Simulation Software folder* and double-click on the *SETUP.EXE* file to install the Crystal Ball 2000 Professional software. Read and follow the online instructions. Leave the registration number empty for now. Use all default settings but when prompted, set Crystal Ball to automatically start every time Excel starts.
4. Open the *Real Options Analysis Toolkit folder* and double-click on the *SETUP.EXE* file to install the Real Options Analysis Toolkit software. Read and follow the online instructions to continue.
5. Contact www.crystalball.com for an extended registration code for both software.

USING THE SOFTWARE

Refer to Chapters 1 and 2 in this book for installing the Real Options Analysis Toolkit software and for information on getting started with Real Options Analysis Toolkit and Crystal Ball 2000.

USER ASSISTANCE

If you have questions about obtaining the fully functional software, contact Dr. Johnathan Mun at JohnathanMun@cs.com.

If you need assistance, contact Technical Support at:

Phone: 800-289-2550
Web: www.crystalball.com

If you have a damaged disk, contact Wiley Technical Support at:

Phone: 201-748-6753
Fax: 201-748-6450
Web: www.wiley.com/techsupport

To place additional orders or to request information about Wiley products, call 800-225-5945.

Index

For information about the CD-ROM see the
About the CD-ROM section on page 291.

WILEY